Globalisation and the Labour Market

Although there have been major globalisation episodes prior to the current one, previous globalisation experiences did not seem as pervasive as the episode which began in the last quarter of the twentieth century. It is claimed that the current globalisation wave is causing social disruption: redistributing income from poor to rich and displacing vulnerable workers. This volume provides a careful investigation into the impacts of globalisation on the labour market.

Globalisation and the Labour Market examines the relative decline in the economic fortunes of unskilled workers in the major industrialised countries over the past 30 years. In the United States and United Kingdom this has resulted in a relative decline in the wages of unskilled workers. In the 'continental' European economies it has tended to manifest itself in the least skilled facing a higher probability of being unemployed or of being unemployed for longer. Many make the case that globalisation was responsible for this. But globalisation is not the only possible explanation. The past 30 years have also been a period of significant technological change – impressive in both its scale and speed. This has increased the demand for skilled workers and made them better off in economic terms.

The contributions to this volume provide a detailed insight into how the labour market impacts of globalisation differ across different firms, industries and countries and how the impacts of technology and trade are intertwined. The analysis contained within this volume will make it invaluable to academic researchers and policy-makers.

Robert Anderton currently works on trade and capital flows issues at the European Central Bank. He is also a professor in the School of Economics, University of Nottingham, UK.

Paul Brenton is a researcher in the International Trade Department at the World Bank.

John Whalley is professor of Economics at both the University of Warwick, UK, and the University of Western Ontario, Canada.

Routledge Studies in the Modern World Economy

Globalisation and the Labour Market

Trade, technology and less-skilled workers in Europe and the United States

Edited by Robert Anderton, Paul Brenton and John Whalley

Routledge
Taylor & Francis Group

LONDON AND NEW YORK

First published 2006
by Routledge
2 Park Square, Milton Park, Abingdon, Oxon OX14 4RN

Simultaneously published in the USA and Canada
by Routledge
270 Madison Ave, New York, NY 10016

Routledge is an imprint of the Taylor & Francis Group

© 2006 Robert Anderton, Paul Brenton and John Whalley, selection
and editorial matter; the contributors, their own chapters

Typeset in Times New Roman by
Newgen Imaging Systems (P) Ltd, Chennai, India
Printed and bound in Great Britain by
Biddles Ltd, King's Lynn

British Library Cataloguing in Publication Data
A catalogue record for this book is available
from the British Library

Library of Congress Cataloging in Publication Data
A catalog record for this book has been requested

ISBN10: 0–415–32012–7
ISBN13: 9–78–0–415–32012–2

Contents

Figures

Tables

Contributors

Lisandro Abrego is a researcher at the International Monetary Fund, Washington DC. Previously, he was at the University of Warwick (UK) at the Centre for the Study of Globalisation and Regionalisation (CSGR) mainly working on issues related to applied general equilibrium analysis.

Robert Anderton is a principal economist at the European Central Bank (Frankfurt) as well as a professor at the School of Economics, University of Nottingham, UK. His current work involves various issues relating to the euro area, such as exchange rate pass-through, the impact of monetary union on trade flows and trade prices, and external shocks affecting the euro area. Before joining the European Central Bank in 1999, he was a research fellow at the National Institute of Economic and Social Research (NIESR) working on a range of research themes, among them are the Exchange Rate Mechanism and European labour markets, the persistence of inflation and unemployment; trade performance and innovation, trade, technology and labour market inequality, and the New Deal for Young Unemployed People.

Paul Brenton is a researcher in the International Trade Department at the World Bank. He was formerly a Senior Research Fellow at the Centre for European Policy Studies (Brussels) where he published widely on a variety of issues such as trade and labour markets, FDI and international trade. Before joining CEPS he was a lecturer at the University of Birmingham. He is the author of *International Trade: a European Text* (with Henry Scott and Peter Sinclair) and *Global Trade and European Workers* (with Jacques Pelkmans).

Ana Rute Cardoso is a senior research associate at IZA Bonn (Institute for the Study of Labor), where she is deputy-director of the Research Program 'The Future of Labor'. She is a research affiliate of the Centre for Economic Policy Research in London. She is currently on leave from the University of Minho, Portugal. Her research interests include earnings inequality and mobility, and the role of employer behaviour and labour market institutions.

Ludo Cuyvers is a full professor at the Faculty of Applied Economics, University of Antwerp, where he is head of the Department of International Economics,

International Management and Diplomacy and Director of the Centre for ASEAN Studies. He is also Chairman of the European Institute for Asian Studies, a Brussels-based think tank. His research interests focus on globalisation through international trade and foreign direct investment and social development in industrial and developing countries, as well as EU trade policies and the development strategies in the countries of South East Asia.

Markus Diehl is a senior economist in the Economics Department of the WestLB AG, Dusseldorf carrying out macroeconomic analysis and forecasting for Japan, China and South Korea. Previously, he was a research fellow in the Development Economics Department at the Institute of World Economics (Kiel, Germany), where he published articles on various topics such as monetary and exchange rate policy, foreign trade and outsourcing, as well as being involved in field research in Vietnam.

Michel Dumont is an assistant professor at the Department of International Economics, International Management and Diplomacy of the University of Antwerp. He teaches international economic issues and international economic organisations. His research focuses on the impact of international competition and technological change on the labour market position of low-skilled workers.

Valerie Jarvis carried out the work published in this book while she was a researcher at the National Institute of Economic and Social Research (London, UK). Her research has involved a wide range of international comparisons – including studies of productivity and industrial organisation, as well as of schooling methods and vocational training.

Eva Oscarsson carried out the research published in this book while she was a PhD student at the Institute for International Studies (University of Stockholm). She now works at the Swedish Ministry of Finance.

Anna Maria Pinna carried out the research for this book while at the Centre for European Policy Studies (Belgium). She has since been associated with the Centre for North South Economic Research, University of Cagliari. In addition to labour market issues, she has also worked on various trade topics such as border effects and trade in intermediate inputs.

Glenn Rayp is a lecturer at the University of Ghent where he is also a member of the Study Hive for Economic and Public Policy Analysis (SHERPPA). His research interests include: income inequality, redistribution and growth, globalisation and regional integration.

Mark Vancauteren carried out the research for this book while at the Centre for European Policy Studies (Belgium) and he has since been associated with the WHU Graduate School of Management (Koblenz) as well the Universite Catholique de Louvain (Institut Recherhes Economiques et Sociales). His research interests cover various topics such as the impact of harmonised food regulations on EU bilateral trade and the intra-European trade of manufactured goods.

John Whalley is a professor of economics at both the University of Warwick, UK, and the University of Western Ontario, Canada. At Warwick he is a co-director of the Centre for the Study of Globalisation and Regionalisation (CSGR), and at Western Ontario he is a co-director of the Centre for the Study of International Economic Relations. He is a fellow of the Royal Society of Canada, and a fellow of the Econometric Society. He is a research associate of the National Bureau of Economic Research (NBER) and is joint managing editor of the journal The World Economy. He has published widely, and is best known for his contributions to applied general equilibrium analysis, and trade and tax policy. He continues to work on WTO and global trade policy issues.

Biographical details of the editors

Robert Anderton is a principal economist at the European Central Bank (Frankfurt) as well as a professor at the School of Economics, University of Nottingham, UK. His current work involves various issues relating to the euro area, such as exchange rate pass-through, the impact of monetary union on trade flows and trade prices, and global impacts on the euro area. Before joining the European Central Bank in 1999, he was a research fellow at the National Institute of Economic and Social Research (NIESR) working on a range of research themes, among them the Exchange Rate Mechanism and European labour markets; the persistence of inflation and unemployment; trade performance and innovation; the Single Currency and European institutional investors' financial asset portfolio allocations; trade, technology and labour market inequality and the New Deal for Young Unemployed People.

Paul Brenton is a senior economist in the International Trade Department at the World Bank. He was formerly a senior research fellow at the Centre for European Policy Studies (Brussels), where he published widely on a variety of issues such as trade and labour markets, FDI and international trade. Before joining CEPS he was a lecturer at the University of Birmingham. He is the author of *International Trade: A European Text* (with Henry Scott and Peter Sinclair) and *Global Trade and European Workers* (with Jacques Pelkmans).

John Whalley is a professor of economics at both the University of Warwick, UK, and the University of Western Ontario, Canada. At Warwick he is a co-director of the Centre for the Study of Globalisation and Regionalisation (CSGR), and at Western Ontario he is a co-director of the Centre for the Study of International Economic Relations. He is a fellow of the Royal Society of Canada and a fellow of the Econometric Society. He is a research associate of the National Bureau of Economic Research (NBER), Cambridge, MA, and the joint managing editor of the journal *The World Economy*. He has published widely and is best known for his contributions to applied general equilibrium analysis and to trade and tax policy. He continues to work on WTO and global trade policy issues.

Foreword

Globalisation may be a relatively recent shorthand descriptor for the process whereby national economies become more integrated, but it is certainly not a new phenomenon. The world has witnessed major globalisation episodes prior to the one we are living through, for instance in the latter part of the nineteenth century. But maybe previous episodes have not been, or seemed, as pervasive as the episode which began in the last quarter of the twentieth century and which continues today.

One reason for this is that change happens more quickly now and we know about the consequences more quickly. Another reason is the perception that the current globalisation wave is causing more social disruption: redistributing income from poor to rich, displacing more vulnerable workers, disenfranchising developing countries in international fora. Although, as even the most ardent pro-globalisation fanatic would concede, the globalisation process results in redistributions, much of what we hear is often based on rhetoric and assertion rather than patient and careful research. More of this is needed, which is why this particular volume was worth commissioning and publishing.

The focus of this volume is the relative decline in the position of unskilled workers in the major industrialised countries over the past 30 years. In the United States and the United Kingdom this has manifested itself in a relative decline in the wages of unskilled workers or, put differently, in a rising premium to skilled labour. In the 'continental' economies it has tended to manifest itself in the least skilled facing a higher likelihood of being unemployed or of being unemployed for longer. A good scientific case can be made to support the argument that globalisation was responsible for this – the industrialised countries are skill abundant; therefore more trade with countries abundant in unskilled labour will leave 'Northern' unskilled workers worse off. But globalisation is not the only possible explanation. The past 30 years have also been a period of extraordinary technological change – extraordinary in both its scale and speed. This has increased the demand for skilled workers and in economic terms increased their lot.

A great deal of research has been undertaken to try to establish whether, broadly speaking, trade or technology is the key driver behind the relative decline in the fortunes of the unskilled. The consensus thus far is that it is more technology, in the form of skill-biased technical change, than trade. Broadly speaking, that is also the conclusion of this volume. However, it is not quite that simple, and to end on this glib summary would understate the contribution of this volume by an order of magnitude. Two features mark it out as a substantive contribution. First, it is not a single study of a single country using a single methodology. The focus is multi-country and the contributors deploy a range of methodologies: econometric, computable general equilibrium and survey-based case studies. That is unusual and makes for a rich range of analysis. Second, these studies recognise something which most do not: globalisation and technological change are interacting rather than separate forces. Modelling these interactions is tricky – it is much easier to model them separately! Happily this volume does not just go for the easy option and we have a deeper and richer evidence base as a consequence.

This is an excellent contribution to the literature on globalisation and labour market adjustment. The editors are to be congratulated on assembling such a worthwhile collection of chapters, which will be useful both to academic researchers and analysts in the policy-making community.

David Greenaway
Professor of Economics, Pro-Vice Chancellor
and Director Leverhulme Centre for
Research on Globalisation and
Economic Policy,
University of Nottingham

1 Globalisation and the labour market

Robert Anderton and Paul Brenton

Introduction

This book is a detailed investigation into the causes of the deterioration in the relative economic fortunes of less-skilled workers across various countries, with a focus on the role of globalisation. Over the past thirty years, the decline in the wages and employment of less-skilled workers relative to skilled workers in Europe and North America has coincided with an acceleration in 'globalisation'. As described by Greenaway and Nelson (2000), the rapid pace of globalisation is indicated by the strong growth in both world trade and foreign direct investment (FDI) which, in turn, have been stimulated by various factors such as: reductions in trade barriers; drastic declines in the costs of communication and transportation; and the internationalisation of production.

Although it is now widely held that the main cause of this rise in inequality seems to be a shift in demand towards higher skilled workers, this book aims to shed light on whether it is trade or technology that is primarily responsible for this demand shift. More specifically: has the rapid growth of labour-saving technological progress reduced the relative demand for less-skilled workers; or has increased international trade with low-wage countries – that is, nations with an abundant supply of low-skill and low-wage labour – decreased the demand for low-skilled workers in the advanced industrialised countries? This is not a new question and is part of an ongoing debate which has stimulated a large amount of research on this issue.[1] So far, the majority of studies conclude that it is technology (i.e. skill biased technical change) rather than trade that has been the main cause of growing inequality in the labour market.

Research on this issue has been steadily evolving, initially using rigid traditional approaches but more recently applying richer methodologies accompanied by more appropriate and sophisticated datasets. This has been partly in response to the realisation that actual inequality outcomes and other economic developments have not always been in line with the expectations of traditional models – the real world has turned out to be far more complex! This book tries to move the analysis further forward by including papers which not only widen the methodologies used but also fine tune the analysis by suitably matching the data and techniques used with the questions being asked. It also tries to give the trade explanation for inequality a 'fair hearing' by thoroughly investigating the trade mechanisms and recognising the important interactions between globalisation, trade and technology. Accordingly, this chapter begins by describing the traditional trade theories and their weaknesses as well as the benefits of newer approaches. Against this background, the motivation for this book is then further explained along with descriptions of the individual chapters and their value-added.

Traditional analysis

The traditional framework for analysing the mechanisms by which trade may influence wages is the Heckscher–Ohlin–Samuelson (HOS) model incorporating the Stolper–Samuelson theorem. This approach assumes high-skilled workers are abundant in the advanced countries, with low-skilled workers prevalent in the newly industrialising countries and emerging market economies. If trade opens up between the advanced countries and the rest of the world, the theorem predicts that the former group of countries will export high-skill-intensive products and import low-skill-intensive goods. Because of the downward pressure exerted by low-priced imports from newly industrialising/emerging market economies, this implies that the price of low-skill-intensive manufactures relative to high-skill-intensive will decline in the advanced economies. As a result of the decline in relative prices, the theorem predicts that the wages of low-skilled workers relative to that of high-skilled workers will decline in the advanced industrialised countries.[2]

How well does the HOS model describe the stylised facts? At first sight, the theorem seems to correspond with the observed decline in the relative wages of the less-skilled. But the key condition that there must first be a decline in the relative price of low-skill-intensive goods is not clearly evident in the data. For example, Lawrence and Slaughter (1993) investigate developments in US import and export prices and discover that, if anything, the price of low-skill-intensive products rose relative to products using significant amounts of skilled labour (implying, within the HOS framework, that trade contributed to greater equality of wages in the US).[3] Meanwhile, Anderton and Brenton (1999a) show that developments in product prices for broad industrial sectors in Germany and the UK also do not provide evidence of the changes in relative prices required for the HOS theorem to explain rising inequality. However, they did find that the relative price of imports of unskilled labour-intensive products did fall in the UK in the 1980s. That is, if low-wage countries had not increased their share of UK imports then the import prices of low-skilled products would have been higher. Even for high-skilled sectors, such as machinery, trade with the low-wage countries has depressed UK import prices, but by much less than that for unskilled-intensive products. The key point remains, however, that increased trade with low-wage countries does not necessarily translate into changes in relative prices. One reason may be that companies in advanced industrialised countries might respond by upgrading the quality of their products in low-skill-intensity sectors in order to escape increasing import competition from low-wage countries, thereby putting upward pressure on domestic output prices in these sectors. Another relevant point highlighted by Anderton and Brenton (1999a) is that price outcomes within broad sectors usually defined as low-skill-intensive, such as textiles, are far from homogeneous.

These points – and, indeed, some of the chapters in this book – highlight the problems of empirically testing the HOS theorem, particularly in terms of defining and precisely measuring an industry in terms of its skill-intensiveness. For example, if the industry sectors which are usually assessed as low-skill-intensive actually differ across their subsectors in terms of their skill requirements, then increased trade with low-wage countries could lead to a decline of the unskilled-intensive activities and the expansion of skill-intensive activities within the sector. Accordingly, the aggregate relative price of the sector may not change much, while the relative employment of skilled labour will increase in the sector even in the absence of technological advances. Furthermore, the HOS prediction that the demand for labour would fall only in the unskilled-intensive-sectors seems at odds with the fact that the demand for unskilled workers relative to those with skills has fallen across virtually all sectors in many advanced industrialised countries.

Different approaches

It therefore seems that the strict application of the standard HOS and Stolper–Samuelson theories omits the intricacies of the ways firms and industries in advanced economies adjust to increased competition from low-wage countries. In particular, traditional trade theories such as the HOS theorem primarily explain movements in relative wages *across* industries, whereas industrialised countries have experienced a dramatic fall in the relative wages and employment of unskilled workers *within* sectors. Therefore, the impact of globalisation appears to be more complicated than is allowed for within the confines of standard factor proportions trade theory. As a consequence, researchers started to look more carefully at how firms within sectors respond to the more intense competition provided by increased imports from low-wage countries. One explanation of how trade with low-wage countries may push down the relative wages and employment of unskilled workers *within* industries is provided by the notion of 'outsourcing' (see, for example, the seminal papers by Feenstra and Hanson, 1995 and 1996a,b). Outsourcing occurs where firms take advantage of both the low-wage costs of relatively labour abundant countries and modern production techniques – whereby the process of manufacturing a product can be broken-down, or fragmented, into a number of discrete activities – and move the low-skill-intensive parts of production abroad, but continue to carry out the high-skill-intensive activities themselves.[4] Once the low-skill activities have been performed, the goods are then imported back from the low-wage countries and either used as intermediate inputs or sold as finished goods. Hence, trade with low-wage countries via this route will shift demand away from less-skilled towards skilled workers in advanced industrialised countries, and put downward pressure on the relative wages and employment of low-skilled workers *within* industries.

Casual but direct evidence suggests that outsourcing plays a significant role in modern production. For example, Nike employs a relatively small number of persons in the US for marketing and other headquarter services, whereas far more people are employed in low-wage countries producing shoes that are sold to Nike.[5] In their case study analysis, Anderton and Schultz (1999) show that outsourcing of production to low-wage countries is quite common in the medical equipment industry in both Germany and the UK and involves *finished* goods as well as *intermediate* inputs.[6]

So, theory and case study evidence support the notion that outsourcing may have played a substantial part in the wage and employment prospects of unskilled workers in industrial countries. Is this substantiated by statistical evidence across a range of industries in different countries? Early pioneering work by Feenstra and Hanson (1995 and 1996a,b) used US industry import shares as a proxy for outsourcing in the US. Although they found that the growth of imports explained a notable part of the increase in inequality in the US, Feenstra and Hanson proxied outsourcing by US imports from *all* countries, which implicitly captures the outsourcing of production activities to high- as well as low-wage countries. However, there is no obvious reason why firms would outsource *low-skill-intensive* activities – which is the key mechanism by which outsourcing may affect the demand for the less-skilled – to advanced industrialised countries which are relatively abundant in skilled labour.

By contrast, papers such as Anderton and Brenton (1999b,c) and Anderton *et al.* (2002) explicitly identify imports *solely from low-wage countries* and use this as a variable for explaining changes in the relative wages and employment of the low-skilled, and thereby more accurately proxy outsourcing to low-wage countries. Using these more accurate measures, the impact of trade on inequality becomes clearer and is more pronounced.[7] These papers also show that it is important to disaggregate the analysis by industry as outsourcing might be more pervasive in some industries than in others. For example, the scope for outsourcing partly depends on the degree to which production of the final good can be fragmented into discrete stages which embody substantially different factor intensity ratios. This, in turn, will be determined by technological conditions in the industry in question. Hence, whether outsourcing is more prevalent in high or low-skill-intensive sectors is an empirical question.[8]

More recent papers also demonstrate that using appropriate empirical definitions of outsourcing can have an important bearing on the significance and magnitude of outsourcing on inequality. For example, Hijzen *et al.* (2004) proxy UK international outsourcing by imports of intermediates using detailed data from input–output tables for fifty manufacturing industries. This measure shows that international outsourcing has had a strong negative impact on the demand for unskilled labour in the UK over the period 1982–1996. Strauss-Kahn (2003) also uses input–output tables, but constructs a measure of vertical specialisation – defined as the share of imported inputs in production – and investigates its impact on labour demand in France. Her estimates show that vertical specialisation contributed 11 to 15 per cent of the decline in the share of unskilled workers in

French manufacturing employment for the 1977–1985 period and for 25 per cent of the decline during 1985–1993.

In summary, the incentives and the potential to outsource may be greater in either high or low technology/skill sectors, and will depend upon a variety of factors which may differ between countries. It follows that outsourcing and its impact may be quite different across countries, particularly if their labour markets are fundamentally different. One would expect adjustment to increased competition from low-wage countries to occur mainly via changes in the relative wages of the less-skilled in the flexible labour markets of the US and UK, while relative employment is more likely to be affected in the more rigid labour markets of continental Europe.

The contribution of this book

The key message from the earlier analysis is that assessing the impacts of trade and technology on inequality requires flexibility and diversity in terms of the theoretical and empirical approaches used. This is where the motivation for this book becomes clear as the individual chapters make a valuable contribution to research on this issue as they continue the evolution of ideas, methodologies and data applied to this question. They apply a wide variety of economic methodologies – ranging from econometrics, general equilibrium models and case studies – across a broad range of countries in order to answer the above questions on the 'globalisation–trade–technology–inequality' debate. By analysing the wage and employment experiences of less-skilled workers across different countries and industries, the book not only attempts to improve our knowledge of the mechanisms by which globalisation and technology might cause inequality, but also seriously contributes to our understanding of how policy-makers might help industries and less-skilled workers to successfully adjust to globalisation and new technology.

The individual chapters constitute a very detailed analysis using, for example, highly disaggregated bilateral trade data combined with detailed industry-level data. This allows distinctions to be made which are important from a theoretical viewpoint, such as distinguishing between, say, high and low-wage country import suppliers, or between skilled-intensive and unskilled-intensive industries. In addition, case studies are undertaken whereby information gained from, for example, visits to manufacturing plants provide detailed information on the impact of technology and globalisation at the firm-level.

In Chapter 2, Anderton and Oscarsson investigate the reasons behind the increase in inequality between skilled and less-skilled workers in the US by assessing the impact of imports and technological change on the wage bill and employment shares of skilled workers. Using highly disaggregated bilateral trade data, which allows the crucial distinction between imports from high- and low-wage countries at a highly detailed industry level, the authors' econometric results show that rising imports from low-wage countries seem to explain a significant part of the rise in US inequality in low-skill-intensive sectors, while technological change (proxied by R&D expenditure) explains the rise in inequality in high-skill-intensive sectors. The authors also find that the technology-based explanation for rising inequality in high-skill sectors is actually partly a trade-based explanation due to mechanisms such as 'defensive innovation'.[9]

In Chapter 3, Ana Rute Cardoso adopts a less traditional approach by econometrically analysing the impact of trade and technology on the job creation and job destruction of skilled and unskilled workers in Portugal during the 1980s and 1990s. Several variables explaining job flows are included in the econometric specification, namely: competitive conditions in international product markets (proxied by industry import and export prices), technological conditions (proxied by the share of computer related professionals in the industry) and firm attributes that can capture institutional factors, such as the type of ownership of the company, its age, size and location. The results show that technology indicators seem more relevant determinants of job flows than competitive conditions in international product markets. Indeed, firms in technologically more advanced industries have expanded job opportunities for the skilled labour force (as job creation took place at a faster pace than job destruction), while the net employment of unskilled workers in these sectors remained unchanged. Regarding the impact of international trade, import prices are found to have no impact on job creation or job destruction for the unskilled or on job creation for the skilled. Consequently, there is no evidence of the much discussed possible impact of falling import prices on the jobs of the less skilled in Portugal. By contrast, rising export prices for Portugal – pointing to an increase in the quality of Portuguese exports – have been associated with an increase in the relative employment of skilled workers as rates of job creation have been significantly greater than job destruction for skilled workers (with job creation offset by job destruction for the unskilled). Accordingly, the results therefore point to an economy slowly increasing its specialisation in skilled labour-intensive activities in response to developments in Portuguese trade.

Ludo Cuyvers, Michel Dumont and Glenn Rayp, in Chapter 4, investigate the impact of trade with low-wage countries on the wages and employment of various EU countries. The authors' econometric approach assesses the impact of trade on European wages using a panel econometric approach based on data for 10 countries, 12 sectors (ISIC two-digit level) and 12 years (1985–1996). The results show that only at lower levels of statistical significance does international trade seem to have influenced income inequality among workers, particularly with respect to trade *vis-à-vis* Asia. By contrast, a Generalised Leontief cost function approach revealed more convincing evidence of a significant influence of international trade on employment demand. For virtually all EU countries, the import competition elasticity of low-wage countries with respect to labor demand is statistically significant and negative. However, the effect of technological change on labour demand is found to be greater than the trade impact, implying that technological innovation matters more for employment than the globalisation of trade.

Yet another informative methodology is applied in Chapter 5 where Lisandro Abrego and John Whalley assess the possible impacts of trade and technology on labour market inequality using Calibrated General Equilibrium (CGE) models.

They argue that the exploration of the outcomes of alternative structural models within a CGE framework, rather than reduced form econometrics based models, may be the best way forward to sort out trade and technology effects on wage dispersion. They find that in a differentiated-goods CGE model with perfectly competitive labour markets, increased wage inequality is basically the result of technological change, with trade playing a more limited role. By contrast, incorporating labour market imperfections into the model for unskilled labour significantly changes this result, increasing the relative contribution of trade.

The next three chapters are based on case studies of selected industries carried out using various methodologies. Chapter 6 (by Paul Brenton, Anna Maria Pinna and Mark Vancauteren) is a very detailed study of the footwear industry and assesses how producers in a selection of EU countries have adjusted to increased competition from low-wage countries. In the standard HOS model, globalisation should lead to a reallocation of resources in OECD countries from low-skill-intensive (i.e. import competing) industries to skill-intensive sectors in which these countries have a comparative advantage. However, for many unskilled intensive sectors such as footwear, the ratio of exports to output has increased in line with the import penetration ratio, while in the standard HOS model countries either import or export products, not both. Hence, even in low-skill-intensive sectors product differentiation exists, which provides another means of adjustment to globalisation not possible within the standard model (i.e. the within sector adjustment to produce different and higher quality products). Second, there appears to be a range of experience across countries in the evolution of low-skill-intensive sectors. In a number of OECD countries some of these sectors have maintained employment and output whilst in other countries production has declined dramatically. If the trade shock from globalisation is common across countries then this suggests that a variety of responses to globalisation are available to firms in OECD countries. Brenton *et al.*'s case studies of the low-skill-intensive footwear industry provide many illustrations of these various mechanisms across a number of European countries.

Markus Diehl in Chapter 7 analyses international trade statistics and input–output tables in order to assess whether international transactions in intermediate inputs in the automobile industry, and mechanisms such as outsourcing, have become more important over time. Detailed results are presented in case studies of four major producers – the US, Japan, Germany and the UK – which show that the share of imported inputs in the gross output value of the motor vehicle industry has grown significantly over the past two decades. Moreover, some low-wage countries have become important exporters of automobile parts, but this trade is regional rather than global. However, Diehl concludes that these developments in the automobile industry and its subsectors are linked to changes in the relative wages of low-skilled workers in this sector.

In Chapter 8, Valerie Jarvis examines the degree of outsourcing and its relation to output quality in the British and German ceramic tableware industries and provides original insights into how technology and trade with low-wage countries affect both production and labour requirements at the firm-level. In contrast to the data-based analyses of the earlier case studies, this study entailed *on-site visits* to more than twenty tableware manufacturers across the two countries involving semi-structured interviews with factory owners, production managers and directors. Significant cross-country differences were found in the ways in which firms typically use technology and low-wage foreign suppliers to supplement their in-house production. Among the larger German firms, the preferred method tended to be the full production of finished products in German-owned (or part-owned) and technician-supervised factories located in low-wage countries. By contrast, the larger British firms tend to buy-in finished items from low-wage country suppliers, to be simply repackaged and marketed alongside domestic output. For many German firms, outsourcing beyond the German border involved sub-contracting the less-skilled labour-intensive elements of decoration activities to specialist lower-cost facilities of the nearby Czech Republic and Poland. In Britain, the lack of availability of a conveniently located supply of lower-cost labour for partial processing has led to an increased reliance on technological innovation, where applicable, as a means of reducing labour costs in the labour-intensive activities. Jarvis finds a somewhat smaller price advantage among low-wage country producers relative to those German and British producers in the *lower-quality grades* of production (with larger price differentials existing in the higher-quality grades), suggestive of a greater impact of competition from low-wage countries in lower quality product markets.

But the responses of tableware manufacturing firms operating in Britain and Germany to this increased competition have been notably different – and perhaps of differing long-term viability. In Britain, the producer's response has been largely one of seeking to *confront head-on* the impact of greater price competition, either through removal of many of the costly labour-intensive processes by means of increased investment in new technologies or the direct importation of low-wage country-produced output for marketing alongside domestically manufactured ranges. The response of the average German producer in this industry has been to seek to *move away* from direct price competition by seeking to produce a higher-quality product, and to accentuate the quality differences of German-made output in the eyes of the consumer. Both tendencies imply a considerable – and continuing – decline in demand for lower-skilled labour in both Germany and Britain. In summary, this chapter tends to support the notion that the HOS theorem is too restrictive for real world complexities. In particular, it is difficult to define industries as unskilled-intensive as this example shows that even at the individual product-level production is differentiated into high- and low-skill-intensive segments. Furthermore, this level of detail helps us to understand how different firms react differently to globalisation, leading to possibly different policy responses.

What are the appropriate policy responses if globalisation is a significant cause of the deterioration in the economic fortunes of the less-skilled? This is the central question of Chapter 9 in which Paul Brenton argues that anti-globalisation measures such as trade barriers and restrictions on long-term capital flows are inappropriate responses to the problems of inequality and social exclusion.

The reason is that trade and capital movements bring substantial economic benefits – hence income redistribution policies which preserve the gains from trade are better suited to addressing the problem of rising inequality. Accordingly, intervention that constrains trade will be one of the least effective mechanisms in combating inequality as such policies will reduce economic welfare. Brenton also argues that poor labour standards in developing countries are not a relevant policy issue in the debate on inequality: first, the impact of low labour standards in developing countries on workers in industrial countries is marginal; second, the effective international implementation of core labour standards will not undermine the ability of developing countries to compete on the world market; and third, it is unlikely that increased global competition will lead to the downward convergence of labour standards.

Although the overall conclusion arising from this volume is that technological progress seems to be the main factor explaining the decline in the relative demand for less-skilled workers, the majority of chapters find that trade has also played an important role in the deterioration in the economic fortunes of the less-skilled over the 1980s and mid-to-late-1990s. Furthermore, many of the studies either find that the rise in technological change has been partly driven by rapid rises in international trade and globalisation (e.g. 'defensive innovation'), or that producers have simply moved into the production of higher-quality products in order to escape direct trade competition with low-wage countries. Accordingly, the technology-based explanation for rising inequality is, on closer analysis, frequently partly a trade-based explanation, making it difficult to assess their individual contributions to the growth in labour market inequality.

Acknowledgement

The research in the majority of the chapters in this volume has been carried out as part of the TSER project on 'Globalisation and Social Exclusion'. Financial support from the European Commission is gratefully acknowledged. The views expressed in this chapter are the authors and do not necessarily reflect those held by the European Central Bank.

Notes

1 See, for example: Wood (1994); the Summer 1995 and Spring 1997 issues of the *Journal of Economic Perspectives*; Feenstra (1999); Dewatripont *et al.* (1999); Brenton and Pelkmans (1999); Greenaway and Nelson (2000); *Review of International Economics*, 8 (3) (2000); Feenstra (2001); Choi and Greenaway (2001).
2 See Sachs and Schatz (1996) who look at developments across industries in the context of traditional trade theories using the HOS model incorporating the Stolper–Samuelson theorem.
3 Sachs and Schatz (1994) argue that the trend in the price of computers explains the decline in the relative price of skill-intensive products in the US. However, even when the impact of computer prices are taken out, there is no clear relationship between changing prices and skill intensity in the US.

4 'Moving the low-skill-intensive parts of production abroad' does not necessarily mean that the firm is involved in outward FDI, it can also mean that the low-skill parts of production are closed down and replaced by imports – of either intermediate or finished goods – from low-wage countries.

5 Outsourcing is documented as a feature of many industries such as: footwear (Yoffie and Gomes-Casseres, 1994); textiles (Waldinger, 1986; Gerefii, 1993); and electronics (Alic and Harris, 1991).

6 For example, the domestic production by some UK firms of simple surgical instruments is frequently supplemented by importing *finished* products from low-wage countries and reselling them on the domestic market after carrying out simple tasks such as quality control procedures and packaging. Some of the price differentials in this sector are extremely large: for example, simple scalpels sold by UK firms for £25 can be purchased from Pakistani companies for £1. Hence the price incentives to outsource can be substantial.

7 Anderton and Brenton (1999) estimate that outsourcing may account for around 40 per cent of the rise in the wage-bill share of skilled workers and approximately one-third of the increase in their employment share in the UK textiles sector. Meanwhile, Anderton *et al.* (2002) find that outsourcing to low-wage countries accounted for around 25 per cent of the average sectoral increase in the wage share of skilled workers in Sweden and for around 15 per cent of the increase in the employment share.

8 For a strong theoretical treatment of how various shocks may affect the degree of outsourcing see Kohler (2004).

9 Other relationships between trade and innovation are described in Glass and Saggi (2001). For example, they claim that outsourcing to low-wage countries can lower the marginal cost of production and thus increase profits, thereby creating greater opportunities for innovation.

2 Inequality, trade and defensive innovation in the United States

Robert Anderton and Eva Oscarsson

Introduction

The United States experienced a considerable increase in inequality during the 1980s, with the major increase in inequality occurring *within*, rather than *across*, industries.[1] Although several studies have investigated the possible causes of this decline in the relative economic fortunes of the less-skilled in the United States their conclusions differ quite considerably. For example: Feenstra and Hanson (1995 and 1996a,b) claim that increased imports explain much of the rise in US inequality; Machin and Van Reenen (1998) find that the main cause is skill-biased technological change; and Haskel and Slaughter (1997) argue that it is the *sectoral* bias of skill-biased technological change that matters.

This chapter contributes to this debate by focussing on the relationship between US labour market inequality, US imports and technological innovation, and also investigates whether trade also influences technological change via 'defensive innovation'. In contrast to most previous studies – which investigate the impact of US imports on inequality but do not distinguish between import suppliers – we examine whether the impact of imports from high-wage industrialised countries differs from that of imports from low-wage countries.

The section on Movements in US inequality of the chapter looks at aggregate movements in US inequality. The section on Trade, technology and inequality within high- and low-skill-intensive sectors, describes developments in trade and technology indicators for three industry groups – representing high- and low-tech sectors – while the section on Econometric results econometrically estimates the extent to which these factors explain the trends in US inequality. This is followed by a discussion of what drives technological innovation (proxied by R&D investment expenditure) and, in particular, empirically investigates whether import competition has any impact on innovation. Finally, the chapter summarises our results and suggests issues for further work.

Movements in US inequality

It is now widely held that the main cause of the decline in the economic fortunes of the less-skilled seems to be a shift in demand towards higher skilled workers.[2]

Two main explanations are frequently offered for such a demand shift: first, that labour-saving technical progress has reduced the relative demand for less-skilled workers; second, that increased international trade with Low-Wage Countries (LWCs) – that is, nations with an abundant supply of low-skill and low-wage labour – has decreased the demand for low-skilled workers in the advanced industrialised countries. These impacts from trade may come about via Stolper-Samuelson effects or by mechanisms such as 'outsourcing'.[3] Regarding the impact of innovation, there are various routes by which skill-biased technical progress may reduce the relative wages and employment of the less-skilled. For example, technical progress which is biased towards reducing the use of unskilled labour will tend to increase the share of skilled, relative to unskilled, labour in production. Such falls in the relative demand for unskilled workers – regardless of whether the cause is trade or technology – will tend to push down their wages and employment relative to the skilled. Using non-production workers as a proxy for higher-skilled labour, and production workers to represent the less-skilled, Figure 2.1 shows the wage and employment shares for skilled workers within US manufacturing from the early 1970s to the mid-1990s.

As indicated by Figure 2.1, the increase in US inequality has not occurred at a constant rate. This was highlighted by Feenstra and Hanson (1996a,b) who pointed out that there was a particulary large increase in inequality in the United States in the *early* 1980s. Given that this period corresponds with a recession in the United States, the behaviour of the wage share is not surprising as the relative demand for non-production workers is generally countercyclical. However, two questions remain: why was the change in the wage share so abnormally large in the early 1980s; and why did it not return to its previous level after the recession?

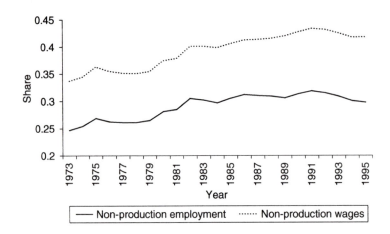

Figure 2.1 Wage and employment shares for non-production workers in the US.

Source: US Census of Manufactures and Annual Surveys.

Notes
Wage bill of non-production workers divided by total wage bill for manufacturing sector. Employment of non-production workers divided by total employment.

The trade-based explanation of inequality may offer some explanation. For example, the hysteresis-type behaviour of the wage and employment shares of non-production workers corresponds to a period when the US dollar temporarily appreciated by around 40 per cent which, in turn, corresponds to a period of possible hysteresis in trade performance.[4] Baldwin (1988) and others argue that the high level of the dollar during the early 1980s caused a surge in US imports, and a fall in US import prices (in dollars), neither of which were reversed when the dollar depreciated back to its previous level from 1986 onwards.

Table 2.1 shows values at key points in time for the wage and employment shares of US non-production workers, total import penetration and R&D expenditure as a percentage of GDP.[5] The latter variable shown as R&D is frequently used in inequality analysis as a proxy for technological change and its behaviour over time lies behind many of the claims that technology has caused an increase in inequality in a number of countries.[6] The table clearly shows that the *major* rise in US inequality – proxied by the wage and employment share of non-production workers – occurred between 1978 and 1986 and roughly corresponds with the period of the appreciation of the dollar. Similarly, US import penetration rose at a more rapid rate during this period, but carried on rising – albeit at a much slower pace – even though the dollar depreciated by around 40 per cent from 1986 onwards (which is consistent with hysteresis-type behaviour).

However, R&D expenditure (as a percentage of GDP) also follows a similar profile. It seems that technological change accelerated extremely rapidly during the early 1980s and then slowed down somewhat from the mid-1980s onwards, but R&D expenditure then remained at a significantly higher level relative to the previous decade (which is again consistent with hysteresis-type behaviour). The increase in both R&D expenditure and import penetration ratios in the early 1980s are shown in Figure 2.2. US Imports are also broken down into imports from high-wage countries (OECD) and low-wage countries (non-OECD).

Table 2.1 US non-production workers' wage and employment shares, import penetration and R&D[a]

Year	Non-production wage share[b]	Non-production employment share[c]	Import penetration[d]	R&D/Output ratio[e]
1974	34.5	25.4	5.8	2.19
1978	35.1	26.1	8.0	2.13
1986	41.3	31.2	12.2	3.51
1993	42.5	30.9	13.9	2.94

Notes
a All figures are in percentages.
b Wage bill of non-production workers divided by total wage bill for manufacturing sector.
c Employment of non-production workers divided by total employment.
d Imports divided by US imports plus domestic production of manufactures.
e R&D expenditure in manufacturing divided by manufacturing output.

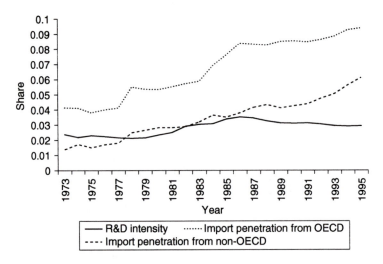

Figure 2.2 R&D and import penetration in the US.

Source: OECD ANBERD database and OECD trade database.

Notes
Imports divided by US imports plus domestic production of manufactures. R&D expenditure in manufacturing divided by manufacturing output.

What can we conclude from Table 2.1, Figures 2.1 and 2.2? If our choice of explanations for the rise in US inequality is only between trade or technology then the above evidence seems to suggest that there is more support for the trade-based explanation than suggested by previous studies. This is not only because import penetration increased when inequality increased but also because the rise in the dollar, and the associated deterioration in the trade competitiveness of US industry, may explain the rapid rise in R&D expenditure via various mechanisms. For example, less-competitive firms – most likely comprising low-tech companies offering low quality products, perhaps associated with minimal R&D spending and a high proportion of low-skilled workers in their labour force – would be squeezed out of business (as the dollar appreciation made US imports much cheaper). These possible *compositional* effects imply that, after a considerable 'shake-out' brought about by the dollar appreciation, US industry would subsequently consist of a higher proportion of high-tech firms and the average R&D–output ratio would therefore rise (and be associated with a higher proportion of high-skilled workers if the technology is skill-biased). In addition, the deterioration in competitiveness may have encouraged US manufacturers to '*innovate defensively*', that is, faced with strong competition from low-cost imports, firms may attempt to escape fierce import price competition by upgrading the quality of their manufactures via 'product innovation' which, in turn, is achieved by spending more on R&D.[7]

Trade, technology and inequality within high- and low-skill-intensive sectors

Traditional trade theories can help explain movements in relative wages *across* industries, whereas what needs to be explained is the dramatic fall in the economic fortunes of less-skilled workers *within* US sectors. One possible mechanism which may explain how trade with low-wage countries may have caused increased inequality within US sectors is 'outsourcing'. 'Outsourcing' is where firms take advantage of both the low-wage costs of the LWCs and modern production techniques – where the process of manufacturing a product can be broken-down into numerous discrete activities – by moving the low-skill-intensive parts of production abroad to the LWCs but continue to carry out the high-skill-intensive activities themselves. Once the low-skill activities have been performed the goods are then imported back from the LWCs and either used as intermediate inputs or sold as finished goods. Hence, trade with the LWCs via this route will shift demand away from less-skilled towards skilled workers in countries such as the United States, and put downward pressure on the relative wages and employment of low-skilled workers *within* industries. 'Outsourcing' is claimed to be an important activity in industries such as footwear (Yoffie and Gomes-Casseres, 1994, case 7) and textiles (Waldinger 1986; Gereffi 1993), etc. The above articles also illustrate that outsourcing applies to *finished* goods as well as *intermediate* inputs.

Orcutt (1950) may provide one explanation for a possible link between exchange rate movements and 'outsourcing'. Orcutt argues that the *costs of switching* from domestic to foreign suppliers may cause the price elasticity of imports to be bigger for large price changes than for small changes and a similar argument can be made for disproportionately large increases in 'outsourcing'. For example, when considering whether or not to 'outsource', US producers have to take into account the costs incurred when switching from in-house, or other domestic, supplies to foreign suppliers. For instance, when switching to foreign suppliers US producers may have to modify production techniques to be compatible with the newly imported products and spend time ensuring that the new supplier is both reliable and makes a product of the required specifications and quality. Consequently, small changes in the price of foreign goods will not be acted upon as the change in price differential will not cover switching costs. In contrast, a large appreciation of the dollar could result in a substantial differential between the costs of producing 'in-house' (or domestic) goods and imports – which may be at least sufficient to cover the costs of switching. In summary, *switching costs* may cause a *disproportionate* increase in 'outsourcing' during *large* exchange rate appreciations, which may partially explain the 'lumpiness' of changes in the economic circumstances of the less-skilled in the United States. Furthermore, such increases in 'outsourcing' may be difficult to reverse, even if the large appreciation of the dollar is fully reversed, since US manufacturers now have a greater understanding of the benefits of 'outsourcing' and are now familiar with the quality of goods not previously imported. Consequently, the substantial *temporary* appreciation of the dollar may have encouraged US purchasers to *permanently* switch from domestic to foreign goods (which may suggest a disproportionate increase in 'outsourcing' at a time when the economic fortunes of the less-skilled in the US deteriorated very rapidly).

Our method for investigating the causes of US inequality is to econometrically estimate the impact of trade with LWCs on the wages and employment of the less-skilled by using a proxy variable for 'outsourcing' similar to Feenstra and Hanson (1996a,b). Feenstra and Hanson (1996a,b) proxy 'outsourcing' by US imports from *all* countries, which implicitly captures 'outsourcing' of US production to advanced industrialised countries as well as LWCs. However, there is no obvious reason why firms would 'outsource' *low-skill-intensive* activities – which is the mechanism by which 'outsourcing' affects the demand for the less-skilled – to advanced industrialised countries which are relatively abundant in skilled labour. Consequently, a major objective of this chapter is to investigate whether the *source* of imports matters by disaggregating US imports according to individual supplier countries and constructing US import share terms for both high and low-wage countries. Therefore, by explicitly identifying imports solely from *low-wage countries* and using this as a variable to explain changes in the wage share of the less-skilled in the US, we are more likely to accurately capture 'outsourcing' to low-wage countries.

In previous work on the United Kingdom, Anderton and Brenton (1999b) find that the impact of trade with LWCs differs considerably between high and low-skill-intensive sectors. Hence in the following analysis we distinguish between groups of industries which we classify as intrinsically high- or low-skill. In Table 2.2 we look at two groups of industries which can be classed as low-skill-intensive (abbreviated as LSA and LSB) and one group of high-skill-intensive sectors (HS). The first part of Table 2.2 shows that the largest rise in US inequality occurred in all three sectors during the period of substantial dollar appreciation, but that inequality continued to increase, albeit more gradually, through the rest of the 1980s and early 1990s.[8]

The last three columns of Table 2.2 show that R&D expenditure expressed as a proportion of output is extremely small in the low-skill sectors (less than 1 per cent in LSA and LSB). Given that the R&D ratios in the low-skill sectors are very small (seemingly confirming that these are indeed low-technology-intensive industries), it becomes doubtful as to whether it is feasible that movements in R&D expenditure/technology can explain the change in the wage share of non-production workers in these sectors. On the other hand, the technology explanation corresponds to movements in R&D expenditure in the high-skill sectors, particularly the large rise in R&D during the period of the dollar appreciation in the early1980s. In addition, unlike the low-skill sectors, it seems feasible that the large absolute size of R&D expenditure in the high-skill sectors, combined with the significant changes in R&D over time, could have a strong impact on labour-skill requirements in these sectors.

Table 2.2 also shows US imports from LWCs as a proportion of total sectoral imports. Although the relationship between the import share of LWCs in the

Table 2.2 US wage bill share and employment share of non-production workers, import share of low-wage countries (LWCs) and R&D in low- and high-skill-intensive sectors[a]

Year	Wage bill share			Employment share		
	LSA[b]	*LSB*[b]	*HS*[b]	*LSA*[b]	*LSB*[b]	*HS*[b]
1974	24.8	25.8	41.2	14.6	20.3	30.9
1978	25.1	26.3	42.2	14.9	20.3	32.3
1986	27.3	30.3	49.6	17.1	23.4	38.4
1993	28.6	31.7	51.1	17.5	23.7	37.6
	Import share of LWCs[c]			R&D/output ratio		
	LSA[b]	*LSB*[b]	*HS*[b]	*LSA*[b]	*LSB*[b]	*HS*[b]
1974	37.7	26.1	34.9	0.45	0.48	4.24
1978	46.1	26.0	36.6	0.46	0.49	3.85
1986	58.0	30.2	35.8	0.57	0.86	5.79
1993	61.2	33.7	42.8	0.80	0.62	5.42

Notes

a All figures are in percentages.

b LSA = low-skill sector group 'A' comprising ISIC sectors 3200, 3300 and 3400 (i.e. Textiles, Apparel and Leather; Wood Products and Furniture; Paper, Paper Products and Printing). LSB = low-skill sector group 'B' comprising ISIC sectors 3600, 3700 and 3810 (i.e., Non-Metallic Mineral Products; Basic Metal Industries; Metal Products); HS = High-skill sectors comprising ISIC sectors 3500, 3820, 3830, 3850 (Chemical Products; Non-electrical Machinery; Electrical Machinery; Professional Goods).

c Sectoral imports from low-wage countries (LWCs) expressed as a percentage of total sectoral imports.

low-skill sectors and the wage and employment shares of non-production workers is unclear in the early 1970s, there is a large increase in US imports from LWCs during the period when inequality rose more rapidly and the dollar appreciated. Conversely, imports from LWCs for the high-skill sector group remained nearly static between 1978 and 1986 – perhaps indicating that defensive innovation succeeded in reducing import competition from LWCs in this sector (the relatively high import share of LWCs in this high-skill sector also suggests that the degree of low-wage country competition may be sufficient to be a plausible cause of defensive innovation).

Econometric results for the 'inequality' equations (i.e. wage and employment share equations)

In this section, we econometrically estimate the impact of both trade with LWCs and R&D spending on the wage and employment shares of non-production workers in the United States. We use highly disaggregated US wage and production data – converted from US SIC to ISIC REV2 – and define non-production workers as skilled and production workers as less-skilled (source: US Census of

Manufactures and Annual Surveys). Technological change is proxied by R&D expenditure as a proportion of GDP (source: OECD ANBERD database). The capital stock data are from the OECD's International Sectoral Database (ISDB). The bilateral US imports data were supplied by the OECD on an SITC basis and converted to the ISIC REV2 classification. Trade, production and wage bill and employment share data are all disaggregated to the 4-digit ISIC level (hence all variables are on an ISIC basis – further details of the 4-digit sectors used in the analysis are given in the data appendix). In order to provide enough observations for separate 'panel estimation' of our three sectoral groupings, we pool the data across the 4-digit ISIC sectors within the LSA, LSB and HS broad groupings using annual data for the sample period 1973–1993 (imposing, in effect, the same parameters across the different 4-digit sectors).

Following Feenstra and Hanson (1995 and 1996a,b), we seek to assess whether industry import shares have contributed significantly to the determination of the within-sector wage bill and employment shares of low-skilled workers in the United States. Following the approach of Berman *et al.* (1993, 1994), and assuming capital to be a fixed factor of production, we start from a variable cost function in translog form:

$$
\begin{aligned}
\ln C_i = {} & \alpha_0 + \alpha_y \ln Y_i + \frac{1}{2}\alpha_{YY}\ln(Y_i)^2 + \beta_K \ln K_i + \frac{1}{2}\beta_{KK}\ln(K_i)^2 \\
& + \sum_j \gamma_j \ln W_{ij} + \frac{1}{2}\sum_j\sum_k \gamma_{jk}\ln W_{ij}\ln W_{ik} + \sum_j \delta_{Yj}\ln Y_i \ln W_{ij} \\
& + \sum_j \delta_{Kj}\ln K_i \ln W_{ij} + \rho \ln Y_i \ln K_i + \lambda_T T_i + \frac{1}{2}\lambda_{TT}(T_i)^2 \\
& + \lambda_{YT}T_i \ln Y_i + \lambda_{KT}T_i \ln K_i \\
& + \sum_j \phi_{Tw_j}T_i \ln W_{ij}
\end{aligned}
\tag{2.1}
$$

where C_i is variable costs in industry i; Y_i is output in industry i; K_i is the capital stock in industry i; W_{ij} is the price of variable factor j and T_i represents technology in industry i.

Cost minimisation generates the following linear equations for the factor shares (S):

$$
S_{ij} = \gamma_j + \delta_{Yj}\ln Y_i + \delta_{Kj}\ln K_i + \sum_k \gamma_{jk}\ln W_{ik} + \phi_{Tw_j}T_i
\tag{2.2}
$$

whilst differencing (denoted by d) generates

$$
\mathrm{d}S_{ij} = \phi_{Tw_j}\mathrm{d}T_i + \delta_{Yj}\mathrm{d}\ln Y_i + \delta_{Kj}\mathrm{d}\ln K_i + \sum_k \gamma_{jk}\mathrm{d}\ln W_{ik}
\tag{2.3}
$$

assuming homogeneity of degree one in prices imposes

$$
\sum_k \gamma_{jk} = \sum_j \gamma_{jk} = \sum_j \delta_{Kj} = \sum_j \delta_{Yj} = 0
\tag{2.4}
$$

which generates with two variable factors, j and k

$$dS_{ij} = \phi_{Tw_j}dT_i + \delta_{Kj}\,d\ln K_i + \delta_{Yj}\,d\ln Y_i + \gamma\,d\ln\left(\frac{W_j}{W_k}\right) \qquad (2.5)$$

In our empirical application of the earlier model we have two variable factors of production, low-skilled (production) workers and higher-skilled (non-production) workers, and adopt a similar approach to Machin *et al.* (1996) and estimate the following US wage bill and employment share equations:

$$dSW_{it} = \alpha\,d\ln K_{it} + \beta\,d\ln Y_{it} + \rho TECH_{it} + \lambda\,d\ln MS_{it} + \gamma D_t + U_{it} \quad (2.6)$$

$$dSE_{it} = \alpha\,d\ln K_{it} + \beta\,d\ln Y_{it} + \rho TECH_{it} + \lambda\,d\ln MS_{it}$$
$$+ l\,d\ln(W^{hs}/W^{ls})_{it} + \gamma D_t + U_{it} \qquad (2.7)$$

where: SW_{it} is the share of the wage bill of the high skilled ($WB_{it}^{hs}/(WB_{it}^{hs} + WB_{it}^{ls})$), SE_{it} is the employment share of the high skilled (similarly derived as SW_{it}).

WB_{it}^{hs} is the wage bill of the higher skilled (i.e. non-production workers); WB_{it}^{ls} is the wage bill of the lower skilled (i.e. production workers); W^{hs}/W^{ls} is the relative wage rate of high and low-skilled workers; K_{it} is the capital stock; Y_{it} is real output; $TECH_{it}$ is a proxy variable for technological change (proxied by R&D); MS_{it} is the share of the value of domestic demand for the output of industry i accounted for by imports; D_t is a set of time dummies included to capture any company preferences for non-manual or manual workers common across industries for a given year; U_{it} is an error term; Subscript i represents industry i. First differences are denoted by d.

The time dummies capture any changes in firm-level preferences for non-production or production workers common across industries in each year. The MS term represents US imports and can be interpreted as a proxy for outsourcing. In this chapter, we follow the approach of Feenstra and Hanson (1995, 1996a,b) and justify the inclusion of the MS term in the wage bill share equation by arguing that merely including the factors derived from a traditional translog production function will not capture other factors – such as outsourcing – which may influence a firm's demand for skilled labour. Given that outsourcing to low-wage countries is claimed to push the range of activities performed by domestic industry away from low-skill towards high-skill tasks, the MS term can be interpreted as representing a reduced-form relationship between outsourcing and a firm's unit input requirement for skilled labour. As we want to distinguish between the impacts of high- and low-wage country import suppliers, we experiment with two different versions of MS:

1 MSO = US imports from high-wage countries (which we define as OECD countries).[9]
2 MSNO = US imports from LWCs (which we define as Non-OECD countries).

Our final wage-bill share specifications based upon (2.6) above are shown in Table 2.3 below. Note that we do not include the relative wage rates for the two types of labour in our final estimated wage bill share equations mainly because relative wages are unlikely to be exogenous. However, the equation includes a set of macro time dummies, which will capture any firm-level changes in preferences for higher-skilled workers due to absent variables such as relative wages. We estimate two equations for each industry group – the first equation uses US imports from high-wage countries (i.e. OECD countries: 'MSO') and the second uses imports from low-wage countries (i.e. non-OECD countries: 'MSNO'). The results show that the change in output is negatively signed and statistically significant (with the exception of industry group LSA) which conforms with our prior that a short-run decline in output tends to reduce the demand for the less-skilled relative to the skilled. The capital stock term is not statistically significant in any of the equations, which may not be surprising for the low-skill-intensive sectors as they are extremely low-capital-intensive industries. Although the capital stock term has the correct positive sign for the high-skill sector grouping – as we expect complementarities between capital and skill – it is not statistically significant (perhaps because it is dominated by the R&D term). One striking result is that R&D is not statistically significant for the low-skill sectors, but is strongly significant for the high-skill sectors.

The statistical significance of the MSNO terms in the LSA and LSB sectors suggests that increased trade with LWCs tends to increase the wage share of

Table 2.3 US wage bill share equations (dSW_{it})

Equation	LSA	LSA	LSB	LSB	HS	HS
C	0.016	0.0149	0.003	0.0032	0.0006	0.0007
	(2.500)	(2.427)	(0.720)	(0.669)	(0.217)	(0.252)
$d\ln Y_{it}$	−0.013	−0.014	−0.042	−0.043	−0.026	−0.025
	(−0.970)	(−1.001)	(−3.205)	(−3.362)	(−2.580)	(−2.516)
$d\ln K_{it}$	−0.045	−0.041	0.005	−0.007	0.059	0.058
	(−0.977)	(−0.869)	(0.074)	(−0.103)	(1.423)	(1.392)
$(R\&D/Y)_{it-1}$	0.118	0.129	0.008	−0.014	0.043	0.042
	(0.131)	(0.142)	(0.030)	(−0.056)	(3.118)	(3.084)
$d\ln MSO_{it}$	0.004		0.0009		−0.003	
	(1.831)		(0.222)		(−0.924)	
$d\ln MSNO_{it}$		0.003		0.0058		−0.0006
		(2.116)		(2.226)		(−0.480)
N	340	340	200	200	440	440
R^2	0.254	0.248	0.551	0.559	0.358	0.356
SEE	0.011030	0.011075	0.008620	0.008543	0.011043	0.011056

Notes

MSO = US imports from OECD countries for sector groups are expressed as a proportion of total US demand for goods produced in that sector; MSNO = US imports from non-OECD countries for sector groups are expressed as a proportion of total US demand for goods produced in that sector. OLS estimation for annual data sample period of 1974–1993 (full set of time dummies included) using White's heteroskedasticity consistent SEs; 't' statistics are in parentheses.

Table 2.4 US employment share equations (dSE$_{it}$)

Equation	LSA	LSA	LSB	LSB	HS	HS
C	0.010	0.0097	0.0044	0.0042	0.0004	0.0004
	(2.809)	(2.714)	(1.152)	(1.106)	(0.149)	(0.155)
d ln Y$_{it}$	−0.007	−0.008	−0.035	−0.037	−0.023	−0.023
	(−0.727)	(−0.748)	(−3.132)	(−3.298)	(−2.705)	(−2.725)
d ln K$_{it}$	−0.036	−0.033	−0.0004	−0.011	0.051	0.051
	(−1.113)	(−1.005)	(−0.009)	(−0.230)	(1.466)	(1.469)
(R&D/Y)$_{it-1}$	0.212	0.217	−0.004	−0.025	0.041	0.041
	(0.334)	(0.340)	(−0.021)	(−0.134)	(3.305)	(3.304)
d ln MSO$_{it}$	0.0024		0.0014		0.0001	
	(1.897)		(0.461)		(0.055)	
d ln MSNO$_{it}$		0.002		0.005		0.00005
		(2.159)		(2.350)		(−0.046)
d ln (W^{hs}/W^{ls})	−0.107	−0.106	−0.100	−0.099	−0.115	−0.115
	(−8.264)	(−8.080)	(−5.807)	(−6.060)	(−6.528)	(−6.543)
N	340	340	200	200	440	440
R^2	0.529	0.526	0.699	0.706	0.527	0.527
SEE	0.007400	0.007426	0.006554	0.006472	0.009252	0.009252

Notes

MSO = US imports from OECD countries for sector groups are expressed as a proportion of total US demand for goods produced in that sector; MSNO = US imports from non-OECD countries for sector groups are expressed as a proportion of total US demand for goods produced in that sector. OLS estimation for annual data sample period of 1974–1993 (full set of time dummies included) using White's heteroskedasticity consistent SEs; 't' statistics are in parentheses.

non-production workers in the low-skill sectors, but that technological change rather than trade partly explains the rise in US inequality in the high-skill sectors. For the LSA sector grouping, there is also some limited – but less-convincing – evidence that any increase in inequality from increased trade may also be partly due to increased imports from the higher-wage OECD countries, whereas only imports from LWCs increase inequality in the LSB sectors.[10]

Table 2.4 shows the results arising from the estimation of the employment share equation (i.e. equation (2.7)). The results support the conclusions drawn in the wage share analysis that imports from low-wage countries seem to explain part of the rise in US inequality in low-skill-intensive sectors, while technological change (proxied by R&D expenditure) explains the rise in inequality in high-skill-intensive sectors. The relative wage term is strongly significant and, as expected, negatively signed. Finally, the explanatory power of the variables in the employment equations is generally better than the wage equations, and the increase in the R^2 is especially large for the LSA sectors.

It is important to note that the above results may underestimate the impact of trade with low-wage countries on US inequality as we do not include the import *price* in our specifications (due to the lack of reliable trade price data for the United States at this level of disaggregation). Relative import price terms may capture other effects in addition to those captured by the import penetration terms such as the *threat* of increased competition from LWCs (e.g. the fall in the import price of LWC products as the dollar appreciated may have made it easier for firms to obtain agreement from their workforce to restrain the wages, or terminate the employment, of less-skilled workers, etc.).[11]

As mentioned before, previous studies such as Machin *et al.* (1996) do not find a significant impact of trade on the relative wages and employment of the less-skilled in the United States. However, unlike our analysis, they do not use trade data which separately identifies imports from low-wage countries – which is important as mechanisms such as 'outsourcing' only influence inequality via trade with low-wage countries – and their empirical work is at a more aggregate level. Although Feenstra and Hanson (1995) do find that imports have increased US inequality, they too do not distinguish between import suppliers. In contrast, we have shown that when assessing the impact of trade on inequality the source of imports matters, which is consistent with economic theory. For the United States, it seems that using aggregate imports to capture mechanisms such as outsourcing may be misleading and that disaggregation of imports in order to identify low-wage countries is necessary, particularly as the impact of trade on inequality may vary across sectors of different skill intensities.

What drives technological innovation?

Given that R&D seems to explain a large part of the rise in inequality in the high-skill sectors, we now turn our attention to investigating the factors behind the rapid rise in technological innovation, particularly as to whether trade influences technological change. Adrian Wood (1994, 1995) launched the term 'defensive innovation' meaning that some innovation may be driven by the need to stay competitive against increased low-wage competition. He argues that some firms in advanced industrialised countries may have to look for new methods of production that are unskilled labour-saving (i.e. 'process innovation' driven by import competition). As we have argued earlier, 'defensive innovation' may also mean that firms upgrade the quality of their products in order to stay competitive (i.e. 'product innovation' driven by import competition). Another relationship between trade and innovation is hypothesised by Glass and Saggi (2001). These authors argue that an increase in outsourcing to a low wage country lowers the marginal cost of production and thus increases profits, thereby creating greater incentives and/or opportunities for innovation.

Considerable empirical research has been carried out regarding the R&D investment decision of the firm (see Cohen 1989). In the standard Schumpeterian framework, firm size and market concentration are the two major explanatory variables explaining R&D at the firm level. Firm size is thought to be important as bigger firms have scale economies in the R&D function, greater access to risky financing on the capital market as well as a larger volume of sales over which they can spread the fixed costs of innovation, etc. Meanwhile, monopoly power (or market concentration) enables firms to reap profits from R&D investments and also provides a more stable environment for the firm's investment decision.

Using data at the industry level, with the objective of investigating whether trade influences technological change, we estimate a simple R&D function for the US loosely based on the specification used by Hirsch (1992) which includes a mixture of industry and firm-level variables. As optimal investment is a function of output (and thus product prices) and relative factor prices, Hirsch includes firm level data on both the physical capital stock and the R&D stock as well as firm-level profitability to take into account firm-specific differences. At the industry level, Hirsch includes the annualised growth rate in industry output, labour costs per employee, the concentration ratio and the share of imports in domestic sales.[12]

Our industry-data approximation of Hirsch's R&D function is as follows:

$$
\begin{aligned}
\mathrm{d}\ln\left(\frac{I_{it}}{\mathrm{PROD}_{it}}\right) = {} & \alpha_i + \beta_C \mathrm{d}\ln\left(\frac{\mathrm{CAP}_{it-1}}{\mathrm{RPRDV}_{it-1}}\right) \\
& + \beta_W \mathrm{d}\ln \mathrm{RWAGE}_{it-1} + \beta_{\mathrm{RP}}\,\mathrm{d}\ln \mathrm{RPRDV}_{it-2} \\
& + \beta_R \mathrm{d}\ln \mathrm{RR}_{it-1} + \beta_M \mathrm{d}\ln \mathrm{MS}_{it-1} \\
& + \Sigma\delta_m \mathrm{YEAR}_{mt} + e_{it}
\end{aligned}
\tag{2.8}
$$

where: $I_{it}/\mathrm{PROD}_{it-1}$ is R&D expenditure expressed as a proportion of production; α_i is an industry specific intercept (fixed effects); $\mathrm{CAP}_{it-1}/\mathrm{RPRDV}_{it-1}$ is the real capital stock relative to real production; RWAGE_{it-1} is the real average wage; RPRDV_{it-2} is real production; RR_{it-1} is profitability measured as price over unit labour cost; MS_{it-1} is the share of the value of domestic demand for the output of industry i accounted for by imports from low- and high-wage countries respectively; YEAR_{mt} is a set of time dummies; subscript i represents industry i; first differences are denoted by d.

The real average wage is simply total real wages divided by total employment per industry, while the profitability variable is calculated as the producer price divided by labour compensation[13]. Although the data used in the estimation of equation (2.8) are the same as in the share analysis earlier, the industries are more aggregated in this section according to the more limited sectoral breakdown of the R&D data.[14] Table 2.5 shows the results using this specification for the high-skill sectors.[15] Again, we report two sets of results in first difference form: one using import penetration from the high-wage countries and the other using import penetration from low-wage countries.

The first variable – the capital/output ratio – is expected to have a positive sign due to the assumed complementarities between capital and R&D investment. However, we found this variable to be both statistically insignificant and incorrectly signed. Meanwhile, an increasing real average wage could affect investment in R&D both negatively or positively.[16] Although, the results show that the real average wage has no significant impact on R&D investments, the negative sign is indicative of factor substitution between R&D and labour.

A growing market, or increases in real production, is positively and significantly correlated with an increasing R&D intensity, which is what we expect.

Table 2.5 US R&D investment equations (d $\ln(I_{it}/PROD_{it})$) for US high-skill sectors

Equation	HS	HS
d $\ln(CAP_{it-1}/$	−0.324	−0.231
$RPRDV_{it-1})$	(−1.348)	(−0.969)
d $\ln RWAGE_{it-1}$	−0.242	−0.249
	(−1.137)	(−1.123)
d $\ln RPRDV_{it-2}$	0.595	0.572
	(3.567)	(3.517)
d $\ln RR_{it-1}$	0.147	0.088
	(0.686)	(0.404)
d $\ln MSO_{it-1}$	0.107	
	(2.092)	
d $\ln MSNO_{it-1}$		−0.004
		(−0.101)
N	180	180
R^2	0.347	0.332
SEE	0.109926	0.111133

Notes
MSO = US imports from OECD countries (as defined in previous tables); MSNO = US imports from non-OECD countries (as defined in previous tables). OLS estimation for annual data sample period of 1973–1994 using White's heteroskedasticity consistent SEs (fixed effects and full set of time dummies included); 't' statistics are in parentheses.

Meanwhile, the effect of an increase in profitability on R&D investments can be positive or negative. On the one hand, high profits create less pressure for investing in technology in order to transform products (or the production process) in comparison to low profits. On the other hand, high profits make it easier for firms to finance investments in R&D. We find that increases in profitability, measured as price over unit labour cost, are not statistically significant but tend to have a positive sign.

Finally, the key result shown in Table 2.5 is that growing import penetration from high-wage countries has a significant positive effect on R&D investments in the US high-skill sectors, while imports from low-wage countries have no impact. Our previous analysis of the US wage and employment shares within the high-skill sectors showed that trade had no impact on skill upgrading, while technological change was important. It therefore seems that trade also has an indirect effect on skill-upgrading in the high-skill sectors when we take into account its impact on R&D investments.

In summary, we find some evidence that 'defensive innovation' seems to occur in the high-skill sectors. Although it is not driven by import competition from low-wage countries but from high-wage countries, such defensive innovation will also reduce competition from low-wage as well as high-wage countries, thereby partly explaining why imports from low-wage countries seem to have had no impact on US inequality in high-skill sectors. Again, in comparison to other studies, this result therefore places relatively more weight on the trade-based explanation for skill-upgrading than the technology-based explanation. However, more work is needed on this topic before any strong conclusions can be drawn.[17]

Conclusions

An increase in US imports from low-wage countries, helped by the large appreciation of the dollar in the early 1980s, seems to explain some of the rise in US inequality in *low-skill-intensive* sectors. Rapid technological change does not seem to be an important determinant of labour market inequality in these sectors – which is not surprising given the low technological nature of these industries. By contrast, technological change – proxied by R&D expenditure – seems to be strongly positively correlated with the rise in US inequality in our sample of *high-skill-intensive* sectors. We also tried to establish why skill-biased technological change was so rapid during the early 1980s in the US. Given that the technological change seemed to be strongly positively correlated with rising imports – associated with the deterioration in US trade competitiveness due to the appreciation of the dollar over this period – we investigated whether the two were connected by estimating some R&D expenditure equations. We found that growing import penetration from high-wage countries had a significant positive effect on R&D investments in the high-skill sectors over our sample period, while imports from low-wage countries had no impact. Meanwhile, our analysis of the wage and employment shares within US manufacturing sectors showed that trade had no impact on skill upgrading in the high-skill sectors, while technological change was important. Accordingly, it seems that trade may also have had an indirect effect on skill-upgrading in the high-skill sectors when we take into account its effects on R&D investments via 'defensive innovation'. Although it is not driven by import competition from low-wage countries but from high-wage countries, such defensive innovation will also reduce competition from low-wage as well as high-wage countries and therefore partly explains why imports from low-wage countries seem to have had no impact on US inequality in high-skill sectors. In summary, in comparison to other studies, our results place more weight on the trade-based explanation for skill-upgrading in the United States relative to the technology-based explanation. However, further work is needed before any strong conclusions can be drawn regarding the role of defensive innovation in the 'trade and wages' debate.

Data appendix: 4-digit sectors

We group together industries which we classify as high- or low-skill-intensive. In particular, we form two low-skill groups, LSA and LSB, and one high-skill grouping we call HS. LSA consists of ISIC sectors 3200, 3300 and 3400 (i.e. Textiles, Apparel and Leather; Wood Products and Furniture; Paper, Paper

Products and Printing). LSB consists of ISIC sectors 3600, 3700 and 3810 (i.e. Non-Metallic Mineral Products; Basic Metal Industries; Metal Products); HS consists of ISIC sectors 3500, 3820, 3830, 3850 (Chemical Products; Non-electrical Machinery; Electrical Machinery; Professional Goods). We pool the data across 18 4-digit ISIC sectors for LSA, across 10 4-digit ISIC sectors for LSB, and across 22 4-digit ISIC sectors for HS. Our annual sample period extends from 1973 to 1993. Given that we lose one observation because we estimate a first difference model, our estimation period 1974–1993 therefore provides us with 340 observations for LSA (i.e. 17×20); 200 observations for LSB; and 440 observations for HS. The specific 4-digit ISIC sectors used in the estimation of wage and employment shares are as follows:

LSA

ISIC3211	Spinning, weaving and finishing textiles.
ISIC3212	Manufacture of made-up textile goods, except wearing apparel.
ISIC3213	Knitting mills.
ISIC3214	Manufacture of carpet and rugs.
ISIC3215	Cordage, rope and twine industries.
ISIC3219	Manufacture of textiles not elsewhere classified.
ISIC3220	Manufacture of wearing apparel except footwear.
ISIC3231	Tanneries and leather finishing.
ISIC3233	Manufacture of prods. of leather except footwear and apparel.
ISIC3240	Manufacture of footwear except rubber or plastic.
ISIC3311	Sawmills, planting and other wood mills.
ISIC3312	Manufacture wooden, cane containers, small cane ware.
ISIC3319	Manufacture wood and cork products NEC.
ISIC3320	Manufacture of furniture, fixtures except primary metal.
ISIC3411	Manufacture of pulp, paper and paperboard.
ISIC3412	Manufacture of containers and boxes of paper, paperboard.
ISIC3419	Manufacture of articles of pulp, paper and paperboard NEC.

LSB

ISIC3610	Pottery, china and earthware.
ISIC3620	Glass and glass products.
ISIC3691	Structural clay products.
ISIC3692	Cement, lime and plaster.
ISIC3699	Non-metallic mineral products, NEC.
ISIC3710	Iron and steel basic industries.
ISIC3720	Non-ferrous metal basic industries.
ISIC3811	Cutlery, hand-tools and general hardware.
ISIC3812	Furniture and fixtures primarily of metal.
ISIC3819	Fabricated metal prods. except mach. and equip. NEC.

HS

ISIC3511   Basic industrial chemicals.
ISIC3512   Fertilisers and pesticides.
ISIC3513   Syn. resins, plastic mat., man-made fibres exc. glass.
ISIC3521   Paints, varnishes and lacquers.
ISIC3522   Drugs and medicines.
ISIC3523   Soap, cleansing preparations, perfumes cosmetics.
ISIC3529   Chemical products, NEC.
ISIC3530   Petroleum refineries.
ISIC3540   Misc. prods. of petroleum and coal.
ISIC3551   Tire and tube industries.
ISIC3559   Manufacture of rubber products, NEC.
ISIC3560   Plastic products, NEC.
ISIC3824   Manufacture of special industrial mach. and equip. except 3823.
ISIC3825   Office, computing and accounting machinery.
ISIC3829   Machinery and equipment except electrical not elsewhere classified.
ISIC3831   Electrical indust. mach. and apparatus.
ISIC3832   Radio, telecomm. equip. and apparatus.
ISIC3833   Electrical appliances and housewares.
ISIC3839   Electrical apparatus and supplies.
ISIC3851   Prof. scientific and control equip.
ISIC3852   Photographic and optical goods.
ISIC3853   Watches and clocks.

Acknowledgement

This research has been performed as part of the TSER project on 'Globalisation and Social Exclusion'. Financial support from the European Commission is gratefully acknowledged. Oscarsson has also been supported by the Swedish Foundation for International Cooperation in Research in Higher Education. All views expressed in this chapter are the authors and do not necessarily reflect those held by the European Central Bank or the Swedish Ministry of Finance.

Notes

1 We define a rise in inequality as a deterioration in the relative wages and/or employment of the less-skilled.
2 For summaries and collections of papers on the causes of inequality see, for example: the Summer 1995 and Spring 1997 issues of the *Journal of Economic Perspectives; Oxford Review of Economic Policy*, 16 (3) (Special Issue on 'Globalisation and Labour Market Adjustment' edited by David Greenaway and Douglas Nelson); and the *Journal of International Economics*, 50 (1) and 54 (1).
3 Anderton and Brenton (1999a,b) describe both of these trade mechanisms in detail.
4 'Hysteresis' denotes the situation where a *temporary* shock results in *permanent* effects.
5 The years 1974 and 1993 correspond to the beginning and end of our sample period, whereas 1978 and 1986 roughly correspond to dates before and after the dollar appreciation.

6 However, some papers use different proxies for technology (e.g. Haskel, 1996a,b find that increased computer usage can explain the rise in UK inequality).

7 The experience of the United Kingdom during this period is very similar to that of the United States. Between 1979 and 1981, sterling temporarily appreciated by around 30 per cent and was associated with a rise in the UK manufacturing R&D/output ratio from around 1.5 to 2 per cent which remained higher even when the appreciation was subsequently reversed.

8 The higher wage bill share for non-production workers in the HS sectors relative to the other sectors is consistent with our claim that the former sectors are relatively high-skill-intensive. Also note that the sum of the sectors does not add up to the aggregate wage share in Table 2.1 as not all sectors are included in Table 2.2.

9 The OECD countries are defined as those members up to and including 1993 (i.e. excluding later members such as the Czech Republic, Hungary, Poland, South Korea and, probably most importantly, Mexico).

10 However, note that only imports from the LWCs are actually statistically significant at the 5 per cent level of significance for the LSA sector grouping.

11 A relative import price term may also capture the increased opportunities for decreasing labour costs via outsourcing.

12 As the Hirsch study focuses on the effects of collective bargaining on investment activity, it also includes firm dummies indicating the degree of unionisation as well as a variable for union density per industry.

13 Source: OECD STAN database.

14 In this section, the HS sector includes ISIC 3520–3522, 3522, 353 + 354, 355 + 356, 3820–3825, 3825, 3830–3832, 3832, 3845 and 385. The LSB sector covers ISIC 31, 36, 371, 372, 381, 3842 + 3844 and 39. The LSA sector includes ISIC 32, 33, 34 and 3843.

15 We only show the results for the high-skill sectors for two main reasons: first, the R&D equations for the low-skill sectors had poor explanatory power and most of the variables were not statistically significant; second, explaining R&D movements in the high-skill sectors is our main task as, according to our earlier results, it is only in this sector where technology (proxied by R&D) has a significant impact on inequality.

16 Although rising labour costs mean that less money is available for investment, increased labour costs may make the industry less competitive and induce R&D investments aimed at decreasing the need for labour (i.e. factor substitution).

17 The approach we use is designed for firm-level data which makes it somewhat difficult to apply on industry data. A second limitation is that we lack information on two major explanatory variables: firm size and market concentration. Accordingly, in our specification, industry differences in these two variables are picked up by the fixed effects.

3   The impact of increased openness on job creation and job destruction in Portugal

Ana Rute Cardoso

Introduction

Portugal joined the European Community in 1986, setting the stage for increased trade links with its member countries. Indeed, by the end of the 1990s, close to 80 percent of Portuguese imports came from the European Union, while the share of exports was even higher. Also, a few years after accession a boom in foreign direct investment took place.

What has been the impact of this growing openness on the employment prospects for workers with contrasting skill levels? Portugal presented during the 1980s and 1990s one of the lowest unemployment rates in the European Union. By the end of the 1990s, it reached 5 percent, a fact that is more puzzling if one keeps in mind the concentration of the country's labor force in the lowest skill ranks. In fact, compared to the rest of the European Union, Portugal is an economy relatively abundant in low-skilled labor. It could therefore be argued that increased openness toward more developed economies was a major factor rescuing the jobs of low-skilled workers. According to trade theory, growing trade with more developed economies leads a country into specializing in products intensive in low skills, raising the demand for that category of workers and their relative wages.

The aim of this chapter is to check whether increased openness could have contributed to sustain the employment of low-skilled workers in the Portuguese economy. This reasoning would be consistent with that by Marimon and Zilibotti (1998), who argued that Portugal increased its specialization in traditional industries and kept its labor costs low, as opposed to Spain, having therefore managed to keep a low unemployment rate.

The analysis focuses on the yearly dynamics of job creation and job destruction at the firm level, from 1985 to 1998. It distinguishes between skilled and unskilled workers, using a longitudinal data set that matches firms and workers. The role of international trade deserves particular attention when searching for the determinants of job flows by skill level.

The section on Trade and the labor market in Portugal overviews changes in Portuguese trade and its labor market, and the section on Job flows and their determinants briefly describes the data used. Job creation, job destruction and the role of growing openness are discussed in the final section, before concluding comments are presented.

Trade and the labor market in Portugal: an overview of recent trends

Portugal has traditionally been an open economy, since it has been a founding member of the European Free Trade Association (EFTA) (Figure 3.1). After joining the European Community, the relevance of its member countries, in particular Spain, as Portuguese trading partners increased (Figure 3.2), with the trade share of the new industrialized countries declining. Increased openness in these terms could have resulted in rising demand for workers with low skills, raising their relative wages.

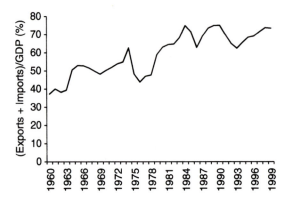

Figure 3.1 Openness of the Portuguese economy, 1960–1999.

Source: Commission Européenne, 1998.

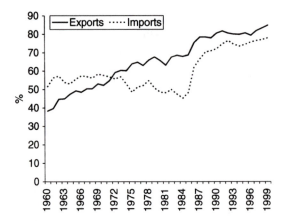

Figure 3.2 Share of the European Union in Portuguese external trade, 1960–1999.

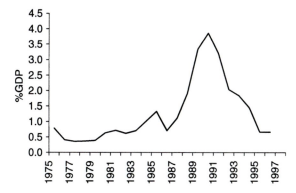

Figure 3.3 Foreign direct investment inflows.

Source: Jimeno *et al.* (2000), citing IMF, Balance of Payments Statistics.

Table 3.1 Employment by skill levels, 1985 and 1998

	Managers, professionals	*Foremen, supervisors*	*Highly-skilled*	*Skilled*	*Semi-skilled*	*Unskilled, apprentices*
1985	3.9	4.5	4.1	41.9	20.0	25.6
1998	7.8	4.2	6.7	45.2	16.9	18.9

Source: Computations based on Portugal, MTS, DETEFP (1985, 1998).

Note
Shares do not sum up to 100 due to missing values.

However, foreign direct investment and the funds channeled to Portugal to promote the modernization of its productive structure could have contributed to raise demand for skills and to a certain upgrading in the skill structure of the working population (Figure 3.3). Note for example that foreign direct investment had a strong export orientation, which had an impact on the profile of Portuguese exports, that slowly shifted away from traditional products such as textiles, clothing, and footwear, toward machinery and transportation material. The share of the latter in exports increased from 16 percent in 1985 to 31 percent in 1997. On the imports front as well, machinery and transport material increased their share (from 23 to 36 percent), due in particular to the strong import-content of exports, and to the growth of investment in general (Portugal, ME, 1996, 1997, 1998, 2000).

A slight improvement in the skill composition of the workforce could be detected (Table 3.1). Meanwhile, the wage premium increased sharply for skilled workers. In particular, university graduates saw their wages relative to high school graduates rise strongly, while their employment figures more than doubled. It should however be noted that, while high wage workers became better off, low wage earners did not lose as much in relative terms as in countries such as the United States, since their wages tended to grow faster than the median wage in the economy.

Portugal has been ranked as one of the OECD economies with highest wage flexibility, since real wages respond to the macro economic conditions, namely the unemployment rate (OECD, 1992), and to the conditions prevailing at the firm level (Cardoso, 2000). Low unemployment rates and high wage flexibility render this economy close to the deregulated *American model*. However, Portugal shares with its European counterparts several aspects of the institutional framework in the labor market. Minimum wages are enforced and collective bargaining is extensively applied. In contrast to the flexibility of wages, employment rigidity has been claimed to be a major characteristic of the country's labor market.

Data sets

The Ministry of Employment gathers annually a linked employer–employee data set, *Quadros de Pessoal*, based on an inquiry that every establishment with wage earners in the private sector is legally obliged to fill in.

A very relevant characteristic of the data set for the purpose of this study is that it reports a direct measure of the skill of the worker, based on the degree of complexity and responsibility of the job performed and the type of knowledge required. The following categories and their roles are defined (Portugal, 1978: 994):

1   *Managers and professionals*: definition of the policy of the company, planning and organization, involving high level of responsibility and requiring knowledge and study of complex technical issues;
2   *Foremen and supervisors*: supervision of a group of workers, according to instructions defined higher up in the hierarchy, requiring thorough training and specialization in one field;
3   *Highly skilled*: performance of complex technical tasks, requiring thorough training and specialization, including theoretical and practical knowledge;
4   *Skilled*: performance of somewhat complex, not repetitive and well defined tasks, according to instructions received, requiring knowledge of their execution plan and training, including theoretical and practical knowledge;
5   *Semi-skilled*: performance of non-complex, usually repetitive tasks, requiring training in a narrow field, including practical, elementary knowledge;
6   *Unskilled*: simple tasks, requiring knowledge that can be acquired in a few days.

The dichotomous classification adopted in this study includes categories 1–4 in the *skilled* workers, and the remaining ones in the *unskilled* group.

The data on trade are gathered by the National Statistical Office. Harmonized chronological series for groups of products are regularly published by the Ministry of the Economy, Trade Directorate, covering information on trade volumes and prices. Paasche indices are computed for prices. Trade volumes are computed using data on values and prices.

Job flows and their determinants

Job flows were quantified using the methodology that is by now standard, defined by Davis *et al.* (1996), and here adapted to consider two different groups of workers (skilled and unskilled). Job creation and destruction are calculated as firm level net employment changes over a period. Job creation occurs when employment at a firm increases and job destruction takes place once employment at a firm decreases. Firms with unchanged employment contribute neither to job creation nor job destruction. Job flows are expressed as rates, dividing through by a measure of the firm size, which is the average of employment in two consecutive periods.[1] The sum of job creation and destruction equals job reallocation, providing a summary measure of the heterogeneity in employment flows across firms.

Job creation and destruction in the Portuguese economy reveals contrasts across skill levels (Table 3.2), with net job creation being much higher for the skilled labor force. For the unskilled labor force, job creation occurred at a fast pace, but it was almost offset by a comparably high rate of job destruction. Therefore, for unskilled workers, job opportunities were reshuffling at a fast pace, as some firms were contracting, and others were expanding their labor force. For the skilled, job destruction was much lower, resulting in a net positive effect.

Consider now the trend among trading industries. Net job creation for the skilled labor force took place across virtually all industries (Table 3.3), with the exception of textiles, where their employment remained almost stable. On the contrary, employment for the unskilled contracted in most trading industries, with the exceptions being footwear, and clothing (where unskilled employment changed little).

To study the determinants of these contrasts in job creation and job destruction across firms, the following factors were inspected: trends in international markets, captured by changes in import and export prices; ownership structure (foreign or national) of the firm; foreign direct investment, proxied by the change in foreign capital at the industry level; technological level of the industry, evaluated by a proxy variable, the share of engineers and computer professionals (engineers, programmers, and operators) in total employment, lagged one year; market structure, measured by the degree of industrial concentration (the share of employment of the twenty largest firms in the industry). Controls for firm specific characteristics such as its size, age, and location were introduced. Industry and year controls were also included. So was the change in the average wage

Table 3.2 Average yearly job flows by skill level, Portugal, 1986–1998

	Skilled			Unskilled		
	Job creation	*Job destruction*	*Net job growth*	*Job creation*	*Job destruction*	*Net job growth*
Yearly average	0.184	0.150	**0.034**	0.213	0.205	**0.008**
Sd. dev.	0.035	0.026	**0.027**	0.024	0.041	**0.050**

Source: Computations based on Portugal, MTS, DETEFP (1985–1998).

Table 3.3 Average yearly job flows by industry and skill, trading industries, Portugal, 1986–1998

	Skilled			Unskilled		
	Job creation	Job destruction	Net job growth	Job creation	Job destruction	Net job growth
Food, bev.	0.172	0.158	0.014	0.167	0.184	−0.017
Leather	0.245	0.219	0.026	0.147	0.172	−0.025
Textiles	0.117	0.125	−0.009	0.102	0.146	−0.043
Clothing	0.187	0.155	0.031	0.225	0.221	0.005
Footwear	0.185	0.144	0.041	0.184	0.140	0.044
Wood, cork	0.186	0.176	0.010	0.171	0.192	−0.020
Paper	0.141	0.127	0.014	0.160	0.182	−0.022
Glass, ceramic	0.146	0.137	0.010	0.160	0.162	−0.002
Chemicals	0.108	0.107	0.001	0.146	0.200	−0.054
Machinery	0.164	0.134	0.030	0.189	0.225	−0.035
Transport equipment	0.112	0.106	0.006	0.169	0.187	−0.019

Source: Computations based on Portugal, MTS, DETEFP (1985–1998).

of the skill group within the firm, since it is a major determinant of labor demand. The model estimates the impact of these forces on job creation and job destruction separately, for each of the skill groups.[2] The detailed results are presented in the appendix in Table 3A.4.

The impact of growing competition in international markets, in particular in the form of declining import prices, has been much discussed in the literature. Nevertheless, there is still no consensus on whether it did contribute to raise unemployment and lower relative wages of unskilled workers in more developed economies.[3] For Portugal, a middle-income country, evidence suggests that declining import prices led to net job destruction for the unskilled labor force, as opposed to net creation for the skilled labor force. Indeed, no significant effect can be detected on job creation for the unskilled, but job destruction increases when import prices fall. For the skilled workforce, on the contrary, declining import prices led to job creation and no relevant impact on job destruction.

When demand for the country's production increases in international markets, leading to higher export prices, the employment prospects of skilled workers increase and those of unskilled workers decline. In fact, for skilled workers job creation increases and job destruction does not react to rising export prices. For the unskilled, instead, both job creation and destruction increase, but the net impact on employment is negative.

Results on the performance of employment across skill groups in response to changing international prices do not therefore support the idea that trade may have rescued the jobs of the least skilled workers in the Portuguese economy. Instead, trends in international trade by themselves have led to an expansion of job opportunities for skilled workers, and a contraction of the employment for the unskilled.

Foreign companies have been net job creators for either skill group. It is interesting to see that foreign direct investment may have spillover effects on the industry. An increase in the foreign capital in an industry may raise the demand for related products or generate imitation effects that lead to the creation of skilled jobs. On the other hand, it contributes to job destruction for the unskilled.

Technological progress is another force driving employment changes that has been much discussed in the literature. Here we can simply consider a proxy for the technological level of the industry, its share of engineers and computer related personnel in total employment. Results indicate that industries with a more advanced technological structure have been, in net terms, creating skilled jobs at a faster pace than technologically less developed industries. For the unskilled labor force, both job creation and job destruction are higher in technologically more advanced industries, with a slight negative impact on overall employment.

The impact of changes in wages follows the predictions by economic theory. It is nevertheless worth noting that the net impact on job creation results from both a decline in job creation and an increase in job destruction.

Conclusion

The analysis of gross job flows at the firm level for skilled and unskilled workers does not lend support to the idea that increased openness was a crucial factor sustaining the employment of low-skilled workers in Portugal, and therefore contributing to the country's low unemployment rate. Indeed, a certain upgrading in the skill composition of the Portuguese working population was brought about by trends in international markets. As competition rises and import prices fall, the unskilled workers in the Portuguese economy see their employment prospects worsen. Skilled workers, instead, see them improve. Better international conditions for exports led to net job creation for the skilled labor force, and net job destruction for the unskilled. Foreign companies have created jobs at a faster pace than national companies, a result that holds for both skill categories.

Appendix

Table 3A.4 Regression of job flows at the firm level across skill groups, trading industries, 1986–1998 (seemingly unrelated regression)

	Coef.	Std. err.
SKILLED		
Impact on job creation		
Exp prices	0.307994	0.018846
Imp prices	−0.14	0.028898
foreign	0.017398	0.002819
FDI	0.000744	0.00014
technology	0.066883	0.002754
Wage change	−0.09624	0.004326

(Table 3A.4 continued)

Table 3A.4 Continued

	Coef.	Std. err.
Sales change	0.009858	0.00079
mkt concent	0.00347	0.000403
sales	−0.00039	9.85E-05
age	−0.0019	4.26E-05
const	0.306167	0.010596
industry dummies	yes	
region dummy (Lisbon)	yes	
year dummies	yes	
Interaction with job destruction dummy		
Exp prices	−0.27386	0.02598
Imp prices	0.108227	0.042084
foreign	−0.03031	0.004187
FDI	−0.00074	0.000197
technology	−0.05577	0.004141
Sales change	−0.01047	0.001146
mkt concent	−0.00169	0.000578
sales	6.24E-05	0.000101
age	−0.00033	6.23E-05
Wage change	0.196354	0.006834
const	−0.14456	0.015694
industry dummies	yes	
region dummy (Lisbon)	yes	
year dummies	yes	

UNSKILLED
Impact on job creation

	Coef.	Std. err.
Exp prices	0.127074	0.021977
Imp prices	−0.0293	0.035871
foreign	0.058826	0.003505
FDI	−7.4E-05	0.000167
technology	0.076448	0.003389
Wage change	−0.02861	0.004318
Sales change	0.010385	0.00098
mkt concent	−0.00238	0.000482
LVT	0.014512	0.003034
sales	−0.00031	3.24E-05
age	−0.0016	5.14E-05
const	0.343571	0.012259
industry dummies	yes	
region dummy (Lisbon)	yes	
year dummies	yes	
Interaction with job destruction dummy		
Exp prices	0.186365	0.029642
Imp prices	−0.13936	0.047399
foreign	−0.04841	0.004675
FDI	0.00105	0.000224
technology	0.018898	0.004595
Sales change	−0.0113	0.001291
mkt concent	0.003007	0.00066
sales	−0.00042	5.38E-05

Table 3A.4 Continued

	Coef.	Std. err.
age	0.000199	6.99E-05
Wage change	0.093563	0.006074
const	-0.21014	0.016729
industry dummies	yes	
region dummy (Lisbon)	yes	
year dummies	yes	

Equation	Obs	Parms	RMSE	"R-sq"	chi2	P
sk	133205	63	0.2517496	0.0745	9980.352	0.0000
unsk	133205	63	0.2876147	0.0783	11184.24	0.0000

Source: Portugal, MTS-DETEFP (1985–1998).

Note
Breusch-Pagan test of independence of residuals across equations: Chi-squared(1) = 25118.899.

Acknowledgment

This chapter has been prepared under the research project "Globalization and Social Exclusion" financed by the European Commission under the Targeted Socio-Economic Research Program (TSER). Data on employment and wages were provided by the Portugese Ministry of Labor, DETEFP, whose cooperation is acknowledged. I am grateful to Cristina Manteu and Sónia for help with the trade data.

Notes

1 The job flow rate therefore ranges from -2 to +2 and it handles contraction and expansion symmetrically.
2 A seemingly unrelated regression model was estimated, with one equation for each skill group and the firm as the unit of observation. A dummy variable achieving the value 1 if job destruction took place was fully interacted with every other regressor, to distinguish between the determinants of job creation and job destruction. The interpretation that follows is based on formal tests on the parameters of the model.
3 See for example Wood (1994, 1995), Haskel and Slaughter (2001), Leamer (1994), Hanson and Harrison (1999), Anderton and Brenton (1999b) versus Baldwin (1995), Desjonqueres *et al.* (1999), Lucke (1999) or Dewatripont *et al.* (1999).

4 International trade and the income position of low-skilled and high-skilled workers in the European Union

Ludo Cuyvers, Michel Dumont and Glenn Rayp

Introduction

Increased trade competition (e.g. of low-wage Newly Industrialized Countries (NIC)) is, in the public debate on the impact of globalization, often rounded up as a usual suspect of the deteriorated income position of low-skilled workers, be it in terms of decreased relative wages in the US or – due to alleged labour market rigidities – in terms of unemployment of low-skilled workers in the European Union. Most academic researchers seem to exculpate international trade and nominate skill-biased technological change for the more probable culprit of increased income inequality (see, for example, Brenton 1999; Haskel and Slaughter 2001). However, Slaughter (2000) argues that despite methodological progress, research has still fundamental limitations with regard to answering how much international trade contributes to rising wage inequality. Moreover, most of the empirical work focuses on the US and is only matched with a limited number of country studies for the European Union.[1] Given the substantial differences in institutional setting and trade patterns of EU countries, economic shocks need not have a symmetric impact within the European Union. It may therefore be debatable to extrapolate the results of the studies on a single EU country, to the whole European Union.

In addition, since labour mobility between the EU member states is very low, the extent to which trade liberalization provokes an asymmetrical economic shock on the EU economy may matter too. This implies that it is also necessary to verify the country heterogeneity of increased trade with low-wage countries, in quantifying the impact of globalization in the context of the European Union.

In this chapter we use data on ten EU countries to estimate the impact of international trade on the inequality between low-skilled and high-skilled workers in the European Union in the period 1985–1995. To assess the impact of international trade on the *relative wages* of low-skilled workers we apply a mandated wage estimation procedure (Feenstra and Hanson 1999; Haskel and Slaughter 2001). This approach fits within the Heckscher–Ohlin–Samuelson (HOS) model, which predicts that trade liberalization decreases the rewards of the production factor(s) a country is poorly endowed with, relative to its trading partners.

Applying a panel data estimation we can account for possible asymmetric effects of trade shocks within the European Union. We furthermore account for heterogeneity of the trading partners by considering three different geographical groups of NICs and by splitting the OECD countries into a group of high-wage EU countries; low-wage EU countries and high-wage non-EU OECD countries. It may be too heroic to assume a priori that NICs of different continents are sufficiently similar with respect to factor endowments and technology, transportation costs and even trade liberalization to have the same kind of impact on the EU economy. By considering OECD countries we can assess to what extent the impact of intra-OECD competition counterbalances the impact of competition from the NICs, on the relative wage of low-skilled workers. Rigidity of EU labour markets may prevent the kind of adjustments the HOS model of international trade predicts. Increased import competition may cause employment rather than wage adjustments in the EU and evidence on the evolution of the relative wage of the high- and low-skilled is not sufficient to assess the impact of globalization. For the latter, one also has to study to what extent international trade with low-wage countries affects relative labour demand.

Under the assumption of sticky wages international trade will induce unemployment of the relatively scarce production factor(s) instead of affecting its relative reward. In order to investigate this, we estimate the demand for high- and low-skilled workers from a flexible cost function within a sticky wage model (e.g. Morrison-Paul and Siegel 2001). From this we compute the elasticity of demand for low- and high-skilled labour, in particular with respect to import competition from the NICs, the OECD high-wage and OECD low-wage countries, which allows us to determine the impact of globalization on relative factor demand.

We will first present the theoretical framework of both models (mandated wage and sticky wage). In the next section, we discuss the estimation results and conclude in the final section. The data that we used in our estimations are described in detail in the data appendix at the end of the chapter.

Trade, wages and employment of low-skilled and high-skilled workers

Trade and wages

The Stolper–Samuelson theorem predicts that, when trade is liberalized, the rewards (in real terms) of the relatively abundant production factors will rise, provided that the relative price of the goods in which a country has a comparative advantage increases. In a small open economy, sector-biased technological change may, however, lead to the same result. If high-skill-intensive sectors experience the highest technological progress the wages of high-skilled workers will rise relative to the wages of low-skilled workers.

Feenstra and Hanson (1999) propose a two-stage extension of the mandated wage procedure proposed by Leamer (1998) in which the impact of international trade on factor rewards can be disentangled from the impact of technological change. The zero profit condition, under perfect competition,[2] results in a relationship between changes in relative product prices and factor rewards. The zero profit condition for a sector is given as:

$$p_i^g = \sum_j a_{ji} w_j + \sum_k b_{ki} p_k^g \quad i, k = 1, \ldots, S \text{(sectors)} \tag{4.1}$$

where p_i^g represents domestic gross output price; w_j the unit cost of the jth production factor; a_{ji} the quantity of factor j used per unit i; p_k the domestic gross output price of intermediate good k and b_{ki} the quantity of intermediate good k used per unit of i. Given labour supply, changes in prices or technology will 'mandate' changes in factor rewards that will restore zero profits in all sectors. This adjustment process can be formalized by differentiating (4.1):[3]

$$\sum_j V_{ji} \Delta \log w_j = \Delta \log p_i + \Delta \log \text{TFP}_i \tag{4.2}$$

V_{ji} denotes the value added share of factor j in sector i, $\Delta \log p_i$ the change in value added prices ($\Delta \log p_i = \Delta \log p_i^g - \sum_k V_{ki} \Delta \log p_k^g$) and TFP_i total factor productivity in sector i.

Small open economies face given international prices and hence all price changes will be exogenous (i.e. of international origin). Factor reward changes can thus be linked to total price changes. For large countries, product prices may be partly determined endogenously. In the first stage of a two-stage estimation procedure Feenstra and Hanson (1999) and Haskel and Slaughter (2001) regress price changes and TFP changes on the underlying determinants, respectively $Z_{\text{pr},i}$ and $Z_{\text{tc},i}$:

$$\Delta \log p_i = \sum_{\text{pr}} Z_{\text{pr},i} \delta_{\text{pr}} + \varepsilon_{\text{pr},i} \tag{4.3}$$

$$\Delta \log \text{TFP}_i = \sum_{\text{tc}} Z_{\text{tc},i} \delta_{\text{tc}} + \varepsilon_{\text{tc},i} \tag{4.4}$$

If the first stage estimates of vectors δ_{pr} and δ_{tc} are regressed on the factor shares, the estimated coefficients $\gamma_{j,\text{pr}}$ and $\gamma_{j,\text{tc}}$ reflect the wage change mandated by trade-induced price changes and technological change:

$$\hat{\delta}_{\text{pr}} Z_{\text{pr},i} = \sum_j V_{ji} \gamma_{j,\text{pr}} + \varepsilon'_{\text{pr},i} \tag{4.5}$$

$$\hat{\delta}_{\text{tc}} Z_{\text{tc},i} = \sum_j V_{ji} \gamma_{j,\text{tc}} + \varepsilon'_{\text{tc},i} \tag{4.6}$$

By including a measure of import competition in the vector $Z_{\text{tc},i}$ an estimate of the influence of international trade on technological change is obtained. Hence, both the direct effect of international competition on the factor rewards, as well as the indirect effect, that is, the effect on factor rewards of trade-induced technological change as pointed out by for example, Wood (1994), can be estimated.

Trade and employment

In an HOS framework wages are assumed to be fully flexible and hence absorb the entire impact of increased trade competition while production factors remain fully employed. The assumption of perfectly competitive labour markets is not reasonable for the European Union, in which most countries are generally characterized by institutional labour market rigidities. We therefore assess the impact of international trade under the assumption of sticky wages, in which case full employment is no longer guaranteed (see Brecher 1974; Krugman 1995a; Davis 1998).

Krugman (1995a) shows in a two-sector model with low-skilled and high-skilled labour as the two production factors, how in a high-skill-abundant country with sticky wages that starts trading with a low-skill-abundant country, production will shift to the high-skill-intensive sector.

Due to the sticky wages, sector technology will not adjust and, as long as the economy does not fully specialize, the demand for low-skilled workers will decline. The free trade equilibrium, in contrast with full-employment autarky, implies unemployment of low-skilled labour.

A small (price taking) country would completely specialize in the production of the high-skill-intensive good, which eventually may restore full employment. A large country may however continue to produce both goods. With constant relative factor rewards, this implies that the relative price of the goods will not change. Hence, we would only expect a shift in supply from domestic to foreign production, determined by the amount the trade partner is willing to offer at the domestic autarkic price ratio.

Estimation procedure and results

Trade and wages

The data allow us to create a panel of 9 EU countries and 12 industrial sectors[4] for which we consider total change (annual average) for 1985–1995. More details concerning the data are given in the Data appendix. Given the size of the European Union, we consider price and technological change as not fully exogenous. Hence, before performing the mandated wage regression, we first have to isolate the share of total change caused by international trade liberalization and technological progress in a two-stage estimation procedure.

Regarding the effect of *import price competition* on domestic price changes, we regress, in the first stage, the domestic price changes on country specific fixed effects, import price changes and the change in total factor productivity (in order to control for the output price effect of technological change):

$$
\begin{aligned}
\Delta \log p_{i,\text{dom}} = {} & \alpha_{0,i} + \alpha_{\text{EUHW}} \Delta \log p_{i,\text{EUHW}} \\
& + \alpha_{\text{OERE}} \Delta \log p_{i,\text{OERE}} + \alpha_{\text{EULW}} \Delta \log p_{i,\text{EULW}} \\
& + \alpha_{\text{ASIA}} \Delta \log p_{i,\text{ASIA}} + \alpha_{\text{CEEC}} \Delta \log p_{i,\text{CEEC}} \\
& + \alpha_{\text{LATIN}} \Delta \log p_{i,\text{LATIN}} + \alpha_{\text{TFP}} \Delta \log \text{TFP}_i + \varepsilon_{i,\text{pr}}
\end{aligned} \tag{4.7}
$$

Table 4.1 Price regression: first stage

Dependent variable	$\Delta \log p_{i,dom}$ (7)
$\Delta \log p_{i,\text{EUHW}}$	-0.13 (-1.78)*
$\Delta \log p_{i,\text{OERE}}$	-0.29 (-2.20)**
$\Delta \log p_{i,\text{EULW}}$	0.26 (2.87)***
$\Delta \log p_{i,\text{ASIA}}$	0.04 (0.69)
$\Delta \log p_{i,\text{CEEC}}$	0.02 (1.37)
$\Delta \log p_{i,\text{LATIN}}$	0.05 (0.76)
$\Delta \log \text{TFP}_i$	-3.64 (-2.49)**
R^2	0.41

Note
The reported results are within estimations (country specific intercepts but common slopes) – heteroscedastic-consistent t-statistics in brackets. *, **, *** denotes significance at respectively 10, 5 and 1 per cent level.

Trade partners are broken down into six country groups (a detailed list of the countries in each group is given in the data appendix): High-wage EU countries (EUHW); non-EU OECD countries (OERE), Low-wage EU countries (EULW); the (South-) East Asian NICs (ASIA), the most advanced Central and Eastern European countries (CEEC) and the Latin American NICs (LATIN) in order to take account of cross-country heterogeneity in import competition and trade liberalization. Table 4.1 shows results of the first stage estimation of equation (4.7) in which we considered common slopes but country specific intercepts to account for the heterogeneity between EU countries (i.e. fixed effects estimation).

The coefficient of import price changes of high-wage EU trade partners as well as the coefficient of import price changes of non-EU OECD countries is negative and significantly so (albeit only at the 10 per cent significance level for the high-wage EU countries). This is the opposite of what one would expect from the Stolper–Samuelson theorem and reflects that the HOS framework, with its focus on differences in factor endowments in explaining trade patterns, is probably not entirely appropriate to explain international trade between high-wage countries with similar relative endowments of production factors.

Hence, the significant negative sign of international trade with regard to both groups of high-wage countries (the OERE in our classification are all high-wage countries[5]) may be explained within more recent trade models, which focus on increasing returns and trade in differentiated products (e.g. Helpman 1984; Helpman and Krugman 1985), but is beyond the scope of this chapter.

More in line with the Stolper–Samuelson theorem, the coefficient of import price changes of the EULW as well as the coefficients of the three NICs groups are positively correlated with EU domestic price changes, but only the first coefficient differs significantly from zero. The coefficient of import price changes of EULW (Ireland, Greece, Portugal and Spain) is the most significant in the first stage of the price regression. Portugal and Spain became members of the European Union in 1986, that is, at the beginning of the period that we consider in our estimations, whereas Greece has only been a member since 1981. Apparently, integrating low wage countries in the European Union did result in significant Stolper–Samuelson price effects in the period 1985–1995 in the other EU countries.[6]

The pass-through of productivity changes to industry prices is negative as expected (e.g. Krugman 1995b; Feenstra and Hanson 1999). Technological change significantly decreased domestic prices. The coefficient is highly significant and clearly dominates the effect of international price competition on domestic price change.

In the second stage, each foreign competition determinant of $\Delta \log p_{\text{dom}}$ is regressed on the factor shares, in order to estimate its contribution to changes in the wages of high- and low-skilled workers:

$$\alpha_j \Delta \log p_{i,j} = V_{\text{HS},i} \Delta \log w_{\text{HS}} + V_{\text{LS},i} \Delta \log w_{\text{LS}} + V_{K,i} \Delta \log w_K + \varepsilon_{i,j} \quad (4.8)$$

(J = EUHW, OERE, EULW, ASIA, CEEC, LATIN)

$V_{f,i}$ denotes the value added shares of production factor f (high-skilled labour, low-skilled labour and capital) in sector i. The factor shares sum to 1 and considering $V_{K,i} = 1 - V_{\text{HS},i} - V_{\text{LS},i}$ as in Lücke (1998) we obtain:

$$\alpha_j \Delta \log p_{i,j} = \Delta \log w_K + V_{\text{HS},i}(\Delta \log w_{\text{HS}} - \Delta \log w_K)$$
$$+ V_{\text{LS},i}(\Delta \log w_{\text{LS}} - \Delta \log w_K) + \varepsilon_{i,j} \quad (4.9)$$

Hence, the coefficient estimate of $V_{\text{HS},i}$ and $V_{\text{LS},i}$ indicates to what extent the remuneration of respectively high-skilled and low-skilled workers diverged from that of capital.

F-tests on the model specification reveal the degree of heterogeneity in the panel. The presence of country-specific intercepts and/or slopes determines the degree of intra-EU heterogeneity with respect to trade competition. If the F-tests support the hypothesis of country-specific intercepts, this would be an indication of country specificity of factor price evolution and hence of income divergence, caused by international trade, within the European Union. A common slopes specification would however point to a homogenous EU pattern of the change in wage inequality between low- and high-skilled workers. If in addition, the hypothesis of country-specific slopes finds support in the data this would point to country differences in the evolution of income inequality, exacerbating the income divergence trend. The latter may be highly problematic given the acknowledged low labour mobility in the European Union.

A last consideration with regard to the estimation procedure concerns inference of the second stage coefficients. The dependent variables in the second stage are generated from the first stage regression instead of being effectively measured. We therefore have to correct the second stage estimated standard errors for the additional variance resulting from the generation of the dependent variables.

Feenstra and Hanson (1997a) propose a procedure to recover the 'true' variances. The proposed correction procedure, unfortunately, sometimes fails to produce positive variance and as a result standard errors cannot always be computed (see Feenstra and Hanson 1999 or Haskel and Slaughter 2001). This seems to point at a negative bias in the corrected variances and hence to indicate an overestimation of the significance of the second stage coefficients. We therefore apply the procedure to correct the second stage variance as proposed in Dumont *et al.* (2005). This correction procedure always results in consistent and positive variance of the second stage parameters. The results of the second stage price regression are shown in Table 4.2.

For the three groups of OECD trade partners the plain OLS specification is rejected at the 10 per cent significance level, but not the fixed effects specification, that is country-specific (absolute) factor reward changes, but a common (EU-) trend in wage inequality (relative factor reward changes). We therefore report the results of the within estimation (i.e. specification with country-specific intercepts but common slopes). For the (South-) East Asian and Central and Eastern European NICs, a plain OLS specification could not be rejected. Apparently international trade with these two groups of NICs had a rather symmetric impact on EU countries. The impact of intra-OECD trade competition on wages seems to be more asymmetric given that a plain OLS specification is rejected for the three OECD groups.

However, none of the coefficients for the two NICs groups are significant, and it would seem that trade with these NICs has not affected (relative) wages in the EU countries. For the Latin-American NICs both the plain OLS and the fixed effects specification is rejected and we therefore do not report the results of this group. International trade with non-EU high-wage OECD countries (e.g. US and Japan) seems to have decreased the relative wages of high-skilled workers in EU countries in a significant way (at the 10 per cent significance level). Hence, the only direct effect of international price competition on wage inequality in the EU, which cannot entirely be rejected, albeit at a low level of significance, is a *dampening* effect on wage inequality between the low- and high skilled. From our data we can see that in the period 1985–1995 the relative wages of high-skilled workers (non-manual workers) actually decreased in a number of EU countries (see Cuyvers *et al.* 2000 for more details). The fact that in a number of EU countries (especially Germany and the UK) relative wages of high-skilled workers increased in this period can explain the asymmetry of trade shocks (i.e. rejection of a plain OLS specification). We conclude from our results in Table 4.2, to the absence of any Stolper–Samuelson effects of trade, especially with the NICs, on the (relative) wages of low-skilled workers in the European Union.

In the first stage of the *total factor productivity growth* regression, we regress TFP change on a proxy for its technological determinants and on measures of international competition. We use the total period change of the sector domestic R&D stock (SRD), the total period change of the non-sector domestic R&D stock (NSRD) and the total period change of the foreign R&D stock (FRD) as determinants of TFP.

Table 4.2 Price regression: second stage

Dependent variable	$\alpha_{EUHW}\,\Delta \log p_{EUHW}$	$\alpha_{OERE}\,\Delta \log p_{OERE}$	$\alpha_{EULW}\,\Delta \log p_{EULW}$	$\alpha_{ASIA}\,\Delta \log p_{ASIA}$	$\alpha_{CEBC}\,\Delta \log p_{CEBC}$
$\Delta \log w_{HS} - \Delta \log w_{K}$	−0.02 (−0.33)	−0.29 (−1.75)*	−0.13 (−1.12)	0.03 (0.65)	0.02 (1.03)
$\Delta \log w_{LS} - \Delta \log w_{K}$	−0.05 (−0.90)	−0.11 (−1.24)	0.03 (0.28)	0.01 (0.57)	0.02 (1.02)
$\Delta \log w_{K}$	F.E.	F.E.	F.E.	$-0.9\ 10^{-3}$ (−0.12)	$0.04\ 10^{-3}$ (0.06)
R^2	0.29	0.22	0.23	0.04	0.01
F-test: common intercept and slopes versus country-specific intercepts and slopes (p-values in brackets)	2.31 (0.00)	1.52 (0.09)	1.55 (0.08)	1.35 (0.16)	0.97 (0.52)
F-test: common slopes versus country-specific slopes, given country specific intercepts (p-values in brackets)	1.16 (0.32)	0.89 (0.59)	0.91 (0.56)	1.45 (0.14)	0.80 (0.69)
F-test: common intercept versus country-specific intercepts, given a common slope (p-values in brackets)	4.48 (0.00)	2.84 (0.01)	2.86 (0.01)	1.07 (0.39)	1.35 (0.23)

Note
Heteroscedastic-consistent t-statistics in brackets, based on standard errors accounting for estimated instead of measured dependent variables as explained in the text-
F.E.: results of fixed effects estimation (country-specific intercepts but common slopes). * denotes 10 per cent significance level.

Grossman and Helpman (1992) consider (international) trade as an important channel of knowledge spillovers. In an empirical estimation of spillover effects, within the Grossman and Helpman framework, Coe and Helpman (1995) construct foreign R&D stocks as the weighted average of trade partners' R&D stocks (with the bilateral import shares as weights) and find evidence of substantial international R&D stocks, especially for small countries.

By using both the domestic sector and non-sector R&D stocks as well as the foreign R&D stock we can assess the extent to which technological change is exogenously (i.e. internationally) determined.

Wood (1994) argues that international trade may induce technological progress and that neglecting this indirect effect of trade may underestimate the actual impact of international trade on wages.

In our specification of the TFP regression we consider international trade as a possible spillover mechanism but by including the import price changes relative to the base period domestic price (in order to avoid a potential simultaneity bias) we also estimate the impact import competition may have in stimulating technological change. The TFP specification for the first stage is:

$$
\Delta \log \mathrm{TFP}_i = \beta_{i,0} + \beta_{\mathrm{srd}} \Delta \log \mathrm{SRD}_i + \beta_{\mathrm{nsrd}} \Delta \log \mathrm{NSRD}_i
$$
$$
+ \beta_{\mathrm{frd}} \Delta \log \mathrm{FRD}_i
$$
$$
+ \frac{1}{P_{\mathrm{dom},i,85}} \Big(\beta_{\mathrm{EUHW}} \Delta \log p_{\mathrm{EUHW},i} + \beta_{\mathrm{OERE}} \Delta \log p_{\mathrm{OERE},i}
$$
$$
+ \beta_{\mathrm{EULW}} \Delta \log p_{\mathrm{EULW},i} + \beta_{\mathrm{ASIA}} \Delta \log p_{\mathrm{ASIA},i}
$$
$$
+ \beta_{\mathrm{CEEC}} \Delta \log p_{\mathrm{CEEC},i} + \beta_{\mathrm{LATIN}} \Delta \log p_{\mathrm{LATIN},i} \Big) + \varepsilon_{i,tc} \quad (4.10)
$$

The results of a fixed effects estimation of (4.10) are reported in Table 4.3.

Table 4.3 TFP regression: first stage

Dependent variable	$\Delta \log \mathrm{TFP}_i$ *(10)*
$\Delta \log \mathrm{SRD}_i$	$0.10 \ 10^{-2}$ (0.34)
$\Delta \log \mathrm{NSRD}_i$	$0.90 \ 10^{-2}$ (0.30)
$\Delta \log \mathrm{FRD}_i$	$0.90 \ 10^{-3}$ (0.10)
$(\Delta \log p_{\mathrm{EUHW},i})/p_{\mathrm{dom},i,85}$	$0.90 \ 10^{-2}$ (1.20)
$(\Delta \log p_{\mathrm{OERE},i})/p_{\mathrm{dom},i,85}$	0.02 (1.86)*
$(\Delta \log p_{\mathrm{EULW},i})/p_{\mathrm{dom},i,85}$	$0.40 \ 10^{-2}$ (0.52)
$(\Delta \log p_{\mathrm{ASIA},i})/p_{\mathrm{dom},i,85}$	-0.01 (-2.40)**
$(\Delta \log p_{\mathrm{CEEC},i})/p_{\mathrm{dom},i,85}$	$-0.20 \ 10^{-2}$ (-0.55)
$(\Delta \log p_{\mathrm{LATIN},i})/p_{\mathrm{dom},i,85}$	$-0.50 \ 10^{-2}$ (-0.93)
R^2	0.35

Note
See Table 4.1.

Table 4.4 TFP regression: second stage

Dependent variable	M_{EUHW}	M_{OERE}	M_{EULW}	M_{ASIA}	M_{CEEC}
$\Delta \log w_{HS} - \Delta \log w_K$	$-0.1\ 10^{-3}\ (-0.04)$	$0.01\ (1.40)$	$-0.2\ 10^{-2}\ (-0.44)$	$-0.01\ (-1.56)$	$-0.5\ 10^{-3}\ (-0.32)$
$\Delta \log w_{LS} - \Delta \log w_K$	$0.3\ 10^{-2}\ (0.87)$	$0.8\ 10^{-2}\ (1.37)$	$0.5\ 10^{-3}\ (0.25)$	$-0.4\ 10^{-2}\ (-0.95)$	$-0.7\ 10^{-3}\ (-0.41)$
$\Delta \log w_K$	F.E.	F.E.	F.E.	$0.4\ 10^{-3}\ (0.12)$	F.E.
R^2	0.32	0.19	0.19	0.04	0.13
F-test 1: see Table 4.2	2.25 (0.00)	1.16 (0.31)	1.44 (0.12)	1.35 (0.16)	0.97 (0.52)
F-test 2: see Table 4.2	0.89 (0.58)	0.69 (0.79)	1.09 (0.38)	1.45 (0.14)	0.79 (0.69)
F-test 3: see Table 4.2	5.07 (0.00)	2.20 (0.03)	2.10 (0.04)	1.07 (0.39)	1.35 (0.23)

Notes
See Table 4.2.
M_R stands for $\beta_R (\Delta \log p_{R,i})/p_{\text{dom},i,85}$ with R = EUHW, OERE, EULW, ASIA, CEEC.

Although all spillover coefficients are positive they are very insignificant. Apparently, when controlling for import price competition we do not find evidence of import-weighted spillovers. The impact of international trade on TFP seems to operate more through import price pressure rather than though facilitating international spillovers.

Increased competition (i.e. lower import prices) of (South-) East Asian NICs significantly raises technological progress in support of the trade-induced technological change argument by Wood (1994). Increased competition of OERE actually seems to decrease TFP. This result might be interpreted that contrary to Asian price competition, competition from OERE is leading EU producers to either develop with non-price responses, or/and relocate production to low-wage economies, such as the Central and Eastern European countries.

The second stage estimation of the impact of the determinants of technological change on factor rewards is reported in Table 4.4.

We do not report the results of the second stage for the three R&D stock components nor for import prices of Latin American NICs as for these variables both a plain OLS and a fixed effects specification are rejected.

None of the coefficients in the second stage of the TFP regression are significant. Although we found a significant impact of price changes of (South-) East Asian and non-EU OECD imports in the first stage regression these effects do not seem to get carried over into the wages of low- or high-skilled workers.

Overall, the results of the two-stage price and TFP regressions do not provide any evidence of international trade with low-wage countries affecting, directly through Stolper–Samuelson effects, or indirectly through trade-induced technological change, the (relative) wages of low-skilled workers in EU countries in the period 1985–1995. Actually, if anything, there are some indications that trade with non-EU high-wage OECD countries decreased the wages of high-skilled workers in the European Union. This intra-OECD competition seems to have affected EU countries in an asymmetric way.

Trade and employment

Our results on the relationship between trade and wages suggest that international trade with the low-wage EU countries and NICs had no negative impact on low-skilled workers' wages. From this, we might conclude to an overall limited effect of globalization on the inequality between low- and high-skilled workers, provided that the effects of trade on employment appear to be equally limited. As mentioned before, many EU countries are often considered to experience labour market rigidities, which may prevent wages from falling to market-clearing levels that ensure full employment. In this section we will estimate the impact of international trade under the assumption that wages are sticky, which may be a more reasonable assumption for the EU. The sticky wage model of international trade entails three basic predictions regarding the influence of trade on employment that can be verified:

- Full employment of the relatively abundant factor and a decline of the demand for the relatively scarce production factor at the aggregate level;
- An increase in the demand for the relatively abundant as well as the relatively scarce production factor in the sectors in which the country has a comparative advantage;
- A decline in the demand for the relatively abundant as well as the relatively scarce production factor in the sectors in which the country has a comparative disadvantage.

To estimate the employment effect of international trade we use a flexible cost function, which characterizes the cost-minimizing behaviour of firms, given technology constraints, without making any assumption about the substitution elasticity between the production factors nor about returns to scale. From the cost function, the demand for factor inputs can be derived and the elasticity of low- and high-skilled labour demand can consequently be computed with respect to trade within the OECD or trade with the NICs. The two most popular flexible cost function specifications are the Translog (e.g. Berndt and Hesse 1986) and the Generalized Leontief (e.g. Morrison 1988). We prefer the latter specification as it allows a closed form solution of the long run equilibrium in a partial equilibrium framework, that is where account is taken of the quasi-fixity of certain production factors due to adjustment costs.[7]

We assume that sector output is produced using three inputs: high-skilled labour, low-skilled labour and capital. Apart from the input factors, we assume that the cost function is also a function of output, import competition and technological change. Though not necessary for estimation or identification, we impose constant returns to scale because the cost function is specified at the sector level. We obtain the following long run equation for each sector, country and year:[8]

$$C = Y\left(\sum_i \sum_j \alpha_{ij} w_i^{0.5} w_j^{0.5} + \sum_i \sum_m \delta_{im} w_i s_m^{0.5} + \sum_i w_i \sum_m \sum_n \gamma_{mn} s_m^{0.5} s_n^{0.5}\right)$$

(4.11)

Y denotes real output, w_i (w_j) is the vector of the rewards of the production factors (the high-skilled workers' wage w_{HS}, the low-skilled workers' wage w_{LS} and the unit capital cost w_K) and s_m (s_n) denote the other determinants of the cost function, that is, imports from high-wage trade partners (high-wage EU countries and non-EU OECD countries: M_{HWC}); low-wage EU trade partners (M_{EULW}) and imports from the Central and Eastern European, (South-) East Asian and Latin American NICs (M_{NIC}) and finally technological change (Tech). The assumption of constant returns to scale in the long run implies that real output Y is omitted from s_m (s_n). The demand for a production factor can be derived, by differentiating the cost function with respect to the factor's reward w_i (using Shephard's lemma): $x_i = \partial C / \partial w_i$. Furthermore dividing by Y yields the following input–output equation for high-skilled labour, low-skilled labour and capital:

$$\frac{X_{HS}}{Y} = \frac{\partial C}{\partial w_{HS}} \frac{1}{Y} = \sum_{j=HS,LS,K} \alpha_{HS,j} \left(\frac{w_j}{w_{HS}}\right)^{0.5} + \sum_m \delta_{HS,m} s_m^{0.5} + \sum_m \sum_n \gamma_{mn} s_m^{0.5} s_n^{0.5} \qquad (4.12)$$

$$\frac{X_{LS}}{Y} = \frac{\partial C}{\partial w_{LS}} \frac{1}{Y} = \sum_{j=HS,LS,K} \alpha_{LS,j} \left(\frac{w_j}{w_{LS}}\right)^{0.5} + \sum_m \delta_{LS,m} s_m^{0.5} + \sum_m \sum_n \gamma_{mn} s_m^{0.5} s_n^{0.5} \qquad (4.13)$$

$$\frac{X_K}{Y} = \frac{\partial C}{\partial w_K} \frac{1}{Y} = \sum_{j=HS,LS,K} \alpha_{K,j} \left(\frac{w_j}{w_K}\right)^{0.5} + \sum_m \delta_{K,m} s_m^{0.5} + \sum_m \sum_n \gamma_{mn} s_m^{0.5} s_n^{0.5} \qquad (4.14)$$

From these three equations, the demand elasticity of factor inputs with respect to factor remuneration can be derived in the following way:

$$\varepsilon_{ij} = \frac{\partial \ln X_i}{\partial \ln w_j} = \frac{\partial X_i w_j}{\partial w_j X_i} \quad i,j = (HS, LS, K) \qquad (4.15)$$

The sensitivity of high- and low-skilled labour demand with respect to the exogenous parameters can be expressed as:[9]

$$\varepsilon_{im} = \frac{\partial \ln X_i}{\partial \ln s_m} = \frac{\partial X_i s_m}{\partial s_m X_i} \quad I = (HS, LS); \ s_m = (M_{HWC}, M_{EULW}, M_{NIC}, Tech) \qquad (4.16)$$

We constructed a panel for this model, consisting of 10 countries,[10] 12 sectors (at the ISIC two digit level except for the machinery sector which is broken down by ISIC three digit sub-sectors) and 12 years (1985–1996). Since in the sticky wage model, factor demand is linked to trade *volume* at the *aggregate* level, we use the national average of the sector import to GDP ratio to proxy import intensity. We allow for a differential impact of trade with high-wage OECD countries, low-wage EU countries and the NICs. We use the knowledge stock (i.e. cumulative discounted and depreciated R&D expenditures) as a proxy for technological change.[11] We apply iterative three stage least squares to estimate the system of equations (4.12), (4.13) and (4.14) for the 12 individual ISIC industries at the EU level, that is, for all countries combined. Lagged values of the variables are used as instruments.

To test the predictions of the sticky wage model, demand elasticity of high- and low-skilled labour with regard to trade and technology variables is computed, at the sector average values of the variables, from the parameter estimates.[12]

The results are reported in Table 4.5 and Table 4.6.

The demand elasticity of high-skilled and low-skilled labour with regard to their proper factor rewards (respectively $\varepsilon_{HS, wHS}$ and $\varepsilon_{LS, wLS}$) has the right sign for all sectors. For all except one sector, capital appears to be a significant substitute for both high-skilled and low-skilled labour (positive sign of $\varepsilon_{HS, wK}$ and $\varepsilon_{LS, wK}$)

Table 4.5 Demand elasticity of high-skilled labour at sector level, 1985–1996

	$\varepsilon_{HS,wHS}$	$\varepsilon_{HS,wLS}$	$\varepsilon_{HS,wK}$	$\varepsilon_{HS,Moehw}$	$\varepsilon_{HS,Meulw}$	$\varepsilon_{HS,Mnic}$	$\varepsilon_{HS,RDS}$
ISIC 31	−0.25***	−0.19***	0.44***	−0.35***	−0.31*	0.48***	0.34***
ISIC 32	−0.93***	−0.01	0.94***	−0.84***	−1.46***	1.72***	0.24***
ISIC 33	−0.58***	−0.32***	0.90***	−1.21***	−0.92***	1.24***	0.37***
ISIC 34	−0.47***	0.09**	0.37***	−0.51***	−0.74***	0.81***	0.10***
ISIC 35	−0.10	−0.17***	0.27***	−0.28***	−0.57***	0.58***	0.08***
ISIC 36	−0.43*	−0.03	0.46***	−0.35***	−0.67***	0.96***	0.06
ISIC 37	−0.23**	−0.06	0.30***	−0.50***	−0.62**	0.83***	0.10
ISIC.381	−0.17	−0.14	0.31	0.22	−0.26	−0.07	0.13
ISIC 382	−0.07	−0.40*	0.46**	−0.29***	−0.36*	0.26	−0.06
ISIC 383	−0.64***	−1.49 10^{-3}	0.65***	−0.60***	−0.54***	1.05***	0.39***
ISIC 384	−0.51***	0.06	0.46***	0.16	−0.59***	1.15***	0.65***
ISIC 385	−0.15	−0.04	0.19***	−0.59***	−0.47***	0.67***	0.19***

Note

*, **, *** denotes respectively significance at the 10, 5 and the 1 per cent level.

Table 4.6 Demand elasticity of low-skilled labour at sector level, 1985–1996

	$\varepsilon_{LS,wHS}$	$\varepsilon_{LS,wLS}$	$\varepsilon_{LS,wK}$	$\varepsilon_{LS,Moehw}$	$\varepsilon_{LS,Meulw}$	$\varepsilon_{LS,Mnic}$	$\varepsilon_{LS,RDS}$
ISIC 31	−0.20***	−0.27***	0.47***	0.33***	−0.36***	−0.05	0.29***
ISIC 32	−6.62 10^{-3}	−0.39***	0.40***	0.22***	−0.24***	−0.19***	−6.60 10^{-3}
ISIC 33	−0.24***	−0.43***	0.67***	−0.17*	−0.25***	0.23**	−5.93 10^{-3}
ISIC 34	0.11**	−0.42***	0.30**	0.109	−0.59***	0.07	0.02
ISIC 35	−0.31***	−0.61***	0.92***	0.49***	−0.95***	0.33**	0.22**
ISIC 36	−0.02	−0.35***	0.37***	0.43***	−0.08	−0.24***	0.11***
ISIC 37	−0.08	−0.36***	0.43***	0.36**	−0.54*	0.42**	0.05
ISIC 381	−0.11	−0.31***	0.42***	0.68***	0.17**	−0.53***	−0.34***
ISIC 382	−0.44*	−0.24***	0.68***	−4.10 10^{-3}	−0.36***	0.21	−0.27***
ISIC 383	−2.11 10^{-3}	−0.43**	0.44***	0.01	−0.23*	−0.03	0.47***
ISIC 384	0.05	−0.35***	0.29***	0.98***	−0.18*	0.37***	0.45***
ISIC 385	−0.09	−1.09***	1.17***	−0.19	−0.47**	0.13	0.54***

Note

*, **, *** denotes respectively significance at the 10, 5 and the 1 per cent level.

whereas high-skilled and low-skilled labour can only be considered significant substitutes in four sectors.

These results for own and cross demand elasticity are consistent with prior assumptions of a well-behaved cost function. The computed elasticity of factor demand with regard to international trade reveals that in all sectors imports from high-wage OECD countries significantly lowered the relative demand for high-skilled workers. The sign of $\varepsilon_{HS,\ Moehw}$ is significantly negative in all but two sectors (ISIC 381 and ISIC 384) and significantly positive for $\varepsilon_{LS,\ Moehw}$ in seven sectors, among which are ISIC 381 and ISIC 384.

Only in one sector (ISIC 33 – Wood and Wood Products) is the sign of $\varepsilon_{LS, \text{Moehw}}$ significantly negative and then only at the 10 per cent significance level.

Trade with the EULW seems to have a negative impact on both high-skilled and low-skilled labour and, surprisingly, seems to have decreased the relative demand for high-skilled workers in 8 out of the 12 sectors.

More in line with expectations is that international trade with the Central and Eastern European, (South-) East Asian and Latin American NICs appears to have lowered the relative demand for low-skilled workers in the EU in all but one sector (ISIC 382: *Non-electrical machinery*) in the period 1985–1995, without however implying an absolute fall in the demand for low-skilled workers in all the sectors of manufacturing.

Compared to the wage effects of international trade competition in the EU, we notice that the effects on employment are much clearer and significant. The breakdown of imports according to geographical origin indicates that most of the effects of import competition are in line with the expectations from a factor endowments model, if we would consider non-EU OECD countries (e.g. the US and Japan) as well endowed with high-skilled workers relative to EU countries. Imports from the latter countries have a negative impact on the relative demand of high-skilled labour in the EU, whereas imports from the NICs have the opposite effect. Import competition with low-wage EU countries has on the other hand a negative effect on labour demand. Because of these partial effects of opposite sign, it is not straightforward to determine the overall impact on (relative) labour demand, nor its degree of country homogeneity. The estimated demand elasticity with regard to international trade with the high wage OECD countries and the aggregated group of NICs seems reconcilable with the first prediction of a sticky wage model (increase in the relative demand of the relatively abundant production factor). However, we do not find any sector-specific pattern that confirms the prediction that labour demand will increase in sectors with a comparative advantage and decrease in sectors with a comparative disadvantage. Our findings are more in line with Feenstra and Hanson (1996a,b, 1997b) who argue – in a flexible wage framework – that adjustments occur *within* sectors rather than *between* sectors.

The last columns of Tables 4.5 and 4.6 show that technological change significantly increased the relative demand for high-skilled workers in seven sectors and significantly increased relative demand for low-skilled workers in only three sectors, which implies some indications of skill-biased technological change.

Conclusions

Two-stage mandated wage estimations of the impact of international trade and technological change on wages in the European Union do not support the view that trade competition from low-wage NICs significantly decreased the relative wages of low-skilled workers in EU countries in the period 1985–1995. Price changes of imports from low-wage EU countries (Ireland, Greece, Portugal and Spain) were significantly positively correlated with domestic price changes in high-wage EU countries but this effect apparently did not carry over to a decrease in the (relative) wages of low-skilled workers.

We do find some indications that international trade with high-wage non-EU OECD countries (e.g. US and Japan) lowered the wages of high-skilled workers in the European Union, though only at the 10 per cent significance level. The significantly negative correlation between non-EU OECD import prices and EU domestic prices does however not warrant a simple Stolper–Samuelson explanation. Intra-OECD competition probably requires an analysis within a more developed theoretical framework. In a number of EU countries the relative wages of high-skilled workers did actually decrease during the period considered. Intra-OECD trade competition appears to have affected EU countries in an asymmetric way.

A mandated wage approach fits within the HOS framework, explaining the effects of international trade under the assumption of flexible wages. If we consider labour market rigidities, often ascribed to EU countries, international trade may cause unemployment of the relatively scarce production factor rather than decreasing its fixed remuneration. The insignificant results of mandated wage estimations for the European Union therefore need not imply that international trade did not affect the relative income position of low-skilled workers.

Therefore, using a flexible cost function, we also estimated the impact of international trade in EU countries under the assumption of sticky wages. From a flexible cost function the elasticity of the demand for low- and high-skilled workers with regard to import competition can be computed.

The results show that trade with the high-wage OERE significantly decreased demand for high-skilled workers in all sectors for a panel of ten EU countries in the period 1985–1996.

Surprisingly, trade competition of the low-wage EU countries significantly decreased the demand for both low- and high-skilled workers, and in 8 out of 12 sectors significantly decreased the relative demand for high-skilled workers. We do find evidence that international trade with the Newly Industrialized Countries significantly decreased the demand for low-skilled workers in the EU in the period 1985–1996 in all but one sector.

If these results seem to support the sticky wage approach for the European Union we also have to acknowledge that the data suggest that the impact of international trade on factor demand is factor-biased rather than sector-biased, that is, that the impact is pervasive over all sectors and there seems to be no asymmetry between high-skill-intensive and low-skill-intensive sectors. Hence, our results might only be fully reconcilable with the sticky wage model in, for example, an extended model in which trade in services is included too and where the manufacturing sector as such may be considered as relatively low-skilled labour intensive.

Data appendix

Labour shares

For the computation of the value added shares of high-skilled labour, low-skilled labour and capital it proved impossible to stick to a single data source to compute the shares for a sufficient number of EU countries for the whole period. In most studies the distinction of high-skilled/low-skilled workers is made by the classification manual/non-manual – production/non-production – operatives/ non-operatives or blue-collar/white-collar. For the period 1985–1991 we used the data on the wage sum of operatives from the UNIDO General Industrial Statistics database. This information was available for Germany, Italy, the UK, Denmark, Spain, Portugal and Finland, although not always for the entire period. The breakdown by operatives/non-operatives is no longer provided by UNIDO after 1991. From 1992 onwards we used data from the Labour Force Surveys (LFS), provided by Eurostat. For some countries the LFS data start in 1992 but for most countries only in 1993. The data source only contains information on the number of workers, not on wages. For data on wages we used Eurostat NewCronos, which contains gross hourly earnings of manual workers and gross monthly earnings of non-manual workers.

The LFS data do not match the OECD data on total employment, which was also established by the OECD. The OECD secretariat adjusted the data to STAN data or data in the OECD National Accounts (OECD 1998: 5). As the LFS data are the results of surveys, we held to the OECD STAN data on total employment and rescaled the ISCO numbers following the white-collar/blue-collar ratio of LFS.

The value added share of non-manuals was computed using the monthly wages of non-manuals and the rescaled numbers of white-collar workers. From this the value added shares of manuals were computed. In general this led to acceptable results, except for Italy. For Italy, data on the number of hours worked by operatives were taken from the OECD Industrial Survey results, which for Italy is only given for 1992–1994. The number of hours worked by operatives (i.e. blue-collar workers in the ISCO classification) and the gross hourly wages of manuals from NewCronos and the total wage sum from OECD STAN allowed us to compute the value added share of manuals. The results appeared to be more reliable. For Belgium we used social security data, on the number of manual and non-manual workers, provided by the National Office for Social Security (RSZ) for the entire period 1985–1996. For Sweden, Eva Oscarsson (Department of Economics-University of Stockholm) kindly provided us with data on employment and wages for the period 1970–1993, as used for example, in Oscarsson (2000).

Wages

Data on monthly wages of non-manual workers were taken from NewCronos. For manual workers this data source gives gross hourly wages. The data on the hours worked per month by manual workers are too scarce to compute monthly wages. For the period 1985–1991 the UNIDO data gives the wage sum of operatives and the number of operatives, which allows for a straightforward way of computing monthly wages of operatives. From 1992 onwards we computed monthly wages of manuals with the wage sum of manual workers (total wage sum-wage sum non-manual workers (LFS + NewCronos)) and the rescaled number of manual workers (LFS).

Price of capital

In Berndt and Hesse (1986) the price of capital is calculated as $P_{Ki,t} = q_{i,t}*(r_t + \delta_i)$ where $q_{i,t}$ denotes the investment deflator of the ith type of capital (e.g. capital in sector i) in year t and r_t denotes the long-term government bond yield and δ_i the depreciation rate of the ith type of capital.

Data on long-term government bond yields were taken from the IMF International Financial Statistics. The same source contains data on fixed capital consumption from which depreciation rates can be computed. Unfortunately this information is given for few countries, sectors and years. Rather than using the sector depreciation rate for just a couple of observations, and disregarding it for most observations, we only used r_t. For $q_{i,t}$ we computed sector-specific deflators from the value added data given in STAN.

Capital stock

Data on capital stocks were taken directly from the OECD International Sector Database (ISDB) or were estimated from ISDB annual investment data using the perpetual inventory method.

Domestic prices

Domestic prices were computed from the OECD STAN data on sector value added.

Unit value import prices

Unit value import prices were computed at the sector level (ISIC). This involved aggregation and conversion. We aggregated data on imports by EU countries from the OECD International Trade by Commodities (ITCS) into six geographical groups of exporting countries: high-wage EU countries (Austria, Belgium-Luxembourg; Denmark; Finland; France; Germany, Italy, the Netherlands; Sweden and the UK); low-wage EU countries (Ireland; Greece; Portugal and Spain); non-EU OECD countries (Australia, Japan; New Zealand; Norway and the US); Central and East European emerging economies (Hungary, Czech Republic and Poland); (South-) East Asian NICs (Hong Kong, Indonesia, Republic of Korea, Malaysia, Philippines, Singapore and Thailand) and Latin American NICs (Argentina, Brazil, Chile and Mexico).

As ITCS data are given for SITC commodity classes and the estimation is done for ISIC sectors we had to convert the data from SITC to ISIC, with a table provided by OECD. Prices were computed for the period 1985–1996. As pointed out by Freeman and Revenga (1999) unit value prices are a 'mishmash' of aggregate prices of commodities. They find however, that sectors that experienced increased import penetration showed relative price declines, which suggests that import price changes are good proxies for import pressure. A caveat of unit value price changes that is often put forward is, that as it concerns aggregates, the changes might reflect a change of the commodity mix rather than a change of commodity prices. To preclude this possibility we computed, following the shift-share approach,[13] unit value prices, keeping the commodity structure fixed.

Total factor productivity

TFP was taken from the OECD ISDB if available. For those countries for which ISDB does not provide data on TFP we computed it, from data on gross fixed capital formation and employment (STAN/ISDB), using the formula given in OECD (1994).

R&D stock

We computed national sector R&D stocks with data from ANBERD, completed with BERD data (both from OECD). The 1973 stock was taken as the initial stock and computed with the formula given by Coe and Helpman (1995). For each sector three R&D stocks were computed: the national R&D stock of the given sector, the total national R&D stock (minus the sector R&D stock) to estimate national inter-sector spillovers,[14] and a foreign R&D stock which was weighted according to the procedure proposed by Lichtenberg and van Pottelsberghe de la Potterie (1996). As it concerns sector R&D stocks the foreign R&D stocks were weighted by total imports over the GDP of the exporting country times the share of the sector in the national output.

Notes

1 See for instance Lücke (1998) for Germany; Oscarsson (2000) for Sweden and Haskel and Slaughter (2001) for the UK.
2 In case of imperfect competition a constant mark-up can be applied.
3 Time subscripts are omitted to simplify the notation.
4 Countries: Belgium, Denmark, Finland, France, Germany, Italy, Spain, Sweden and the United Kingdom. Sectors: Food, drink and tobacco (ISIC 31); Textile, footwear and leather (ISIC 32); Wood, cork and furniture (ISIC 33); Paper, printing and publishing (ISIC 34); Chemicals (ISIC 35); Non-metallic mineral products (ISIC 36); Basic Metal Industries (ISIC 37); Fabricated metal products (ISIC 381); Non-electrical machinery (ISIC 382); Electrical equipment (ISIC 383); Transport equipment (ISIC 384) and Precision instruments (ISIC 385).
5 The Newly Industrialized Countries, which are members of the OECD have been classified in their respective group of NICs and have not been considered in the OECD group.
6 Spain is the only low-wage EU country in the 'mandated wage' panel of nine EU countries.
7 Adjustment costs are not our central concern though, because of degree of freedom limitations at a sufficient level of detail. We use a specification where allowance is made for adjustment costs and quasi-fixed input factors primarily as a robustness check on our results. Capital is often treated as a quasi-fixed input.
8 We omitted the different indices s, c and t for the sake of the legibility of the notation.

9 If at least one input factor is quasi-fixed in the short run, these expressions apply to the short-run. Long-run elasticity would follow from the equilibrium value of the quasi-fixed inputs, which is obtained by equating the price of the quasi-fixed input and its shadow value. They can be calculated by determining the short-run elasticity and by adding the long-run adjustment. The latter comprises the effect of a change in the exogenous variable on the equilibrium stock of the fixed input and the effect of the latter on factor input demand. See also Morrison (1988).

10 The nine countries included in the mandated wage regression (enumerated in note 3) and Portugal.

11 Non-sector and foreign knowledge capital were not included in order to limit the loss of degrees of freedom in this framework where each variable, its square and all its cross-products enter in the specification.

12 Not reported here for the sake of brevity but available from the authors upon request.

13 The shift-share approach decomposes changes in unit value prices into three components: a component that measures which part is due to changes in the commodity mix, keeping commodity prices fixed at their begin of period values; a component measuring the part of unit value price changes that can be explained by changes in commodity prices, keeping the commodity mix fixed at its begin structure; and a last interaction component of changes of the commodity mix *and* commodity prices. We took the second component as a measure for unit value price changes.

14 In principle national inter-sector spillovers could be computed with weights reflecting input–output linkages. Unfortunately input–output tables are only available for a limited number of countries.

5 Using structural models in trade–technology wage inequality decompositions

Lisandro Abrego and John Whalley

Introduction

This chapter explores the use of structural models as an alternative to reduced form econometrics when decomposing observed joint trade and technology driven wage changes into the components attributable to each source. Many papers have been written on the principal sources of increased wage dispersion in the form of an elevated premium paid to skilled labour in OECD countries in recent years, and most focus on increased trade and skill-biased technological change as the two principal causes. Lawrence and Slaughter (1993), Krugman and Lawrence (1993), Leamer (1996), Baldwin and Cain (1997) and others conclude that the role of trade is small; Wood (1994) points to a dominant role for trade. Conclusions in this literature rest largely on reduced form regressions. Some, such as Murphy and Welch (1991), and Borjas, Freeman, and Katz (1991) estimate the factor contents of trade and use these estimates via exogenous (literature based) labour demand elasticities to infer the wage change attributable to trade. They then compare this to observed wage changes. Others, such as Leamer (1996) and Baldwin and Cain (1997) use estimating equations derived from explicit general equilibrium models.

We show how alternative structural models with different properties can be built for decompositional analysis, each consistent with the same joint shock, but with sharply different results. Typically, double calibration to joint observations on relative wage change and trade shocks is required. Using a simple Heckscher–Ohlin type model, close to what is found in some of the trade and wages literature, only small changes can be analysed and these, in turn, offer a wide range of decompositions from alternative data consistent parameterisations. With a product differentiation model, larger changes can be analysed and across alternative parameterisations decomposition results are relatively robust, but with demand side effects entering the model the contribution of trade to inequality is much reduced. Analyses differ over short and longer runs, and alternative labour market structures also influence results. While showing how structural models can be used in the decompositions more so than advocating one particular structural model, we nonetheless suggest that exploration of alternative structural models rather than reduced forms may be the way forward to more satisfactorily sort out trade and technology effects on wage dispersion.

The trade and wage inequality debate

Literature on trade and wages focuses on understanding the quantitative significance of trade in explaining the sharp increase in OECD wage inequality which has occurred during the 1980s because of the associated pressures for protection which arise if trade is deemed to be the main source of increased inequality. This increase in wage inequality has been documented for a number of OECD countries, most notably the US and the UK (e.g. Davis, 1992; Kosters, 1994). The pattern has been observed across different types of workers according to their skills (low vs. high skill), education level (college vs. non-college graduates), and experience. Even among observably similar workers wage inequality has increased (e.g. Davis, 1992). There has also been some documentation of a rise in unemployment in European countries without major increases in wage inequality (Kosters, 1994) as well as of a decline in wage inequality in some key developing countries (Korea, Venezuela, Colombia and Brazil) (Davis, 1992). A large literature has evolved on the explanation of increased wage inequality, especially for the US case.[1]

Two major factors have been identified as responsible for this phenomenon: increased trade with developing countries and technological change biased against unskilled labour. The great majority of research has concluded that unskilled-biased technological change, rather than increased trade, is the main source of the surge in wage inequality.[2]

This literature uses a variety of econometric methods.[3] Early papers focussed on how trade changes labour demand via the factor content of trade (e.g. Borjas *et al.*, 1991; Murphy and Welch, 1991; and Katz and Murphy, 1992). They typically ran regressions which linked labour demand (by type of labour) and trade flows, and then used actual trade flows to infer the changes in labour demand they imply. They then combined these labour demand changes with wage elasticity of labour demand estimates culled from the literature to infer what portion of actual wage changes are due to trade changes. This work generally came to the conclusion that the portion of actual wage change attributable to trade is small.

These estimates, based on factor content of trade calculations, were criticised by Wood (1994) who argued that trade is a considerably more important factor than these analyses show. He argued that, for many products and especially those from developing countries, there is no comparable domestic product, and so factor substitution effects attributed to trade using conventional elasticities are understated. He also argued that technological response to trade will occur in expectation of future trade surges, and so some of what is attributed to technology in factor content analyses should in reality be attributed to trade.

Later papers in the area (Lawrence and Slaughter, 1993; Baldwin and Cain, 1997; Leamer, 1996) took a different approach and worked with estimating equations derived from explicit general equilibrium models of a Heckscher–Ohlin type. Lawrence and Slaughter, for instance, related changes in relative skilled and unskilled wage rates to changes in prices of skilled- and unskilled-labour-intensive products. Highlighting key measurement issues, they suggest that for the US the changes in product prices appear to be opposite from those needed to generate increased wage inequality (i.e. unskilled-intensive product prices rise rather than fall). Their conclusion is that unskilled-biased technical change is the main source of increased wage inequality and that trade is relatively unimportant.

Finally, other work regresses measures of factor shares on measures of outsourcing (Feenstra and Hanson, 1996a,b; Anderton and Brenton, 1999c), concluding that trade may be more important than in earlier analyses. Anderton and Brenton (1999c), in particular, find that trade is more important when only trade with developing countries rather than with all countries is used as an explanatory variable.

Virtually all of these analyses use reduced-form data in their estimations, with little or no work explicitly employing structural models,[4] even though structural models are needed to make a meaningful decomposition of an observed relative wage change into a portion due to trade and a portion due to (skill-biased) technological change. Because the model parameters which are consistent with given reduced-form data are not unique, different parameterisations can generate different decomposition between trade and technological change as sources of an observed combined change in inequality. Some attention to structural models may be required.

An example of a calibrated model for use in decomposition

Here we outline a recent trade and wages decomposition undertaken by Abrego and Whalley (2002). For their decomposition analysis of data for the UK for two years (1979 and 1995), Abrego and Whalley use a model of a small open, price-taking economy of Ricardo–Viner specific-factors form, in contrast to a Hecksher–Ohlin type, fully mobile, factors model. During the period they studied, substantial increase in wage inequality occurred in the UK. Their issue was what portion of the observed change can be attributed to import surges of low-wage goods and what portion to technical change.

Simple Heckscher–Ohlin type models prove unsatisfactory for the task of decomposing wage inequality change into separate trade and technology components if there is near linearity of the production frontier, and associated problems of specialisation. This is a well known numerical property of production frontiers generated from conventional functional forms for production functions and fixed economy wide endowments (see Johnson, 1966). If alternatively a production frontier with sufficient curvature to prevent specialisation were directly specified, the problem would remain that there is no known way to recover sector production functions consistent with such a frontier, and they anyway would be inconsistent with the observed base case equilibrium data.

They treated the UK as a small open, price-taking economy that produced two goods, M and E, both of which are traded at fixed world prices (P_{it}; $i = M, E$), in period t. The production of each good in each period required the use of two mobile factors: skilled labour, S, and unskilled labour, U, along with a sector-specific fixed factor. Production, consumption and trade took place in each of the two time periods, 1 and 2, which they referred to as the initial and terminal periods.

Thus, each good in each period is produced according to a decreasing returns to scale technology:

$$Y_{it} = A_{it}L_{it}^{\alpha_{it}}, \quad i = M, E; \; t = 1, 2 \tag{5.1}$$

where Y_{it} represents output of good i in period t, A_{it} denotes a sector-specific efficiency measure of a composite labour factor input, and L_{it} is use of a composite labour input. α_{it} is the output elasticity with respect to composite labour, assumed to be strictly less than one to yield decreasing returns to scale. Consistent with a Ricardo–Viner approach, (5.1) implicitly defines a fixed factor in production in each sector, with a Cobb–Douglas share $(1 - \alpha_{it})$.

The composite labour input in each sector, L_{it}, is, in turn, a CES aggregate of unskilled and skilled labour, U and S,

$$L_{it} = B_{it}\big[\beta_{it}(\delta_t^U U_{it})^{(\rho_{it}-1)/\rho_{it}} \\ + (1 - \beta_{it})(\delta_t^S S_{it})^{(\rho_{it}-1)/\rho_{it}}\big]^{\rho_{it}/(\rho_{it}-1)}, \quad i = M, E; \; t = 1, 2 \tag{5.2}$$

where B_{it} defines units for composite labour used in sector i in period t, and β_{it} is the CES share parameter in the aggregation function. δ_t^U and δ_t^S are factor-augmenting technical change parameters which capture changes in input quality over time. ρ_{it} denotes the elasticity of substitution in sector i in period t between unskilled and skilled labour.

Combining (5.1) and (5.2) for each sector in each period yields

$$Y_{it} = \gamma_{it}\big[\beta_{it}(\delta_t^U U_{it})^{(\rho_{it}-1)/\rho_{it}} \\ + (1 - \beta_{it})(\delta_t^S S_{it})^{(\rho_{it}-1)/\rho_{it}}\big]^{\alpha_{it}\rho_{it}/(\rho_{it}-1)}, \quad i = M, E; \; t = 1, 2 \tag{5.3}$$

where the units parameter in the consolidated function (5.3) $\gamma_{it} = A_{it}B_{it}$. In (5.3), changes in γ_{it} represent sector-specific, Hicks-neutral technical change, while δ_t^U and δ_t^S reflect factor-biased technical change. In our empirical implementation of this model, we assume that (as in most OECD economies) production of the importable good, M, is intensive in unskilled labour in both periods, that is, $\beta_{Mt} > \beta_{Et}\; \forall t$.

Competitive labour markets were assumed, so that each type of labour is paid its marginal value product, with full employment of each type of labour in each period. The endowments of unskilled and skilled labour, $\overline{U}_t$ and $\overline{S}_t$ respectively, are assumed to be fixed in each time period, while varying across periods.

First order conditions for factor demands implied by marginal product pricing were

$$W_{Ut} = P_{it}\alpha_{it}\beta_{it}\delta_{ut}^{(\rho_{it}-1)/\rho_{it}}Y_{it}^{[\rho_{it}(\alpha_{it}-1)+1]/\alpha_{it}\rho_{it}}\gamma_{it}^{(\alpha_{it}\rho_{it}/\rho_{it}-1)}/U_{it}^{1/\rho_{it}} \\ i = M, E; \; t = 1, 2 \tag{5.4}$$

$$W_{St} = P_{it}\alpha_{it}(1 - \beta_{it})\delta_{St}^{(\rho_{it}-1)/\rho_{it}}Y_{it}^{[\rho_{it}(\alpha_{it}-1)+1]/\alpha_{it}\rho_{it}}\gamma_{it}^{(\alpha_{it}\rho_{it}/\rho_{it}-1)}/S_{it}^{1/\rho_{it}} \\ i = M, E; \; t = 1, 2 \tag{5.5}$$

where W_{Ut} and W_{St} denote unskilled and skilled wage rates respectively, and P_{it} is the (fixed) world price of good i in period t. Given the decreasing returns technology set out in (5.1), payments to unskilled and skilled labour do not exhaust the value of production in either sector, and the remaining factor income implied by (5.1) accrues to the fixed factor in each sector.

They modelled trade shocks in this framework as changes in world prices, which, in turn, typically induced increased import volumes. They considered the shock to be a fall in the relative price of unskilled-intensive to skilled-intensive goods between the initial and terminal years. These generated larger import volumes in the model, adjustment of labour out of the unskilled intensive sector, and increases in exports.

In equilibrium a zero trade balance condition held, that is,

$$\sum_{i=M,E} P_{it}T_{ti} = 0 \tag{5.6}$$

where T_{it} denotes the net trades of the country in the two goods, M and E. The sign convention is that if good i is exported, domestic production less consumption is positive; if good i is imported this difference is negative. Imports and competitive domestically produced goods are treated as homogeneous, as is also assumed to be the case with exports. This homogeneity assumption implies that trade flows involving any good are always one-way, and that one of the goods is exported and the other imported.

Equilibrium in each period in this model is given by unskilled and skilled wage rates such that the two domestic labour markets clear. The value marginal product of each mobile factor in each sector is equal to the corresponding wage rate, as in (5.4) and (5.5), and the fixed factor in each sector i receives the residual return, F_{it}, in period t. Market clearing conditions of this form hold in both periods, that is,

$$\sum_i U_{it} = \bar{U}_t, \quad i = M, E; \ t = 1, 2 \tag{5.7}$$

$$\sum_i S_{it} = \bar{S}_t, \quad i = M, E; \ t = 1, 2 \tag{5.8}$$

The two market-clearing conditions (5.7) and (5.8) determine the equilibrium wage rates for skilled and unskilled labour. The fixed factor in each sector receives the difference between the value of production at world prices and payments to mobile factor inputs. This enters incomes which, in turn, finance goods demands.

Consumption of each good in equilibrium is given by the difference between production and net trade, that is,

$$C_{it} = Y_{it} - T_{it}, \quad i = M, E; \ t = 1, 2 \tag{5.9}$$

where C_{it} denotes consumption of good i in period t. A property of equilibrium in such a model (from Walras Law) is that trade balance will be satisfied.

For the model structure specified earlier, Abrego and Whalley's calibration consisted in choosing values for model parameters such that the model gives, as far as possible, equilibrium solutions consistent with data in both periods. With the small open economy treatment, the demand and production sides of the model are separable. This separability allowed them to concentrate only on production function parameters when calibrating since the focus of their decomposition analysis is on determinants of wage rate change, and does not involve demand side considerations (such as statements about consumer welfare would do). Thus, in the calibration used, the demand side of the model is irrelevant to the outcome of the decomposition of wage inequality change.

Single period calibration typically assumes that the values of elasticities of substitution in production (ρ) are exogenously given, based on separate literature-based estimation of parameters. They also assume that this is the case, but now for both periods. This leaves sixteen production-side parameter values to be determined through calibration; the output elasticities with respect to composite labour, the units terms in sector production functions, CES shares in aggregation functions, and factor-biased technological change parameters, that is

$$\alpha_{it}, \gamma_{it}, \beta_{it}, \delta_t^U, \delta_t^S; \quad i = M, E; \; t = 1, 2 \tag{5.10}$$

If these parameters are to be consistent with the model equilibrium conditions in each time period, the values determined for them must satisfy the first order conditions (5.4) and (5.5), as well as equation (5.3). These equations yield a system of 12 equations in 16 unknowns, and to determine parameter values from it they needed to introduce additional identifying restrictions.

They first set

$$\delta_1^U = \delta_1^S = 1 \tag{5.11}$$

This is a normalization rule for factor-biased technological change terms, and they adopted this because it is only changes in technology parameters over time that are relevant in the model.

They then imposed further restrictions on the model parameterization to yield an equation system for calibration across the two time periods in which the remaining endogenous model parameters are exactly identified. They used three alternative sets of restrictions, each of which yields an exactly identified system of equations from which parameter values for the model are determined. These were

(1) $\gamma_{i1} = \gamma_{i2}, \quad i = M, E$ $\hspace{4cm}$ (5.12)

(2) $\delta_2^U = \delta_2^S = 1$ $\hspace{4.5cm}$ (5.13)

or

(3) $\beta_{i1} = \beta_{i2}, \quad i = M, E$ $\hspace{4cm}$ (5.14)

These three alternatives differ in their implied treatment of technical change over time. Restriction 1 implies that no Hicks-neutral technical change takes place over time. Restriction 2 implies that no factor-biased technical change occurs over time. Restriction 3 allows technical change to be both Hicks-neutral and factor-biased, but rules out any change over time in share parameters in the composite CES labour aggregation function. For each of these sets of restrictions, they calibrate the model and assess the implications for decomposition results. They do not restrict the α_{it} when implementing calibration since these parameter values represent the share of the composite labour input in sectoral income, and must be consistent with the shares implied by the data assembled for each time period.

They used the model calibrated in each of the ways set out above to generate estimates of the contributions of increased trade, factor-biased technical change, and factor endowment change (demographics) to increases in wage inequality in the UK between 1979 and 1995. They captured trade shocks in their analyses as changes in world prices (the relative price of skill intensive to unskilled-intensive goods). These affected trade flows were also endogenously determined in the model. They considered the fall in the relative price of the unskilled-intensive products (in our case, aggregated under M) which took place in the UK between 1979 and 1995. Factor-biased technical change over time was modelled as changes in the factor-augmenting technical change parameters, δ_t^U and δ_t^S. They also considered other production function parameter changes generated by the model and calibration procedures as indicated earlier.

They used the calibrated versions of the model to carry out decomposition experiments using both the exact and inexact calibration procedures described earlier. In the process, changes in model technology parameters were determined over time using two-period data and the various calibration procedures.

Results suggested that there is a relatively small contribution of trade to increased wage inequality over the period. A larger role emerges for factor-biased technical change (procedures 1 and 3), which, in turn, varies significantly depending upon the calibration used. Where changes in share parameters, β_{it}, are not allowed, factor-biased technical change accounts for more than the observed wage inequality change. Factor endowment changes have large negative effects on wage inequality, but these are offset by the positive effects of changes in share parameters under methods 1 and 2, and by factor-biased technical change under method 3.

Trade and wages decompositions in a differentiated goods model

One can also analyse the relative importance of trade and technology in explaining relative wage changes in OECD countries in a trade model with differentiated goods, similar to that set out in de Melo and Robinson (1989), and more recently discussed by Bhattarai *et al.* (1999). In this model, imports and domestically produced goods are imperfect rather than perfect substitutes. The model has two traded and two produced goods, but embodies three goods in aggregate when the consumption side is included, since imports are not produced domestically and the domestically produced good which substitutes for imports in consumption is not traded. On the production side, the model has a domestically produced good – the imperfect substitute for imports – and an exportable. Each of the produced goods uses two factor inputs: low-skill and high-skill labour. Imports, the (non-exportable) domestic good and the exportable enter consumption. Imports and exports are traded at fixed world prices.

As imports and the domestically produced import substitute become perfect substitutes in preferences, in this structure the model approaches the conventional homogeneous goods form, with only two traded and produced goods. The model, therefore, is a generalisation of the conventional homogeneous goods trade model, which stands as a special case when the elasticity of substitution in preferences between imports and the domestically produced import substitute is infinity. For finite elasticities, demand side effects from world commodity price changes will be reflected in substitution in consumption between these two goods.

More formally, denoting consumption of imports by M, the exportable by E, and other domestically produced goods by D, preferences are defined as

$$U(M^C, E) \tag{5.15}$$

where M^C is a composite function of M and D; that is

$$M^C = C(M, D) \tag{5.16}$$

With D and E being the two produced goods, and H and L (high and low skilled labour) the two factor inputs, technology is represented by

$$D^S = D^S(L_D, H_D)$$
$$E^S = E^S(L_E, H_E), \tag{5.17}$$

where D^S and E^S represent production of the (imperfect) import substitute domestic good and the exportable, respectively L_D, L_E, H_D and H_E, denote the use of high- and low-skilled labour in domestic good and export production. In later empirical implementation of the model, technologies are also modelled through CES production functions.

For simplicity, the economy is assumed to be a taker of prices $\overline{P}_E, \overline{P}_M$, for exports and imports. The price of the domestic good, P_D, however, is endogenously determined. Thus, in contrast to a simple homogeneous goods trade model, a product price adjusts to clear the domestic market even in the small-country case. Trade shocks are modelled as changes in world prices, that is, of imports relative to exports.

Given the per unit cost functions for the production of E and D, consistent with zero profits, are given by

$$P_D = g_D(W^H, W^L) \tag{5.18}$$
$$\overline{P}_E = g_E(W^H, W^L) \tag{5.19}$$

where W^H and W^L are the wage rates of high- and low-skilled labour, and g_D and g_E are per unit costs functions for D and E.

Full employment conditions for factors yield

$$f_D^H \cdot D^S + f_E^H \cdot E^S = \overline{H} \tag{5.20}$$
$$f_D^L \cdot D^S + f_E^L \cdot E^S = \overline{L} \tag{5.21}$$

where $f_D^H, f_E^H, f_D^L, f_E^L$ are per unit cost minimising factor demands for H and L in the production of the domestic import substitute and the exportable.

To generate commodity demands, the representative household in this economy maximises the utility function (5.15) subject to the budget constraint

$$P_D D + \overline{P}_M M + \overline{P}_E E^D = W^L \overline{L} + W^H \overline{H} \tag{5.22}$$

where D, E and M denote domestic consumption of the domestic substitute, imports, and the exportable.

In equilibrium, the price of the domestically produced good P_D^*, is determined such that market clearing occurs in D, that is,

$$D = D^S. \tag{5.23}$$

No market clearing in either E or M is required in this model since these are internationally traded at fixed prices. Walras Law, which automatically holds for economies with demand functions generated from utility maximization subject to a budget constraint, also implies that trade balance will hold in equilibrium, that is,

$$\overline{P}_M M = \overline{P}_E E \tag{5.24}$$

where M and E represent imports and exports.

The feature of this structure that is relevant to the trade and wages debate is that changes in world prices of imports can be partially, or even fully, accommodated by changes in import volumes without necessarily impacting the rest of the economy. Hence, if changes in $\overline{P}_M$ occur but yield offsetting changes in M which are consistent with the other equilibrium conditions of the model, trade balance will still hold, but these price changes will have no impact on domestic production. The domestic output of each product will remain the same, as will the use of factors by sector and relative factor prices, and no impacts on the wages of skilled and unskilled labour will occur from a trade shock. More generally, imperfect pass through of world price changes onto domestic product prices in a heterogeneous goods trade model will tend to lessen the impact of trade on wage inequality.

An outcome in which world price changes have no impact on wage inequality will occur when the elasticity of substitution between M and D in preferences (equation 5.16) is unity, since demand-side substitution effects will fully accommodate to the world price change. If this substitution elasticity is close to one, world price changes affecting low-skill-intensive goods will still largely be accommodated by the demand side of the model, weakening the role of trade in explaining increased wage inequality compared to the conventional homogeneous goods model.

Empirical studies yielding import demand elasticities (see, for example, Reinert and Roland-Holst, 1992; Shiells and Reinert, 1993; Marquez, 1994) consistently produce estimates in the neighbourhood of one. The role of trade in explaining recent increases in OECD wage inequality thus seems to be weakened once goods market behaviour considerations are added to conventional trade models.

Long and short run models for trade and wages decompositions

Edwards and Whalley (2002) compare decomposition results from short-run models in which some factors are either immobile or face adjustment costs moving between sectors, to those from a longer-run Hecksher–Ohlin type model where all factors are fully mobile between industries.

Models where not all factors can move easily between sectors (Mayer, 1974; Mussa, 1974; Neary, 1978) have investigated the implications of this feature for relative incomes in a two-factor model (such as whether the Stolper–Samuleson theorem still holds) and are the starting point.

They discuss the case where the factor inputs are unskilled (U) and skilled (S) labour, with U being the factor subject to adjustment costs. In this case, if there is a fall in the world price of the U-intensive good, with S freely mobile between sectors, then since U cannot easily move towards the S-intensive sector in the short run, its wage will rise in the expanding sector and fall more steeply than the goods price in the declining sector. The wage of S will fall in the short run, though by less than that of the U-intensive good. In the longer run, as factor U becomes free to move towards the S-intensive sector where its wage is higher, the output of this sector will expand. Given the shift towards the S-intensive sector, S's wages will rise, while U's wages will fall further in both sectors. This relative wage effect reflecting the shift over time in factors can be more marked than the initial impact effect of the price shock, and is the main factor behind the long-run Stolper–Samuelson influences on relative wages (a fall in the U-intensive good price will reduce U's wage and raise S's wage).

Although U's income will fall sharply in the U-intensive sector when the goods price falls, it will actually fall further, rather than be mitigated, once U becomes free to move to the other sector, as S's share of income gets bid up by the shift of output to the S-intensive sector. This suggests that some of the conclusions of the short-run model may differ from the longer-run H–O model, in that much of the impact of trade on relative factor rewards takes place only as trade and output here are able to change (a magnification effect). Also factor price insensitivity to endowments does not apply when not all factors are able to move, so any short-run study of the causes of changing wage inequality needs to take account of changing endowments, not simply world prices and technology.

They compare the effects of alternatively assuming changes between 1979 and 1995 in the UK using the Abrego/Whalley data (mentioned earlier) that represent either short- or the long-run responses, and they use three calibrations. In a Ricardo–Viner model they have three factors: capital, skilled and unskilled labour. In the other two versions (Heckscher–Ohlin or H–O, and partial mobility) they allocate capital income from the base data proportionately by sector, so the simplified model just has two factors. The H–O model differs from the partial mobility one in that adjustment costs for unskilled and skilled labour are set to zero: calibration based on this assumption means assuming a long-run equilibrium in the economy (i.e. the standard H–O model), whereas adjustment costs for unskilled labour are set at a non-zero level, assuming the economy is at a short-run equilibrium only. This latter treatment means that the adjustment process for the unskilled factor reflects an outcome influenced by short-run adjustment costs.

They solve the model for parameter values given data for the two years, 1979 and 1995 with prices, wages, output and employment set at their observed values. They assume a value for the elasticity of substitution between factors in production σ (we assume the same elasticity for both sectors, to rule out the possibility of factor intensity reversals), and also assume values for the differential between skilled and unskilled wages in the expanding and declining sectors E and M. The unknowns at this stage are the model parameters for each sector and each time period.

In the long-run H–O factors mobile model, the increase in skilled and fall in unskilled factor endowments has no effect, as a factor price insensitivity result (due to Leamer and Levinsohn, 1995) suggests. However, the model shows substantial sensitivity to the change in world prices, which alone accounts for the total observed wage change. There is also substantial factor bias in favour of the skilled factor (skill-bias + 184 per cent and factor quality + 255 per cent), and rise in the skilled share of output. These results fit the observed wage and output changes due to a sizeable sector-biased technical change in the opposite direction (−491 per cent), favouring the unskilled intensive sector M.

The partial mobility model shows different results. The change in endowments has a large effect on relative wages narrowing the gap between skilled and unskilled wage rates. The effect of world prices is reduced, while sector-bias, which still favours the unskilled-intensive good, is also smaller in this model compared to the factors mobile model. The main factor in this model behind the increased inequality is the change in the skill share within industries, with a slightly smaller contribution from factor quality.

Results of these decompositions are different depending upon whether a short-run model, with limited mobility of unskilled labour, or a long-run model is used to explain the observed changes. This emphasises that the assumed model structure applied to the same data in decomposition will substantially affect the perception of the role of trade in wage inequality change.

In the long-run model, the usual H–O result of factor price insensitivity holds, so that the rise in relative supply of skilled labour has no effect on skill premia.

The factor-bias of technical change has no effect (except insofar as the relative quality of skilled labour has risen). In contrast, the effects of observed world price increases are large: on their own these price increases would cause a larger shift in output towards the skill-intensive goods, and a larger rise in skill premia than actually observed. The long-run model can only be made consistent with the observed output and income changes if the sector-bias of technical change (the residual category of the decomposition) is in the opposite direction: for UK total factor productivity in the unskilled-intensive sector to have risen faster than in the skill-intensive sector, so damping the tendency of output to switch.

By contrast, when they use a short-run model for these decompositions, one in which unskilled labour is only partially mobile, the decomposition results are different. The rise in the relative supply of unskilled labour now has a sizeable damping effect on inequality. Factor-biased technical change (leading to a rise in skilled/unskilled input ratios in both sectors) despite rising skill premia will raise relative skilled wages in a short-run model. The effect of trade is less marked in the short-run model, though still quite substantial. The sector-bias in technical progress (which had been large and favoured the unskilled-intensive sector in the long-run model) is relatively minor in the short-run model.

Decomposition in a model with union bargaining

Abrego (2000) performs decomposition analysis using a trade model that incorporates union bargaining, and compares results with fully-flexible labour markets. He uses a differentiated goods model similar to that described in the earlier section on Trade and wages decomposition in a differentiated goods model, to which he adds union Nash bargaining in the market for unskilled labour, allowing for unemployment of this factor. The skilled-labour market is assumed to be perfectly competitive.

The model is calibrated to 1990 UK data on production, consumption, trade and factor use as well as on international price and technology changes over the period 1976–1990. To perform the decomposition exercises, Abrego follows the methodology set out in Abrego and Whalley (2000), except for the modelling of technical change. In line with the findings in the bulk of the empirical, econometric-based literature, he assumes that unskilled labour saving technological change occurs, and takes this as being pervasive, rather than sector-specific. This differs from Abrego and Whalley (2000), where technical change is assumed to be Hicks-neutral, and sector-biased (which can be accommodated by the H–O structure used there). Abrego models skill-biased technological change as a uniform reduction in the share of unskilled labour in each of the two sectors.

His results for the model with fully flexible labour markets confirm previous findings that increased wage inequality is basically the result of technological change, with trade playing only a minor role. The presence of rigidities in the form of union bargaining in the market for unskilled labour changes this decomposition, increasing significantly the relative contribution of trade. For Abrego's central case parameter specification, this change in decomposition is only quantitative, as the dominant factor continues to be technological change. However, for some model parameterisations consistent with existing ranges of empirical estimates for production and preferences parameters, the change brought about by the introduction of union bargaining is also qualitative, as it turns trade into the dominant factor.

The results suggest that, given the amplitude of the range of empirical estimates for some key parameters – such as substitution elasticities in production – decomposition can become ambiguous when labour market rigidities are incorporated. Abrego and Whalley (2000) show that, under fully flexible labour markets, ambiguity in decomposition occurs in a standard H–O model but is unlikely to show up in a differentiated goods model. The fact that it is also present in a more general model lends additional support to the idea that model in which the underlying structure of the economy is explicitly specified are probably better suited for conducting meaningful decomposition of wage inequality outcomes. By its own nature, their reduced-form counterparts are indeed unable to discriminate between alternative economy structures or paramaterisations.

Conclusion

In this chapter, we have explored the use of general equilibrium based structural models as an alternative to reduced form econometric models when decomposing observed wage changes into the components attributable to different sources, typically trade surges and technical change. The chapter illustrates the use of a variety of general equilibrium models of international trade for decomposing wage inequality change under different calibration procedures. It shows how alternative structural models, each consistent with the same wage inequality outcome, can yield sharply different results.

While showing how structural models can be used in the decompositions more so than advocating one particular structural model, this chapter suggests that the exploration of alternative structural models, rather than using econometric-based reduced-form counterparts, may be the way forward to more satisfactorily sort out the relative contribution of trade and technology to recent increased wage inequality.

Acknowledgement

The research in this chapter has been carried out as part of the TSER project on 'Globalisation and Social Exclusion'. Financial support from the European Commission is gratefully acknowledged.

Notes

1 See, for instance, the surveys by Burtless (1995); and Brenton (1999). Also see Deardorff and Hakura (1994).

2 Exceptions to this conclusion include Borjas, Freeman and Katz (1991); Wood (1994); and Feenstra and Hanson (1996a,b). The latter identify outsourcing as a significant cause.

3 Francois and Nelson (1998) are seemingly the other authors who use an applied general equilibrium model to look at the effects of trade and technology on wage inequality. They set out a modelling approach, rather than analyse decompositions in detail.

4 An exception is Leamer (1996), where a structural form is estimated.

6   Adjustment to globalisation

A study of the footwear industry in Europe

Paul Brenton, Anna Maria Pinna and Marc Vancauteren

Introduction

Most of the economic literature on globalisation has concentrated upon the impact of trade upon relative wages and relative employment opportunities for unskilled relative to skilled workers in OECD countries.[1] This has been based upon the observed worsening of the fortunes of less-skilled workers in many industrial countries and the textbook Hechscher–Ohlin–Samuelson (HOS) model of international trade. This theory, including the Stolper–Samuelson link between changing product prices and changing relative wage rates, has been widely adopted despite rather shaky empirical support. In this framework globalisation leads to a reallocation of resources in OECD countries from import competing, low-skill-intensive industries to the high-skill-intensive sectors in which these countries have a comparative advantage. Most economists conclude that the role of policy in this context is to assist this reallocation by providing training and increasing the quantity of skilled labour.

However, a number of observed features suggest that this paradigm is inappropriate for a complete appraisal of the impact of globalisation in OECD countries. First, for many of the unskilled intensive sectors, as the import penetration ratio has increased so has the ratio of exports to output. In the standard HOS model countries either import or export products, not both. Hence, even in low-skill-intensive sectors product differentiation exists. This then provides another means of adjustment to globalisation not possible within the standard model, the within sector adjustment to produce different and higher quality products. Second, there appears to be a range of experience across countries in the evolution of low-skill-intensive sectors. In some OECD countries certain sectors have maintained employment and output whilst in other countries production has declined dramatically. If the trade shock from globalisation is common across countries then this suggests that a variety of responses to globalisation are available to firms in OECD countries.

Industrial adjustment to globalisation is the focus of this chapter. Here we concentrate upon one particular sector, footwear, which bears the characteristics of a typical low-skill intensive manufacturing sector where comparative advantage has decisively shifted to low-wage labour abundant countries. We do not provide a comprehensive overview of developments in the footwear sector but highlight a number of key issues which are apparent from an analysis of footwear but which do not often figure in general discussions of globalisation. We concentrate upon how adjustment to globalisation has taken place in those European countries which were major footwear producers at the start of the 1970s and discuss the diversity of experiences across Europe. We start with the standard trade model and analyse the changes in trade flows which have affected the footwear industry in Europe. We then proceed to discuss the main changes in the industry which are apparent over the last 20 years. We first look at developments in employment, distinguishing between skilled and unskilled workers, before looking at changes in wages and some data concerning the nature of unemployment of footwear workers in one EU country; Belgium. Finally, we look for evidence of strategies used by firms to successfully adjust to the increased international competition from low-wage countries, including discussion of productivity growth, technological adaptation, upgrading of product quality and finally the development of industrial districts and flexible organisation.

Globalisation and EU trade in footwear products

Traditional trade theory, in the form of the Stolper–Samuelson theorem, suggests that changes in the relative price of unskilled labour intensive products, such as footwear, lie at the heart of traditional explanations of the link between trade, changes in relative wages and structural adjustment. Much of the empirical literature on this issue has failed to find convincing evidence that the price of products, such as footwear, has fallen relative to the price of products skilled-intensive products, such as machinery (Lawrence, 1996; Lucke, 1997; Slaughter, 1998; Anderton and Brenton, 1999a).

One possible explanation for these results is the sectoral producer prices which as typically analysed are unable to capture the relevant trade shock faced by the industrialised economies because they are too aggregated. Wood (1997, 1998), for example, argues that heterogeneity of goods in standard statistical definitions of sectors and changes in quality over time (which maybe correlated with the skill intensity of production) could engender substantial errors into available producer price series. If sub-sectors within industries are different, in terms of requiring different amounts of skilled and unskilled labour, then more open trade may reduce the prices of some goods but raise the prices of others, leaving the industry aggregate price unchanged. This is likely to be the case for footwear when thinking of standardised mass-produced varieties and fashion sensitive high quality shoes, for example. Ideally, one would use highly disaggregated series on producer prices to address this issue, but unfortunately they are not available. Wood points instead to changes in the prices of imports and exports, which do suggest a rising relative price of skilled-intensive products in the 1980s (but not in the 1970s).

However, Brenton and Pinna (2000), who use highly disaggregated import data to separate out changes in quality (defined as movements to higher value products) from pure price movements within the bundle of imported footwear products, suggest there was no change or even a decrease in the import prices of the skilled intensive machinery industries relative to footwear. Thus, the traditional trade theory link from falling relative prices to falling relative wages is difficult to support in the case of footwear, but these authors do find support for falling relative import prices for textiles and for clothing.

Imports used in the earlier exercise were measured at the border and hence the calculated prices did not capture tariffs and the impact of non-tariff barriers. Thus, even if border prices did not change, producer and consumer prices may have fallen if trade barriers have been reduced. However, in the EU there has been little change in the degree of tariff protection of footwear producers over the past thirty years. Footwear remains a relatively highly protected industry. The average tariff on EU imports of industrial products is now around 3 per cent whilst for leather footwear the tariff is 8 per cent and for footwear with non-leather uppers the tariff is currently equal to 17 per cent. In 1976 the tariff on finished leather footwear was 8 per cent whilst that on non-leather footwear was 20 per cent, the latter has only declined since 1994.

In addition to customs duties, imports of footwear into EU countries have often been subjected to non-tariffs measures including quantitative restrictions and voluntary export restraints and anti-dumping measures. Prior to the creation of the Single Market in the EU there were a number of bilateral trade restrictions on imports of footwear. For example, the French and Italian footwear industries pleaded successfully with the Commission to be allowed to impose VERs in the mid-1980s on imports of non-leather footwear from Asian countries, specifically Taiwan and Korea. The Commission justified this action on the basis that different types of footwear are substitutable in demand and that the sharp rise in imports of synthetic and textile footwear contributed directly to the fall of more than 70 million pairs in Community production of leather footwear.[2] The removal of border and customs formalities that was necessitated by the Single Market implied that bilateral restrictions could no longer be maintained. Thus, the bilateral restrictions on imports into Italy and France were reformed into an EC-wide quota system, though this has subsequently been removed.

Evidence for the UK suggests that non-tariff trade barriers have not been successful in preserving total employment in the footwear sector and have been an extremely expensive means of protection. Brenton and Winters (1993) and Winters and Takacs (1991) model the effects of a number of quantitative restrictions imposed by the UK in the late 1970s and early 1980s on imports of non-leather footwear from the Far East and imports of leather footwear from Central and Eastern European countries. Their findings suggest that in 1979 (when all of these restrictions were in place) the total cost of a job saved in the UK footwear sector was nearly 12 times annual wages every year for each year that the protection was in place.

This all suggests that trade liberalisation in the form of reductions in tariffs or removal of NTBs cannot be at the heart of explanations of the decline in footwear employment in Europe. In addition the view that high tariffs and non-tariff barriers are a useful tool to protect domestic industries from low-cost foreign competition or to allow time for adjustment to the new competition receives little support from the experience of footwear. We now proceed to look in more detail at changes in the quantity of footwear imported into the EU market.

Import penetration and export intensity in the EU footwear sector

According to Wood (1995), developed countries have shifted from 'manufacturing autarky', in which they produced all the manufactures demanded domestically (skilled-labour-intensive and unskilled-labour-intensive products) to specialisation in the production of the skilled-intensive activities within all sectors and reliance upon imports from developing countries to supply their needs of labour intensive commodities. Thus, not all types of footwear that are imported compete with domestically produced shoes. In this framework, a fall in the world price of the imported unskilled intensive products would no longer affect skilled and unskilled workers as factors of production in industrial countries. Relative wages are not tied to relative world prices and instead both benefit from a lower price of goods they consume. Relative wages are only determined by domestic factor demand and supply conditions. Hence, trade volumes and not relative product prices matter. The trade effect on wages and employment in the industrial countries has to be measured by calculating the quantities of skilled and unskilled labour embodied in imports and export flows. According to this view, wages in the footwear sector have been driven down because footwear activities (not only finished pairs of shoes, but especially components) formerly undertaken by unskilled workers in industrial countries are increasingly being purchased from low-wage developing countries.

Figure 6.1 shows the trend in the quantity (metric tons) of footwear traded within the EU12 market (intra-EU) and imported by the EU12 from the extra-EU region. It is clear that the trend rate of growth of imports from both external and EU countries increased after the mid-1980s but that the rate of growth of extra-EU imports was greater than that of internal EU trade.[3] Hence import penetration of the EU footwear market from external sources increased considerably after the mid-1980s.

In the 1990s, for the first time, the volume of footwear imported from outside of the EU has exceeded internal trade in footwear. Imports from non-EU countries increased by 41 per cent between 1976 and 1981. Between 1986 and 1994 extra-EU imports rose by 168 per cent whilst the volume of EU production increased by 25 per cent and domestic consumption was 43 per cent higher.

Figure 6.2 illustrates import penetration as well as the export intensity ratio for each of the main EU producing countries, Italy, Germany, France and the UK, along with Spain and Portugal, whose shares of European production have increased since the 1980s. The Italian, UK, German and French markets have been increasingly penetrated by imports since the mid-1970s whilst in Spain and Portugal import penetration increased considerably only after 1986.

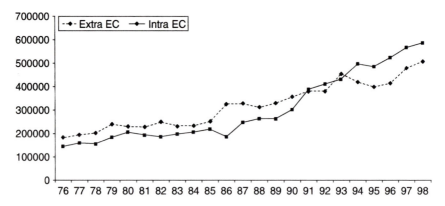

Figure 6.1 EU12 intra-EC and extra-EC and imports of footwear by volume, 1976–1998.
Source: Comext Database.

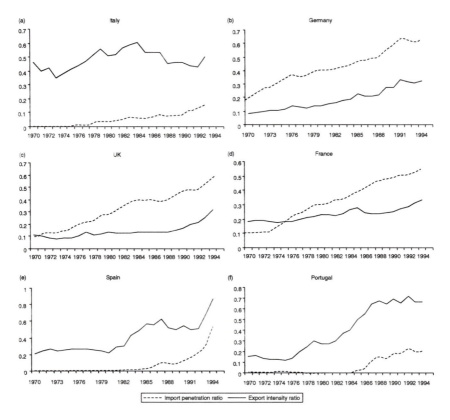

Figure 6.2 Import penetration and export intensity in the European footwear industry:
(a) Italy; (b) Germany; (c) UK; (d) France; (e) Spain; (f) Portugal.

Source: OECD STAN Database.

In all of these European countries the share of production devoted to exports has risen, with this increase being particularly strong for Spain and Portugal. In 1994, Spain exported more than 80 per cent of total production, whilst at the beginning of the 1980s only 20 per cent of production was exported. Italy has seen some variability in the amount of production exported but was already a major exporter of footwear in the early 1970s. Nevertheless, a substantial proportion of Italian footwear output continues to be exported. Moving to the remaining countries, the common picture is one of a concurrent increase in import penetration and export intensity. For the UK, France and Germany a substantially higher proportion of output is now exported relative to the 1970s.

Clearly, this rise in the export propensity reflects in part the decline in the amount of production of footwear in Europe. However, it is clear that EU producers are now exporting more footwear than 20 years ago: the volume of footwear exported has increased. This is difficult to reconcile with standard trade theory. Loss of comparative advantage should affect sales in all countries not just those in the domestic market. The trade data also show that the volume of footwear exported outside of the EU has grown faster than exports to other EU countries. Hence the explanation for rising exports cannot be increased trade between members behind a protective external wall.

This growth in the amount of EU footwear that is exported entails that EU producers are selling shoes that are differentiated from those of the low wage producers who have increasingly penetrated the EU domestic market and/or that the amount of outsourcing of footwear has increased. Some information on this issue can be gleaned from comparing the volume of exports of footwear measured in tonnes and the volume of exports measured in pairs. In the EU trade statistics finished shoes are recorded in both pairs and tonnes, whilst parts of footwear tend to be measured only by weight. Over the past 20 years exports of footwear measured in tonnes and measured in pairs have both increased but the amount of tonnes of exports has grown at a much faster rate than exports of footwear measured in pairs. Thus, unless there has been a substantial increase in the weight per pair of shoes exported (unlikely unless exports have been concentrated upon boots with an ever increasing size of steel toe cap), then not only has there been an increase in exports of finished differentiated footwear from Europe but there has been a more significant increase in outsourcing, where parts are exported from the EU for further processing abroad. We return to the issue of outsourcing later.

To consider more carefully how the increase in import penetration may have affected the nature of production of EU footwear we proceed to consider the geographical composition of EU imports, and in particular, how the share of low-wage countries has changed. Figure 6.3 illustrates the trend in the share of EU12 imports of total footwear from the NICs (4 Asian tigers), RoA (rest of Asian countries), CEEE (Central Eastern European Economies) and RoW (rest of the World trade). The data show a clear increase in the penetration of imports from less-developed, low-wage regions in the period after the mid-1980s, which coincides with the rapid increase in the volume of EU imports of footwear identified

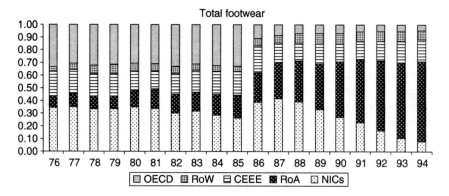

Figure 6.3 Shares of extra-EC12 imports by region of origin.

in Figures 6.1 and 6.2. This occurred first, at the expense of the OECD countries and has subsequently been associated with a decline in the share of the NICs themselves. This reflects in part the relocation of activity in Asia away from the NICs towards countries such as the Philippines and Thailand but, in particular, China.

Until 1985, trade with OECD countries accounted for around 30–35 per cent of total extra-EU12 imports. This share has subsequently been reduced considerably to less than 10 per cent. Such changes in the composition of imports may reflect, at least partially, another aspect of the globalisation process whereby firms in OECD countries have relocated their production to low-wage regions. Sales by OECD firms of finished products in the EU market which are produced in low-wage locations overseas will be recorded as imports from the developing country where production took place.

Thus the past 15 years have seen important changes in the magnitude of import penetration on the EU footwear market and that of each member country. This has been accompanied by substantial adjustments in the source of extra-EU imports. At the more detailed product level the data confirm a substantial increase in the penetration of imports of final footwear products by low-wage countries and the re-sourcing of parts and components away from OECD countries to the Central and Eastern European countries and to countries in Asia (excluding the NICs).

We now address how exports of the different categories of footwear have developed, and in particular, finished products relative to parts and components. Much of the discussion on how globalisation has affected labour market outcomes in OECD countries has concentrated upon the impact of the increased availability of cheaper products imported from low-wage economies. However, a world of more integrated economies implies not only the possibility to export the national variety of a product but also the option to partially or completely relocate domestic production to low-wage locations. The two developments are linked if relocation occurs as a defensive strategy to the availability of cheaper imports.

Finished footwear products exported from the EU are mainly sold in other OECD countries, although the importance of the OECD has been declining and the Central and Eastern European countries have risen in prominence as a market for finished EU footwear. Changes in the geographical composition of exports of parts and component segments follow the same pattern but their magnitude has been much greater. For example, uppers of leather and other parts made of leather were mainly exported to OECD countries during the 1970s and the first part of the 1980s, but by 1994 less than 20 per cent of EU12 exports were directed to the OECD region. In 1994 the majority, over 70 per cent, of such parts and components were exported to Central and Eastern European countries. These changes in the geographical structure of exports of parts and components may be linked to the relocation of production out of the EU12 in response to increasing import competition from low-wage regions, which brings us to the issue of outsourcing.

Outsourcing occurs when firms take advantage of low-wage costs in labour abundant countries by moving the low-skill-intensive parts of the production process abroad, but continue to carry out the high-skill activities themselves in the domestic economy. Trade with low-wage countries via this route shifts employment away from less-skilled workers in industrial countries and puts downward pressure on the relative wages and employment of less-skilled workers within industries. The phenomenon has been investigated by Feenstra and Hanson (1996a,b) using data on imports of intermediate inputs by domestic firms. The underlying intuition is that intermediate inputs are associated with unskilled labour activities which domestic firms choose to move abroad to cheap labour locations as a response to more intense import competition from low-wage countries.

One feature that is apparent for the EU is that the value per unit of imports of parts and components is greater than the unit value of exports of parts and components, both in total and for various sub-categories. Such a difference, moreover, has increased over time. This is consistent with the view that an important feature of manufacturing trade over the last two decades has been the increasing division of the value chain (Krugman, 1995b) and the relocation of certain activities (the most unskilled-intensive) to low-wage economies. Here the evidence suggests that the value-added embodied in European exports of parts and components of footwear is less than that embodied in European imports of footwear parts and components, suggesting that additional value to parts and components is added outside of Europe. We now proceed to look at how the domestic nature of the footwear industry in Europe has changed over the past 30 years in the light of these developments in trade.

Changes in employment and wages in the footwear sector

Employment in footwear

Table 6.1 shows the tremendous changes in the use of labour in the footwear sector that have occurred since 1970. However, it is clear that the pattern of

Table 6.1 Change in total labour input in footwear in selected countries: 1970 = 100

1997	US	Italy	Spain	Portugal	UK	Germany
1970	100	100	100	100	100	100
1980	78.92	97.52	121.36	108.21	91.49	62.54
1985	51.96	96.18	104.40	124.02	68.81	54.07
1990	37.74	91.53	61.92	n.a.	52.27	36.50
1995	29.65	101.14	53.15	n.a.	42.32	20.8
1997	31.85	101.78	57.16	n.a.	42.98	19.56

Source: ISIS.

changes in labour input varies substantially across countries. In the UK, the US and Germany the amount of persons employed in footwear has been declining continuously since 1970. For these countries between one-tenth and one-third of the jobs in footwear in 1970 had been lost by 1980. Employment loss continued throughout the 1980s and by 1997 the number of footwear jobs in the US was only 32 per cent of the level in 1970. In Germany in the same year employment in footwear was less than one-fifth of the level of 1970, whilst in the UK only 43 per cent of the number of jobs at the start of the period remained.[4]

For Italy, employment in footwear remained roughly constant throughout the 1970s and early 1980s. Between 1985 and 1992 there was a 10 per cent reduction in the level of employment in the Italian footwear sector. However, there has subsequently been an increase in employment with a return to the numbers employed in the early 1970s. For Spain the level of employment in the footwear sector increased during the 1970s and then declined from 1980 to 1988 with some subsequent stabilisation. Between 1985 and 1988 one-third of footwear jobs in Spain was lost. The period of employment loss in Spain coincides with accession to the EU and there is some evidence of a period of relocation by Spanish footwear manufactures to Portugal during this period. Footwear employment in Portugal itself has increased continuously since 1970. In 1989 the number of footwear jobs in Portugal was double the number which existed in 1970.[5]

In addition to looking at changes in total employment it is also important, as trade theory suggests, to consider changes in the relative employment of skilled and unskilled workers in the footwear sector. Unfortunately, the available data do not clearly define skilled and unskilled workers and so, in common with other studies of globalisation, we have to use definitions based upon manual and non-manual workers (Table 6.2).

In all countries except Portugal and Italy, there has been a substantial loss of manual employment in the footwear industry. This loss of manual employment has occurred consistently since the 1970s although it has generally been more pronounced in the period since 1985, when import penetration has increased most strongly. The final rows of Table 6.2 show a substantial decline in the ratio of unskilled to skilled footwear workers in all countries, including Italy where the fall in the employment of unskilled workers has been less significant, even though there was a much higher ratio of unskilled to skilled workers in Italy at the start

Table 6.2 The composition of employment in footwear: manual and non-manual workers (number)

	Germany		Spain		Portugal		Italy		UK		France	
	Manual	Non-man	Manual	Non-man	Manual	Non-man	Manual	Non-man	Manual	Non-man	Manual	Non-man
1970	78,450	11,250	45,510	7,125	14,050	2,120	88,531	7,300	76,000	12,900	65,210	8,972
1975	61,025	9,425	55,320	8,560	15,242	2,255	79,251	7,200	70,727	11,150	58,464	8,845
1980	47,850	8,250	48,700	6,250	17,604	2,450	79,250	7,100	70,285	11,050	50,337	7,412
1985	41,250	7,250	36,250	4,985	25,045	2,564	78,250	6,920	54,287	6,885	40,524	6,432
1990	26,147	6,596	26,786	4,659			68,412	8,812	40,343	6,125	33,414	7,994
1995	14,152	4,521	24,202	5,802			77,121	15,213	31,250	6,372	25,847	5,451
1997	13,252	4,293	23,654	5,594			72,221	11,421	30,145	8,064	24,510	4,854
Percentage changes												
1970–1985	−47,42	−35,56	−20,35	−30,04	78,26	20,09	−11,61	−5,21	−28,57	−46,63	−37,86	−28.31
1985–1997	−67,87	−40,79	−34,75	12,22			−7,70	65,04	−44,47	17,12	−39,52	−24.53
Ratio of manual to non-manual												
1970	6.97		6.39		6.63		12.13		5.89		7.27	
1997	3.08		4.23				6.32		3.74		5.05	

Sources: Eurostat, ILO, ISIS.

of the period relative to other countries. In Spain, Italy and the UK there has been an absolute increase in the employment of non-manual workers since 1985, whilst manual employment has continued to plummet. This is difficult to reconcile with standard trade theory, where given the fall in the price of unskilled labour, the unskilled/skilled labour ratio is expected to increase. It may reflect a somewhat different response to international competition since the mid-1980s. The observed increase in the relative use of skilled labour could reflect an attempt by European footwear producers to upgrade their production and to concentrate upon the production of high quality footwear and/or upon design-intensive activities. We return to this issue later, when we discuss evidence of upgrading from data on exports by EU footwear producers. It may also reflect the impact of outsourcing, which we suggest above has been an important feature of the adjustment to globalisation, as low-skill-intensive activities are moved overseas whilst the skill-intensive parts of the production process are retained in Europe.

Developments in wages

Globalisation may lead to social exclusion even for workers who remain employed if there is a significant deterioration in their relative and more importantly their real wage. Here, in Table 6.3 we present the available data on percentage changes in wages for the unskilled and changes in salaries for the skilled workers employed in the footwear sector in various countries during the 1980s and early 1990s. In most cases the average wage of the unskilled footwear worker has increased proportionately less than the average salary of skilled workers. This is as one would expect. Intense competition from low-wage sources of supply would be expected to put downward pressure on the relative wage of the unskilled footwear workers in Europe. However, in Germany the returns to skilled and unskilled workers have risen at similar rates whilst in Portugal the unskilled footwear worker has fared much better than the average skilled footwear worker.

It is also important to compare the wage performance of footwear workers relative to that of other workers employed in manufacturing. Table 6.3 also shows changes in wages and salaries in manufacturing as a whole. These data demonstrate that in Germany, the UK, Italy and Spain unskilled footwear workers have done less well in terms of wage increases than other workers in manufacturing. In Portugal, France and the US unskilled footwear workers have received larger increases in wages than unskilled workers in general. Similarly, in all countries for which data are available, with the exception of France and the US, skilled workers in footwear have obtained lower increases in salaries than skilled workers on average in manufacturing.

The final rows of Table 6.3 also show that, with the exception of Spain over the short 5-year period for which data is available, wages of unskilled workers employed in the footwear industry in Europe have increased at a faster rate than the general price index since 1980. In this sense we find no evidence from these data that unskilled footwear workers in Europe or the US have suffered from the compression of real wages experienced by unskilled workers in general in the US.

Table 6.3 Changes in wages and salaries in footwear and in manufacturing, 1980–1994

	United States		Germany		Portugal		UK		Spain		Italy		France	
	Unskill	Skill	Unskill	Skill	Unskill	Skill	Unskill	Skill	Unskill	Skill	Unskill	Skill	Unskill	Skill
Percentage change in wages and salaries in footwear 1980–1994	100.4[a]	110.3[a]	64.13	64.66	659.18	542.6	146.51	165.53	24.69[b]	39.06[b]	101.02[c]	122.84[c]	132.27	146.7
Percentage change in wages and salaries in manufacturing: 1980–1994	73.6[c]	93.2[c]	76.96	75.48	512.5	796.09	168.33	195.30	92.59[b]	91.59[b]	127.1[c]	141.1[c]	120.80	121.0
Percentage change in consumer price index: 1980–1994	75.27[c]		51.28		560.19		115.66		31.16[b]		93.62[c]		94.31	

Sources: EUROSTAT, US Bureau of Labour Statistics and IMF *International Financial Statistics*.

Notes
a 1980–1993 All footwear, leather-related products except rubber footwear.
b 1989–1994.
c 1980–1993.
a 1983–1994.

More surprisingly the data do suggest a decline in the real wage of skilled footwear workers in Portugal. So, although unskilled footwear workers in Europe have not suffered a real wage reduction, in general, their wage relative to that of other unskilled workers in Europe has fallen.

For footwear it is clear that the group of production or unskilled workers is far from homogeneous, as is often assumed in discussions of the impact of globalisation. The process of making footwear can be broken down into distinct stages of production. Accordingly, this division of production stages has brought about a division of labour, which requires a variety of skills from within the unskilled labour force. For example, the cutting of the leather, in which the varying texture of the material must be taken into consideration, is the most highly skilled and best paid job within the group of production workers in the factory. This is further illustrated by Table 6.4, which shows the range of wage costs for manual workers according to skill types in both Belgium and Italy.

It would appear that wage levels reflect the skill intensity of manual workers in the leather footwear industry. Cutters, vampers, Goodyear stitchers, and so on, are of the highest order of skill and receive the highest hourly wages. This reflects not only that the nature of the job is quite complex, but also that it takes years of experience to work up to full efficiency (Blim, 1983). In Italy those at the highest levels within the group of production workers receive almost 60 per cent more in hourly wages than those at the bottom of the skill spectrum. In Belgium the ratio is smaller at around 16 per cent. Table 6.5 looks at the picture over time and presents the ratio of the wages of the most skilled manual workers (level 1) to those classified as less skilled. The lack of significant change in these ratios over time reflects the institutional structure of wage setting in both of these countries.

Table 6.4 Hourly wages for Italian and Belgian labourers according to level of skills in the leather footwear industry in 1999 (in EURO)

Level	Classifications	Italy	Belgium
1	Cutting parts of the upper and the sole, stitching of the inside sole, Goodyear stitchers	8,55	8,78
2	Stretching the completed upper over a wooden form (the last)	7,97	8,56
3	Attaching the sole to the upper, tying up out-soles	7,21	8,56
4	Includes all tasks of level 1,2,3 at the experience level between 3 and 6 months	6,89	8,26
5	Includes all tasks of level 1,2,3 at the experience level of 0–2 months	6,6	8,06
6	Completely perforating, stitching of front-feet, inspecting the shoe, tempering heel stock, pulling out tacks	6,33	7,99
7	Not-completely perforating and stitching, polishing and packing	6,05	7,89
8	Includes all tasks of level 6,7 at the experience level of 0–2 months	5,43	7,59

Sources: Committee of Social Affairs (Belgium 1997), FILTA (1999).

Table 6.5 Ratio of hourly wages for Italian and Belgian labourers according to level of skills in the leather footwear industry, 1981–1999 (skill level 1 = 1)

	Skill level							
	1	2	3	4	5	6	7	8
Italy								
1999	1	0.93	0.84	0.81	0.77	0.74	0.71	0.64
1995	1	0.94	0.85	0.83	0.80	0.77	0.74	0.69
1989	1	0.98	0.90	0.85	0.82	0.80	0.76	n.a.
1985	1	0.92	0.86	0.84	0.81	0.78	n.a.	n.a.
1981	1	0.90	0.83	0.81	0.78	0.76	n.a.	n.a.
Belgium								
1999	1	0.97	0.97	0.94	0.92	0.91	0.90	0.86
1995	1	0.97	0.96	0.94	0.92	0.91	0.90	0.88
1989	1	0.97	0.96	0.94	0.92	0.91	0.89	0.88
1985	1	0.97	0.96	0.94	0.91	0.90	0.89	0.87
1981	1	0.97	0.95	0.93	0.91	0.90	0.88	0.86

Sources: Committee of Social Affairs (Belgium 1997), FILTA (1999).

If there has been a change in the relative demand for these different types of manual workers it is likely to have been reflected in changes in employment since wage adjustment appears constrained. In addition, if outsourcing reduces the employment of the least skilled within the group of production workers at a greater rate than employment of the more skilled cutters then the average recorded wage for production workers could rise.

It is also apparent that footwear produced within the key categories of leather, plastic, rubber and textile shoes is far from homogeneous. Thus, the extent to which production workers employed in the footwear industry in Europe compete with unskilled labour elsewhere in the world depends on the quality of the shoes produced. Higher quality shoes and more elaborate footwear styles require better workmanship and so the need for firms to retain those with the highest degree of skills among the production workers. In general, most EU countries producing leather footwear have oriented their production towards skilled labour, while EU firms producing synthetic shoes have sought to exploit the large endowment of low skilled, low wage labour in developing countries such as China, South Korea (CEC, 1997). In other words, where the quality of the footwear is important and it reflects the quality of the labour input then the forces pushing towards locali-sation of production can outweigh those of globalisation. At the same time these considerations also suggest that where quality is important the scope for mecha-nisation of the tasks of the production workers is likely to be limited.

Unemployment of footwear workers

The 'trade and labour' debate, both in the US and Europe, has firmly focused on the issue of how much inequality, either in terms of wages or unemployment, can

Table 6.6 Duration of unemployment in footwear and total manufacturing[a] in Belgium

	Less than 1 month	1–3 months	3–6 months	6–12 months	**STU/TOTU[b]**	**LTU/TU[c]**
1. Cutting, stitching and pinning-footwear						
1988	0.02	0.04	0.03	0.17	0.25	0.75
1998	0.04	0.03	0.04	0.05	0.16	0.84
2. Not completely perforating and stitching and polishing-footwear						
1988	0.07	0.06	0.14	0.12	0.40	0.60
1998	0.03	0.04	0.08	0.14	0.28	0.72
3. Spinning, weaving and knitting-textiles						
1988	0.03	0.04	0.05	0.10	0.22	0.78
1998	0.02	0.05	0.06	0.09	0.22	0.78
4. Manuals-total industry						
1988	0.04	0.06	0.07	0.13	0.30	0.70
1998	0.04	0.06	0.07	0.14	0.31	0.69
5. Non-manuals-total industry						
1988	0.05	0.07	0.09	0.22	0.43	0.57
1998	0.06	0.07	0.08	0.18	0.39	0.61

Source: Belgian Federal Ministry of Labour.

Notes
a based on number of job searchers registered.
b ratio short term unemployed/total unemployed.
c ratio of long term unemployed/total unemployed.

be attributed to increased competition from low-wage countries. None of the other dynamics of labour markets linked to social exclusion, such as the length of unemployment for those who are made redundant, or the mobility of different types of workers between wage classes, has been directly considered in relation to the emergence of less-developed countries in international markets.

An important element in the extent to which the decline in employment opportunities for manual workers in the footwear sector translates into social exclusion is the adjustment costs that such workers face in obtaining employment elsewhere in the economy. If workers released by the footwear sector are quickly re-employed in other sectors then the decline in employment in the footwear sector is unlikely to be a significant factor creating social exclusion.[6] On the other hand if footwear workers spend long periods without work, due perhaps to the sector specificity of the skills that they possess or locational factors, then the social costs of the decline in the footwear industry will rise.

Table 6.6 illustrates the duration of unemployment of two groups of manual footwear workers in Belgium and compares these with a group of manual workers in the textiles industry and then with all manual and all non-manual workers in Belgium. As shown in the table above differing wage levels reflect the skill intensity of manual workers in the footwear industry which suggests a degree of heterogeneity within the manual labour force employed within the footwear sector. We have selected the two groups of manual workers with the highest and lowest levels of skill according to the wage rate; respectively, those involved with (1) cutting, stitching and pinning and (2) those manuals who are partially involved in the stitching, and undertake perforating and polishing.

Table 6.6 shows the proportion of total unemployment in each category of worker by duration. We distinguish primarily between short-term unemployment, defined as those unemployed for twelve months or less, and the long-term unemployed, those without a job for more than one year. Thus, for footwear workers previously employed in cutting, weaving and pinning 75 per cent of the total number of unemployed had been without a job for more than one year in 1988. The principal conclusions which emerge from these data for Belgium are that

- Since 1988 the proportion of unemployed manual footwear workers who have been unemployed for more than one year has increased whereas the proportion of total unemployed manual workers in Belgium who are long-term unemployed has remained constant.
- A higher proportion of the more skilled manual footwear workers becomes long-term unemployed than do the least skilled manual workers. Those footwear workers who have the lowest level of skill find alternative employment more quickly than those manual workers with higher skills and higher wages. What is not apparent is whether this reflects skill specificity or wage inflexibility of this group of manual workers.
- The duration of unemployment of the least skilled footwear workers is, on average, less than that of the group of manual textile workers.
- The duration of unemployment of non-manual workers in Belgium is considerably less than that of manual workers.

It is also interesting to note that there may be considerable differences in the unemployment propensities of different skill categories of manual workers. For example, in Belgium in 1991 for every cutter and pinner, the most skilled manual worker, employed in the footwear sector there were more than two unemployed persons who previously worked as cutters and pinners in footwear. On the other hand, for every 8 finishers, the least skilled of the manual workers, employed in the footwear sector there was 1 unemployed former footwear finisher. Further, the ratio of employed to unemployed increased between 1981 and 1991 for finishers but declined for cutters and pinners. A similar feature is apparent for the textiles industry in Belgium: the ratio of employed to unemployed is higher for the least skilled manual workers and the propensity for the more skilled production workers to be unemployed has increased during the 1990s whilst that of the least skilled production workers has declined.[7]

So, for the footwear sector we find a degree of heterogeneity within the group of workers classified as manual both in terms of wage rates and unemployment duration. In Belgium, those manual footwear workers who receive the highest wage rates are also likely to experience longer terms of unemployment. This finding, which needs to be supported by data for other countries and other industries, is suggestive that training programmes which seek to upgrade the skills of manual workers to aid their re-entry into employment, could be more efficient if targeted at particular groups of manual workers, those which have a higher degree of skill which may be highly sector specific.

Responses to increased international competition

We now proceed to look at certain key factors which have affected the perfor-mance of the footwear industry in Europe in the light of globalisation and how European footwear producers have reacted to increasing foreign competition. We concentrate upon technological change, the upgrading of product quality and reorganisation of the industry to adopt flexible production methods and the devel-opment of industrial districts. In the earlier section, we showed that, in general, adjustment of the labour input in Europe has taken the form of reductions in the quantity employed and that large changes to the relative price of labour employed in footwear are not apparent.

We start by looking at technological change. In much of the debate over the causes of increasing inequality between skilled and unskilled workers the focus is upon identifying the relative impact of trade relative to technological change. However, improvements in technology may be both a cause of increased trade flows, by allowing the outsourcing of low-skill activities, for example, as well as a defensive response by producers in industrial countries to increasing competi-tion from low-wage countries. Here we simply seek to identify the extent of tech-nological change in the footwear sector.

Technological change

Measuring technological change is obviously very difficult. One simple approach is to look at the share of equipment in total investment and to check, as one might suspect, that the share of equipment increases substantially during periods in which technological change transforms the production process. Table 6.7 shows that, in general, the share of investment devoted to machinery has not changed substantially when the 1990s are compared with the early 1970s, although the data for certain countries show quite high volatility from year to year.

Table 6.7 Index of the share of investment in machinery in total investment in footwear (1970 = 100)

	Germany	Portugal	Spain	UK	Italy
1970	100,00	100,00	n.d.	100,00	100,00
1975	127,12	109,04	n.d.	104,17	104,40
1980	112,10	88,27	n.d.	104,17	109,24
1985	126,38	100,00	n.d.	100,96	84,36
1990	91,47	98,83	95,81	142,66	98,28
1994	112,99	28,68	96,93	90,00	118,20

Source: ISIS.

Table 6.8 The use and impact of computer-aided technologies in the footwear industry (percentage of respondents)

	France		Germany		Italy		UK		Portugal	
	CAD[a]	CAS[b]	CAD	CAS	CAD	CAS	CAD	CAS	CAD	CAS
In use	67	73	85	46	23	10	41	64	9	4
Negative impact on employment	20	33	38	38	12	20	9	55	9	13
Requires new abilities	67	40	85	31	40	30	59	45	48	43
Positive impact on quality	60	80	85	69	29	28	50	77	43	43

Source: DG V-EU data 'Social Study on the European Footwear Industry' (questionnaire).

Notes
a Computer-aided design.
b Computer-aided stitching.

Further indicators of technological development are provided in Table 6.8 which shows the responses of 250 firms to a survey carried out in 1999 concerning the application of two new technologies, computer-aided design (CAD) and computer-aided stitching (CAS). The responses suggest that the use of CAD, which is related to the design of the product, is far more widespread than the more production related technology, CAS. The data also suggest important differences across countries in the application of these technologies.

In general, CAD and CAS are applied more widely in France, Germany and the UK than in Italy and Portugal. In Germany, 85 per cent of respondents report that they are applying CAD techniques whilst 46 per cent of respondents are using computer-aided stitching. In the UK, nearly two-thirds of respondents confirm that they are using CAS. In Italy and Portugal these technologies appear to be much less widely applied, perhaps reflecting the nature of the sector in these locations; a large number of small firms and the preponderance of fashion-oriented leather-uppered footwear. Only 10 per cent of respondents in Italy and 4 per cent of respondents in Portugal report that they are using CAS techniques.

The questionnaire also asked respondents if the application of these technologies had had a negative impact upon employment. About 40 per cent of German firms, just over half of UK firms and one-third of French firms responded that the use of CAS had reduced employment. Responses in France and the UK suggest that the use of CAS has a more significant negative impact upon employment than application of CAD; only 9 per cent of UK respondents reported that CAD reduced employment levels. For Germany the same proportion of firms report a negative impact of CAD on employment as reported a negative employment impact of applying CAS.

Thus, we observe that loss of employment in footwear has not been evenly distributed amongst European countries. On the basis of the available data we find that those countries which had the lowest levels of labour productivity in footwear at the start of the period in 1970 experienced the sharpest falls in employment in footwear. In addition, there is some indication that these countries have more widely adopted the most recent technological advances that are relevant to the sector. We can, however, say nothing about the direction of causality concerning these developments or the extent to which the application of these technologies represents a response to more intense international competition.

Quality upgrading

We noted earlier that at the same time as import penetration ratios have increased so have export to output ratios. This is not possible to reconcile with traditional trade theory where products are assumed to be homogeneous wherever they are produced. Clearly, with the magnitude of the wage differentials between the EU countries and the developing countries, it is unlikely that EU producers could compete in the same market segments. Thus, one response from EU producers to intense international competition from low-wage countries would be to differentiate their product in terms of higher quality and in terms of design and fashion. It is interesting to note that the success of this response is likely to depend in part upon access conditions in other industrial countries. The principal markets for high quality footwear will be the OECD countries. Thus, in principle constraints upon exports of footwear to other OECD countries may constrain adjustment to more intense competition from low-wage countries. Here the role of regional integration may be important in the face of high barriers in other rich country markets.

A recent survey of global buyers of footwear products (Schmitz and Knorringa, 1999) highlights the importance of innovative design in the ability of Italy to compete with other countries who exhibit superiority in terms of price, such as China, India and Brazil. This study also shows the importance of flexibility in meeting orders in influencing buyers decisions. Italy's leading position in the industry is maintained by 'first, its innovative design capability, and second, its strong component industry' (Schmitz and Knorringa, 1999, p. 13), this is enhanced by fast response and high quality in supplying relatively small orders. China on the other hand is considered as a place of cheap shoes of reliable quality. China is also seen to be strong in responding to massive standardised orders.

Assessing the extent of quality upgrading is difficult. Data on production is collected at too aggregate a level to be useful. Given this, Brenton and Pinna (2000) look at upgrading of the exports of European countries as reflecting possible strategies by domestic footwear producers to increase the quality of their output. Using detailed (8-digit) trade data these authors take quality upgrading to be a shift within the bundle of commodities exported towards higher value products. This analysis provides little evidence of a marked upgrading of the bundle of footwear products exported by EU countries in the 1980s and 1990s when import competition has become more intense. In fact exports of most of the EU countries, including Italy, to other OECD markets were downgraded after 1988.

Brenton and Pinna (2000) find no evidence of more intense import competition from low-wage countries in the footwear sector being statistically associated with export upgrading. The only significant correlation that they find suggests a positive relation between movements in the pure price of imports (after correcting for quality upgrading) and changes in pure price of exports. Thus, where import competition has been strongest in terms of pure prices there appear to have been smaller pure price increases of exports.

Thus, to date, despite much survey and anecdotal support, there is no comprehensive evidence from industry or trade data of quality upgrading being used as a response to globalisation in the footwear sector in Europe. However, the approach above will not pick up increases in quality which occur for all of the most detailed product categories. Hence, the Italian advantage in innovation in design could result in a higher quality of all the footwear produced in Italy. This will not appear as quality upgrading in the export bundle unless there is a shift to products which have a higher value at the start of the period under investigation.

Industrial districts and flexible organisation

Clearly the response to globalisation, and to greater competition generally in the footwear sector, has not been uniform across EU countries. In some countries, such as Germany, investment abroad has played a very important role and domestic employment has declined sharply. Elsewhere, in Italy, for example, domestic output and employment have been maintained. An important aspect of the apparent success of the footwear industry in Italy is the way that the industry has become organised, and in particular the adoption of flexible production methods and the emergence of locational concentration of firms in industrial districts. It is to this issue that we finally turn.

Storper and Scott (1990) define flexible production as the '*variety of ways in which producers shift promptly from one process and/or product to another, or adjust their output upward and downward in the short run without strongly deleterious effects on productivity*'. This flexibility can be achieved within the firm and between firms. The former can be derived from the use of general-purpose equipment and machinery and through the more effective adjustment of labour inputs. Flexibility between firms is achieved from the fragmentation of the production process into many units in different firms. This provides for rapid change in the combinations of vertical and horizontal linkages between the various units and allows for quick adjustment of output levels and of product specifications. It is clear that the footwear industry in Italy has benefited from a high degree of specialisation based upon the division of the production cycle, with several firms specialised in different phases of production (Rabellotti, 1995). Crucial in this structure is a well-developed network of backward-linked firms producing components and raw material. This organisation of the sector has led to a high degree of flexibility and ability to adjust to changing market conditions.

Flexibility in production is often closely linked with labour flexibility. Storper and Scott (1990) identify three main areas where employers seek flexibility from the labour input: (i) to make wage rates adjustable downwards and to determine wages on a worker-by-worker basis rather than with occupational groups (ii) redeployment of the workforce (internal flexibility) across the shop-floor and (iii) develop strategies that allow for rapid adjustments in the quantity of labour input (external flexibility). The latter can typically be achieved through labour turnover, including temporary lay-off and recall, through the use of more temporary workers, more part-time workers and via subcontracting. Internal flexibility of labour can be associated with a higher level of job security if firms seek to retain the high level of firm specific human capital that is involved. External flexibility will in general have an adverse effect upon employment security, although again cases can be found where, for example, high levels of subcontracting stabilise the level of production.

In such an industry, skilled workers will typically be required to move frequently from task to task and from job to job. However, this is not usually associated with long periods of unemployment. Unskilled labour, on the other hand, whose wages are generally low, often face considerable employment instability. Thus, although flexible production methods have been an important response to changing international conditions, and seem to have played a crucial role in the success of the footwear industry in Italy, there are significant implications for labour, primarily unskilled labour, in terms of employment security.

Flexibility in production often results in rapid increases or decreases in labour input and has led firms to increase the number of workers, temporary or part-time, who enjoy lower levels of employment security. This results in income variation for workers over time due to their changing access to employment. Finally, workers with lower levels of employment security are likely to have less bargaining power than more secure workers. Thus, production and labour flexibility may have played an important role in widening wage differentials between skilled and unskilled workers.

Flexible production methods result from the fragmentation of the production process into many specialised units linked together in a network of supplier–buyer and subcontracting relationships. The close inter-relations between suppliers entails that many firms tend to be located in close proximity which has led to the development of industrial districts. Rabellotti (1995) provides evidence of the nature of footwear districts from two Italian regions; Brenta and Marche. Of fundamental importance to these districts is the presence of strong backward-linkages. That is, the existence of a well-developed system of suppliers and subcontractors which can provide a wide variety of products with short delivery times. This has a number of advantages including, smaller stocks of inputs for producing final shoes, the progressive reduction of the time between order and delivery, and an increase in the capacity of final shoe producers to diversify their products. Collaboration between the suppliers of inputs and the producers of shoes is an important aspect of the way that footwear industrial districts are organised since it allows fashion decisions to be taken together.

The Italian footwear districts are characterised by a high level of subcontracting with a wide network of enterprises specialised in particular aspects of the production process. According to Varaldo (1988), more than 80 per cent of Italian footwear firms subcontract the production of soles, insoles and heels, around 70 per cent subcontract the production phases of edging and sewing of uppers and about half of the firms subcontract the cutting phase. This splitting up of the production process allows the use of specialised machines and specific labour skills for particular tasks and provides for larger scale economies than are possible in shoe production itself. In the survey of Rabellotti (1995) the key reason for subcontracting is to reduce costs. Nearly three quarters of the surveyed firms report this as the catalyst for their decision. In addition, for 50 per cent of the firms subcontracting is seen as an important means of increasing flexibility. As subcontractors are more specialised, and are more able to reap the available economies of scale, they are seen as providing better products at lower cost and with shorter delays.

Most of the shoe producers surveyed in Italy chose subcontractors within the same area. The key issue in terms of our discussion of globalisation, is why it is in Italy that subcontracting has mainly been allocated to other firms in the region and not overseas to even lower cost suppliers. A key feature of industrial districts is the maintenance of stable and continuous linkages between shoe producers and subcontractors. Despite having been given prominence in a number of previous studies of industrial districts, local government was of little importance in the footwear districts of Italy.

Several authors observe a link between the characteristics of the local labor market and industrial clusters. The learning process which usually takes place inside the firm, becomes a collective process in the industrial district, based on common knowledge which accumulates in people rather than in firms. Knowledge, which is transmitted from one generation to the next, enhances local innovation through labour mobility, which circulates the know-how of one firm to the other.

Interestingly, the Italian model of the industrial district in the footwear sector is not replicated elsewhere. In the case of Mexico, Rabellotti (1995) observed a substantial difference in the linkages between firms. The relationship between suppliers and manufacturers are mainly 'market linkages', simply based on a factor of price and not through cooperation, as in Italy. Hing (1998) explores regional clustering in Taiwan and focuses on the existing key role of trading companies, which did not play an important role in Italy. The connection of these companies with international markets helped to keep Taiwan's small and medium sized shoe manufacturers up to date with rapidly changing fashion trends and technologies. Trading companies serve as a hub of information regarding managerial, technical and financial conditions in shoe factories.

In conclusion, a key feature of the footwear industry in Italy has been the increasing flexibility of production and the strong links between producers of components and the producers of final shoes within industrial districts. This has enabled Italian producers to maintain market share and output in the high quality, design intensive, and fashion sensitive part of the footwear market. The flexibility of production and labour input have enabled footwear firms to respond quickly to changing demands and to efficiently and effectively meet small scale orders for quality footwear. Clearly, such a response to increased competition would not be appropriate in the case of the mass production of standardised shoes. Nevertheless, the use of subcontracting to local firms and the flexibility of small firms have been a crucial aspect of the success of the Italian footwear industry. The response elsewhere in Europe, for example in the UK, of increasing firm size has not provided a basis for effective competition in the global market.

Nevertheless, the precise role that flexibility and industrial districts play in relation to social exclusion is not yet entirely clear. Flexibility in the use of labour often means the increasing use of temporary, part-time and cottage workers. The lack of employment stability for these workers can be reflected in rising wage differentials compared to skilled workers with higher job stability. In addition, these are workers who can miss the social safety net which is in place for permanent, full-time workers.

Conclusions

Footwear is often perceived as a standard labour-intensive manufactured product in which comparative advantage has decisively shifted from OECD countries to low-wage developing countries. In Europe as a whole there has been a substantial contraction of the sector over the past thirty years with a considerable loss of jobs. However, this decline is not uniform across EU countries. Italy, for example, has been able to maintain employment in footwear roughly at 1970 levels throughout the subsequent period.

What is apparent is that developments in the footwear sector have varied across EU countries. It would seem that Germany, for example, has been characterised by a substantial shift to production in overseas locations and the outsourcing of parts of the production process. Countries such as Italy, for example, have not shifted production overseas in this manner and have instead maintained domestic output and employment levels. An important feature of this has been the shift to ever-higher export intensities at the same time as import penetration has increased. Thus, one might conclude that globalisation, as well as creating additional competitive pressures in the domestic market, provides increased opportunities for sales overseas. An important part of the response to low-wage competition in countries which have maintained domestic output and employment would appear to be success in reorienting sales towards foreign markets. A key element in the relative success of the industry in countries such as Italy has been the move towards more flexible modes of production and the development of industrial districts. The role that policy can make in facilitating this adjustment is something which requires further attention.

Finally, this study highlights that even within a fairly standard sector such as footwear, unskilled or manual labour appears to be far from homogeneous. Within this group of workers there are significant differences in wages paid to certain types of workers. One interesting finding, which needs to be further substantiated, is that those manual workers with the highest level of skills and the highest wages tend to experience longer periods of unemployment than the least skilled footwear workers. This would suggest some attention be given to the need to target retraining schemes amongst unemployed manual workers and that within the group of unskilled workers there may be particular market imperfections which reduce the flexibility of certain types of manual workers and so raise the costs of adjustment for these workers to new economic conditions.

Acknowledgement

This work has been prepared under the research project 'Globalisation and Social Exclusion' financed by the European Commission under the Targeted Socio-Economic Research (TSER) Programme.

Notes

1 See Wood (1998) and Slaughter (1998) for an overview.
2 Commission of the European Communities, Official Journal no. 161/16, 27.
3 The dip in intra-EU trade after 1993 may reflect the change in the measurement of trade after the creation of the Single Market.
4 The data for Germany incorporate the eastern part of the country after 1990, hence there was an even greater decline in employment in the western part of the country in the 1990s than is shown in these data.
5 Due to an apparent change in the recording of footwear employment in Portugal after 1989 we cannot continue the employment series into the 1990s. Recorded employment in 1990 was double that recorded in 1989 yet output remained at roughly the same level.
6 Unless the quality of these new jobs, in terms of wages and other conditions, is considerably inferior to those in the footwear sector and this contributes to the problem of social exclusion.
7 These data come from: NIS, Belgium: 'Volkstelling' (Census), 1981–1991 (ten-yearly survey, data available for 1961–1971–1981–1991) and Ministry of Labour.

7 International trade in intermediate inputs

The case of the automobile industry

Markus Diehl

Introduction[1]

Globalization is a process of economic integration that involves international trade, international capital flows, the international diffusion of technologies and the organization of production networks on an international scale. The development of "international production sharing activities" (Yeats, 1998) has been an evolving process. Historically, the earliest forms of this process involved the production of primary commodities in developing countries, processing in industrial countries and (partly) re-exportation of the final good. Escalation in import tariff systems of industrial countries and high transaction costs have contributed to this exchange pattern. In the second half of the twentieth century, a different form of production sharing emerged. This involved the relocation of some (mostly labor-intensive) stages of the production process to low-income countries within multinational enterprises or enterprise networks. For example, electronic components produced in industrial countries were assembled in Southeast Asia for international firms, and wearing apparel was assembled virtually all over the world from textiles produced in third countries.

Until recently, this process of increasing interdependence through international input–output relations did not attract much attention in the economics profession. In most textbooks on international trade, the international division of labor is still depicted as specialization of countries in final goods. However, some contributions[2] to the "trade-and-wages debate" highlighted the increasing relevance of international trade in intermediate goods and the consequences of 'international outsourcing'[3] for the labor markets in high-income countries. The main argument is that, due to increasing import competition from low-wage countries, those stages of the production process in advanced countries that are relatively unskilled-labor-intensive are deployed to other countries. Hence, domestic goods prices are affected not only by world market prices for competing final goods, but also by the changes in prices of imported inputs and the resulting substitution of imported inputs for domestic value added. This causes the domestic production process (i.e. the remaining value adding stages) to change its factor intensity, and this also affects domestic factor prices. In contrast, many empirical studies attribute higher skill intensity only to technology, which could be mistaken if outsourcing is important. Hence, international outsourcing could possibly provide an explanation for unskilled-labor saving technical progress, hitherto treated as exogenous (Diehl, 1999).

The automobile industry is essentially an assembly industry. It brings together an immense number and variety of components, many of which are manufactured by independent firms in other countries. There are three major processes prior to final assembly: the manufacture of bodies, of engines and transmissions, and of other components (e.g. electrical components, braking systems, wheels, tires, windscreens, exhaust systems). How far vehicle manufacturers carry out the separate parts of the production sequence themselves varies considerably. Moreover, the automobile industry is often regarded as one of the most fragmented and hence most global manufacturing industries (see Nunnenkamp, 2000 for references). This assumption is usually corroborated with firm-level case studies. If the magnitude and nature of global production sharing is to be assessed at the industry level, one faces the difficulty that production data are not sufficiently disaggregated to analyze intrasectoral changes. This is in contrast to the analysis of international trade data which sufficiently differentiate between components and final goods (Appendix Table 7A.16). The revision of the International Standard Industrial Classification of the UN (ISIC, Rev. 3; effective 1995) makes it somewhat easier to assess the relevance of internationally traded inputs (Appendix Table 7A.17).

The next section provides a broad overview of global trends in the production and international trade of automobiles and automobile parts. It will be shown that the automobile industry in major countries has undergone a process of vertical disintegration, but international trade in automobile parts has not increased significantly faster than trade in finished vehicles. The intrasectoral and geographical pattern of international trade in automobile parts is analyzed in more detail in the third section with case studies for four major automobile producers (the United States, Japan, Germany, and the United Kingdom). It will be shown that the cost share of imported intermediate inputs has increased in general. Low-wage countries have gained in importance as suppliers of automobile parts although the bulk of international trade in automobile parts is still between high-income countries. Distributional effects of globalization in the automobile industry are assessed in the fourth section. The final section concludes.

Production and trade of automobiles and automobile parts: global trends

Between 1960 and 1995, the world production of automobiles has almost tripled. At the same time, major changes occurred in the global distribution of the industry (Vickery, 1996; Dicken, 1998: chapter 10). The share of Japan in the total passenger car production of the world increased from only about 1 percent in 1960 to about 18 percent in 1999,[4] whereas the share of the United States decreased from more than half of the world total to about 25 percent (Table 7.1).

Table 7.1 Production of automobiles, 1960 and 1999

	1960				1999			
	Passenger cars		Trucks and buses		Passenger cars		Trucks and buses	
	1,000 units	Share in total	1,000 units	Share in total	1,000 units	Share in total	1,000 units	Share in total
Canada	325	2.6	71	2.2	2,821	6.0	224	2.6
France	1,175	9.3	194	6.1	2,784	5.9	386	4.5
Germany	1,817	14.4	238	7.5	5,307	11.3	377	4.4
Italy	620	4.9	50	1.6	1,410	3.0	291	3.4
Spain	41	0.3	10	0.3	2,209	4.7	644	7.5
United Kingdom	1,354	10.7	458	14.5	1,787	3.8	186	2.2
United States	6,696	52.9	1,198	37.8	11,761	25.0	1,263	14.7
Australia	166	1.3	33	1.0	303	0.6	18	0.2
China PR	n.a.	n.a.	n.a.	n.a.	565	1.2	1,259	14.6
India	19	0.2	26	0.8	649	1.4	168	2.0
Japan	165	1.3	308	9.7	8,100	17.2	1,795	20.8
Korea Republic	n.a.	n.a.	n.a.	n.a.	2,362	5.0	481	5.6
Malaysia	n.a.	n.a.	n.a.	n.a.	257	0.5	16	0.2
Taiwan	n.a.	n.a.	n.a.	n.a.	246	0.5	104	1.2
Argentina	11	0.1	49	1.5	225	0.5	80	0.9
Brazil	37	0.3	97	3.1	1,049	2.2	235	2.7
Mexico	n.a.	n.a.	n.a.	n.a.	1,391	3.0	142	1.6
Czech Republic	n.a.	n.a.	n.a.	n.a.	348	0.7	27	0.3
Poland	n.a.	n.a.	n.a.	n.a.	521	1.1	19	0.2
Russia	100^a	0.8	400^a	12.6	947	2.0	229	2.7
Turkey	n.a.	n.a.	n.a.	n.a.	218	0.5	74	0.9
Total	12,650^b	100.0	3,167^b	100.0	47,136^c	100.0	8,610^c	100.0

Source: Ward's 1964 Automotive Yearbook; VDA, International Auto Statistics 2000; own calculations.

Notes
a Estimated.
b Total of the countries reported.
c Corrected for double counting (cf. VDA).

Even more dramatic was the decline of the UK automobile industry. Its share declined from about 11 percent of the world total in 1960 to a mere 4 percent in 1999. Within the EU, Germany and France remain the dominant producers with 11 and 6 percent of the 1999 world total, respectively. Their shares have declined by less then the UK share over this period. The most impressive growth in automobile production in Europe occurred in Spain, whose share in world total increased from only about half a percent of the world total in 1960 to about 5 percent in 1995.

Outside the triad (Japan, the United States and Western Europe) some important locations for automobile production have emerged. One center is Latin America where Mexico, Brazil, and Argentina together account for about 6 percent of world total. Another more recent location is South Korea with about 5 percent of world total. A third center is the former Soviet Union and Eastern Europe. In the former Soviet Union automobile production is in serious disarray, whereas the former state-owned automobile industries in Poland, the Czech Republic, Hungary, and Slovenia are in various stages of transition, commonly through joint ventures with foreign manufacturers. In most of the other developing countries, the bulk of automobile production is simply assembly of imported components, although the "local content" varies significantly (ILO, 2000). In some cases, for example, Thailand, the automobile industry consists only of assembly of completely knocked-down (CKD) vehicles imported from the home plants.

Another important element of the globalization of the automobile industry is the increasing role of international trade. Both export orientation and import market penetration in the major producer countries have steadily increased during the last three decades. For example, exports of the large Western European countries and Mexico have increased to levels of 40 percent of domestic production or more (Table 7.2). By contrast, the export orientation of large countries, especially the United States, is only moderate. Significant increases were

Table 7.2 Export orientation[a] in the motor vehicle industry,[b] 1970–1995

	1970	1975	1980	1985	1990	1995
United States	9.7	16.2	15.6	11.2	15.1	16.2
Japan	9.1	18.1	26.9	33.4	24.7	21.7
France	30.5	40.2	40.7	45.4	43.4	43.7
Germany	31.9	35.3	37.6	44.9	40.7	38.0
Italy	30.8	36.1	26.0	23.7	27.3	49.5
Spain	n.a.	n.a.	19.8	33.8	38.9	n.a.
United Kingdom	26.5	29.9	34.0	30.4	35.1	35.3[c]
Korea Republic	n.a.	n.a.	n.a.	n.a.	n.a.	26.0
Mexico	n.a.	n.a.	n.a.	n.a.	26.8	56.0

Sources: OECD, STAN; own calculations.

Notes
a Exports in percent of gross output value.
b ISIC (Rev. 2) section 3843.
c 1994.

Table 7.3 Import market penetration[a] in the motor vehicle industry,[b] 1970–1995

	1970	1975	1980	1985	1990	1995
United States	13.0	16.7	23.7	26.1	30.2	28.7
Japan	0.7	1.0	0.9	1.0	3.5	4.0
France	17.5	22.2	28.0	36.7	38.8	39.4
Germany	11.3	13.4	14.9	17.7	22.8	24.1
Italy	21.0	22.5	29.9	27.2	33.7	49.6
Spain	n.a.	n.a.	10.7	20.1	35.9	n.a.
United Kingdom	7.0	16.6	32.7	41.7	45.8	45.6[c]
Korea Republic	n.a.	n.a.	n.a.	n.a.	n.a.	8.5
Mexico	n.a.	n.a.	n.a.	n.a.	7.5	29.0

Source: OECD, STAN; own calculations.

Notes
a Imports in percent of apparent domestic consumption.
b ISIC (Rev. 2) section 3843.
c 1994.

recorded for the case of Japan (mainly in the 1970s), Spain (1980s) and South Korea (1990s). Import market penetration has reached levels of 30 percent or above in most countries (Table 7.3), in some countries at a spectacular speed (UK in the 1970s, Spain in the 1980s, Italy and Mexico in the 1990s). By contrast, import penetration is still at a very low level in Japan and South Korea, and relatively moderate in Germany. Differences in the respective indicator values are probably related to the existence of "national champions" rather than to trade protection, except for the case of South Korea where import barriers have only recently been removed.

At this aggregate level, however, the question cannot be answered whether the increasing role of international trade is only due to intra-industry trade in finished vehicles or to an increasing trade in intermediate products.[5] Only the latter would support the hypothesis of emerging international production networks. The case studies (next section) shed some light on this issue.

A rough indicator for the relevance of externally supplied components is the degree of vertical integration, that is, the ratio of value added to total production value. By this indicator, the automobile industry moved gradually towards external sourcing over the period 1970–1995 (Table 7.4). In 1970, most industrial countries had a value added share of 35 percent or higher, with the notable exception of the United Kingdom. The share was in the range of 25–30 percent 25 years later. Some countries proceeded very fast in this restructuring process, most notably Italy, South Korea, and the United States. However, this trend is not necessarily related to *international* outsourcing. External inputs are provided either by specialized domestic suppliers in the same industry (e.g. car bodies or combustion engines), by domestic suppliers in other industries (e.g. outsourcing of administrative activities to specialized suppliers of business services), or by suppliers from abroad. Input–output tables with separate transaction tables for domestic and imported inputs can be used to address this issue (see next section).

Table 7.4 Vertical integration[a] in the motor vehicle industry,[b] 1970–1995

	1970	*1975*	*1980*	*1985*	*1990*	*1995*
United States	39.6	30.0	25.7	30.4	21.4	26.4
Japan	33.8	31.7	28.6	28.4	26.8	28.1
France	35.6	36.1	35.1	28.9	31.0	29.4
Germany	38.8	36.8	35.4	34.6	30.8	30.1
Italy	42.5	37.4	28.1	25.1	25.6	24.6[c]
Spain	n.a.	n.a.	37.4	27.5	30.4	n.a.
United Kingdom	25.5	24.7	30.5	27.6	7.0	22.5[c]
Korea Republic	36.5	25.7	20.4	25.5	26.4	26.1
Mexico	26.6	23.2	27.7	30.3	25.1	25.8

Sources: OECD, STAN; own calculations.

Notes
a Value added in percent of gross output value.
b ISIC (Rev. 2) section 3843.
c 1994.

A first impression of the relevance of international production networks can be gained from world trade data, disaggregated by product category. During the period 1980–1995, world trade in automobile parts accounted for about one-third of total world trade in automobile products (Table 7.5). This ratio has remained relatively stable which, at first sight, does not support the hypothesis of increasing international sourcing activities. However, three qualifications are in order:

- The ratio is given in nominal terms. To the extent that the price of parts has increased by less than that for finished vehicles, the magnitude of international sourcing is underestimated.
- The growth of international trade in some automobile parts, namely engines, has outpaced that of trade in finished vehicles over the whole period, whereas international trade in other parts (e.g. chassis with engines mounted) stagnated. The latter is probably due to the bulky character of this product which does not allow mass shipments at competitive prices.
- Global production networks may have expanded even if the share of automobile parts in total trade remained virtually constant after the previously mentioned corrections. To some extent, automobile parts are delivered to assembly plants[6] abroad which were established for re-export rather than for the respective domestic market. In that case, exports of finished automobiles and imports of parts increase at the same pace.

A second impression of the relevance of international production networks can be gained from the geographical pattern of world production and trade in automobile parts. A comparison of the relative position of countries in 1995 reveals some interesting aspects (see Table 7.6):

- The major producers of automobiles are at the same time the major producers of automobile parts. About two-thirds of all parts are produced in the United States, Japan, and Germany.

Table 7.5 World imports of automobiles and parts thereof, 1980, 1990, and 1995

Products	Code (SITC Rev. 2)	(Billion US$)			Annual average rate of change (percent)	
		1980[b]	1990	1995	1980–1990	1990–1995
Passenger motor vehicles excluding buses	781	59.5	162.5	232.0	+10.5	+7.4
Motor vehicles for transport of goods	782	19.2	35.7	47.0	+6.4	+5.7
Buses and tractors for semi-trailers	783	4.0	6.2	15.8	+4.5	+20.5
Trailers, transport containers etc.	786	2.4	4.9	6.8	+7.3	+6.8
Total vehicles		85.1	209.3	301.6		
Combustion engines for motor vehicles	713.2	4.7	14.8	23.0[e]	+12.0	+9.3
Parts for combustion engines[a]	713.9	5.3	12.3	19.6	+8.8	+9.7
Chassis fitted with engines	784.1	2.9	2.7	2.6	−0.8	−0.6
Car bodies, parts and accessories for motor vehicles	784 ex. 784.1	30.7	71.1	114.9	+8.8	+10.1
Electrical equipment for motor vehicles parts	778.3	3.0	7.4	11.0	+9.4	+8.1
Total parts		46.6	108.3	171.1		
Total vehicles and parts (thereof: parts) (%)		131.7 35.3	317.6 34.1	472.7 36.2	+9.2	+8.3
Memo: total world exports (thereof: manufactures)	0–9 5–8 less 68	2,001 (1,085)	3,437 (2,423)	5,012 (3,745)	+5.5 (+8.4)	+7.8 (+9.1)

Sources: UN, International Trade Statistics Yearbook 1982 and 1997; OECD, ITCS.

Notes
a Includes parts of engines for other transport equipment (except aircraft).
b Only market economies.

- The relative importance of the production of parts in a country can be measured by their value share in the total output of the automobile industry (second column). Accordingly, the production of automobile parts is relatively important in Japan, China, Mexico, and Portugal (share of 40 percent or more), whereas it is less important in countries like Sweden and Belgium (share below 20 percent).[7]
- The relative importance of international production networks can be measured by the trade intensity of automobile parts (i.e. the ratio of exports

Table 7.6 Production and international trade of automobile parts, 1995

	Production of bodies and parts (*ISIC 3420, 3430*)		Exports of parts for motor vehicles (*SITC 784*)		Imports of parts for motor vehicles (*SITC 784*)		Memo: total automobile production (*ISIC 3410–3430*)
	Million US$	*Percent[a]*	*Million US$*	*Percent[b]*	*Million US$*	*Percent[b]*	*Million US$*
Austria	1,778	27.7	1,355	76.2	1,693	95.2	6,425
Belgium	3,137	15.4	3,075	98.0	6,230	198.6	20,337
Canada	13,341	18.3	7,683	57.6	14,714	110.3	72,899
France	19,873	22.6	10,324	51.9	5,731	28.8	88,075
Germany	46,308	26.5	21,932	47.4	12,926	27.9	174,799
Italy	12,580	34.1	6,053	48.1	2,492	19.8	36,837
Japan	212,715	50.6	19,656	9.2	1,455	0.7	420,540
Netherlands	2,354	34.4	1,575	66.9	2,593	110.2	6,848
Sweden	2,715	14.8	3,688	135.8	2,507	92.3	18,332
United Kingdom	12,892	29.2	5,240	40.6	9,272	71.9	44,210
United States	128,521	35.7	23,817	18.5	21,156	16.5	360,079
Australia	n.a.	n.a.	302	n.a.	1,168	n.a.	n.a.
China PR	15,488	51.1	378	2.4	897	5.8	30,305
Korea Republic	16,762	36.8	667	4.0	1,304	7.8	45,496
Taiwan	4,598	n.a.	1,334	29.0	1,542	33.5	n.a.
Thailand	n.a.	n.a.	140	n.a.	3,022	n.a.	n.a.
Argentina	n.a.	n.a.	546	n.a.	1,169	n.a.	n.a.
Brazil	n.a.	n.a.	1,471	n.a.	1,486	n.a.	n.a.
Mexico[c]	8,803	41.5	2,308	26.2	1,343	15.3	21,204
Czech Republic	n.a.	n.a.	488	n.a.	438	n.a.	2,880
Hungary	470	37.3	250	14.1	160	9.0	1,260
Poland	n.a.	n.a.	124	n.a.	753	n.a.	3,589
Portugal	1,771	40.4	354	20.0	1,026	57.9	4,380
Russian Fed.	n.a.	n.a.	197	n.a.	287	n.a.	9,512
Slovenia	n.a.	n.a.	145	n.a.	356	n.a.	n.a.
Spain	9,158	25.8	4,186	45.7	6,063	66.2	35,434
Turkey	n.a.	n.a.	182	n.a.	768	n.a.	n.a.

Sources: OECD, ISIS; EUROSTAT, DAISIE; UNIDO, Industrial Statistics; UN, Yearbook of International Trade Statistics 1997; Statistical Handbook of the Republic of China (Taiwan) 1998; VDA, International Auto Statistics 1999; own calculations.

Notes
a Share in total production of the automobile industry.
b Ratio to production of bodies and parts.
c 1994.

or imports to domestic production of parts). High values for both indicators (e.g. for the case of Canada and Western Europe) can be interpreted as intra-sectoral specialization in open markets. The interpretation of low values of both indicators (e.g. Japan, South Korea and China) is less clear: they may indicate either restricted market access or a high degree of vertical integration in the domestic industry. Low export orientation may also reflect insufficient international competitiveness.

- There are large differences with respect to the balance of international trade in automobile parts and components, even within the group of high-income countries. Large net exporters are Japan, Germany, France, Italy, Mexico, and

Sweden, whereas trade is almost balanced in the United States. Large net importers are Canada, Spain, United Kingdom, Belgium, Thailand, Australia, Argentina, Portugal, and the Netherlands. To some extent, this supports the hypothesis of international production networks since large-scale assembling activities for subsidiaries of multinational enterprises are located in the countries in the group of net importers.

- Some low-income countries have become important suppliers of parts on a regional level (e.g. Mexico for the United States and Spain for Western Europe). Moreover, the international orientation of the Eastern European automobile producers has changed significantly in the mid-1990s. However, exports of parts from low-income countries do not account for a sizable share of total imports of high-income countries. The share of Latin America, Asian DCs, Eastern Europe and the EU periphery[8] in global imports of the triad was roughly one-sixth in 1995.

All in all, the analysis of aggregate data provides only limited insights. Thus we proceed to a more detailed analysis by means of case studies in the next section.

International trade in automobile parts: case studies

Since the 1970s, major changes in the ways in which automobiles are developed and manufactured have occurred (Hartley, 1992). One is the increasing use of just-in-time methods, another trend is the increasing use of entire sub-assemblies ("modules") rather than individual components. Such modules may be made by the assembler but in many cases they are made by outside suppliers. The source of such changes is the leading Japanese producers. Womack *et al.* (1990) use the term "lean production" to contrast with the mass production techniques which have pervaded the industry. In their view,

> lean production combines the best features of both craft production and mass production – the ability to reduce costs per unit and dramatically improve quality while, at the same time providing an even wider range of products and even more challenging work.
>
> (Womack *et al.*, 1990: 277)

A major requirement of flexible production forms is that the relationship between the customer and suppliers of modules has to be extremely close in functional terms, with design and production of components being carried out in very close consultation. These new organizational methods may have biased international production networks towards geographical proximity. The analysis of international trade in automobile parts by region will shed some light on this issue.

Information derived from input–output tables can be used to analyze the role of international outsourcing.[9] The share of imported inputs in the gross output value of the motor vehicle industry increased significantly in 1970–1990 (Table 7.7). It reached about 20 percent in the United Kingdom and about 10 percent in Germany and in the United States, but was still very low in Japan. To some extent, this increase is matched by a decrease of the value added share, but the share of inputs purchased from domestic suppliers has also decreased, most notably in the United Kingdom. The only exception is Japan where the share of domestic inputs has increased. This reflects the fragmentation of the production process in the Japanese motor vehicle industry through multi-tier customer–supplier relationships (Smitka, 1991).

Inputs produced by the automobile industry of other countries account for only about half of all imported inputs. At first sight, this could be interpreted as substitution of foreign suppliers of non-specific materials for domestic suppliers rather than as a reorganization of the production process within the automobile industry. However, even though many inputs for the motor vehicle industry are produced in other industries (e.g. electrical equipment, windscreens, plastic materials; cf. Appendix Table 7A.16), they still are designed according to the specific needs of the motor vehicle industry. Hence, the increase of the imported inputs share clearly supports the hypothesis that international outsourcing in the motor vehicle industry has become more relevant.

In the following, international trade in automobile parts is analyzed in detail for four major automobile producers (the United States, Japan, Germany and the United Kingdom). Three indicators are considered: first, the commodity structure of international trade in automobile products; second, the export orientation and the import market penetration of the automobile industry by subsectors; and third, the composition of imports of automobile parts[10] by region. Whenever possible, information about the trade policy of the respective country (including regional free trade agreements) and about firm strategies is added to explain specific developments. The first indicator will be used to identify the type of parts which are increasingly traded internationally. The second indicator will be used to find out whether imports and/or exports of intermediate products have gained in importance for these countries. The third indicator will be used to identify whether the relevance of low-income countries as suppliers of intermediate inputs has increased; moreover, it allows to test the hypothesis that globalization is largely a phenomenon on the regional rather than the global level.

An important objective of the case studies is to test indirectly whether the increasing trade in automobile parts has contributed to the labor market developments in these countries, that is, the increased unemployment of less-skilled workers in Europe and the increased skill premium in the United States. If automobile parts are mainly imported from other high-income countries, international outsourcing cannot be used as the main explanation for the labor market developments in high-income countries. However, this must not be the case if low-income countries have gained considerable shares in the market for automobile parts.

Table 7.7 Cost components[a] in the motor vehicle industry,[b] 1970–1990

	Germany			United Kingdom			Japan			United States		
	1970[c]	1978	1990	1968	1979	1990	1970	1980	1990	1972	1982	1990
Domestic inputs	58.4	53.2	57.3	65.5	52.0	49.9	68.6	73.5	77.4	62.3	64.6	59.8
Thereof: from motor vehicle industry	17.1	15.1	15.3	24.4	7.0	7.3	25.5	28.8	43.9	24.2	21.7	21.8
Imported inputs	6.4	8.1	11.7	3.9	11.7	20.8	0.7	1.1	1.3	3.9	6.5	10.2
Thereof: from motor vehicle industry	2.0	3.5	5.4	0.5	5.4	8.0	0.0	0.1	0.3	2.2	3.6	6.1
Value added	35.2	38.8	31.0	30.6	36.3	29.4	30.7	25.4	21.3	33.9	28.9	30.0

Sources: OECD-DSTI; Statistisches Bundesamt, Input-Output-Tabellen.

Notes
a In percent of gross output value.
b ISIC (Rev. 2) section 3843.
c Own calculations from revised 1970 input–output table for Germany.

The case of the United States

During the last two decades, the United States was a large net importer of finished vehicles whereas the trade in automobile parts was almost balanced (Table 7.8). Automobile parts accounted for more than half of the exports of all automobile products but only for less than 30 percent of total imports. However, imports of automobile parts have grown significantly faster than exports. Consequently, the United States has become a net importer of engines and electrical equipment for vehicles in 1995.

The liberal US trade regime made room for this development. Import tariffs on automobile products are very low in the United States, ranging from 0 to 4 percent in general. Higher rates, up to 25 percent, apply only for trucks (GATT, 1994). However, voluntary export restrictions on Japanese passenger cars to the United States were terminated only in 1994 (WTO, 1998).

Within the automobile industry, the production of parts was always more export-oriented than other subsectors, recording an export share of about one-quarter of domestic production (Table 7.9). This may be explained by the long standing cooperation between firms in the United States and in Canada which accounts for the bulk of the US parts exports. By contrast, the import market penetration for automobile parts was lower than for finished vehicles.

The regional structure of US imports of automobile parts has recorded two significant shifts.

First, the share of Japan has increased since the early 1970s (Figure 7.1). This was due to increased Japanese production and assembly in the United States, initially based on supplies of parts from the home country (Payne and Payne, 1990). In the early 1990s, imports from Japan accounted for about 40 percent of

Table 7.8 US trade with motor vehicles and parts, 1980 and 1995

	Code (SITC)	Exports (billion US$)		Change[a] (percent)	Imports (billion US$)		Change[a] (percent)
		1980	*1995*		*1980*	*1995*	
Cars	781	4.3	16.8	+9.6	18.0	66.1	+9.1
Trucks	782	2.1	5.3	+6.2	2.1	10.2	+11.1
Buses	783	0.5	1.4	+7.6	0.2	2.2	+16.0
Trailers	786	0.2	0.9	+9.1	0.0	0.6	+21.1
Engines	713.2	0.9	3.7	+10.2	0.8	6.3	+14.7
Parts thereof	713.9	1.6	3.4	+5.0	0.9	3.3	+9.5
Parts and accessories	784	7.6	23.8	+7.9	5.5	21.2	+9.4
Electrical equipment	778.3	0.3	1.5	+10.1	0.3	2.0	+14.3
Total		17.5	56.8	+8.2	27.8	111.9	+9.7
(thereof: parts[b]) (%)		59	57		27		29

Sources: OECD, ITCS; own calculations.

Notes
a Annual average rate of change for the period 1980–1995.
b Share of engines and parts thereof, parts and accessories and electrical equipment in total trade.

Table 7.9 Export orientation[a] and import penetration[b] in the US automobile industry[c]

	Export orientation			Import penetration		
	1985	*1990*	*1995*	*1985*	*1990*	*1995*
Automobiles and engines[d]	9.5	10.0	11.4	34.1	29.9	29.3
Automobile bodies and trailers[d]	0.7	1.7	2.1	1.5	1.4	1.6
Automobile parts and accessories[d]	25.6	25.7	24.4	24.1	27.5	22.7
Total automobile industry	12.5	12.9	13.9	29.4	27.2	25.5

Sources: OECD, ITCS; EUROSTAT, DAISIE; own calculations.

Notes

a Exports in percent of domestic production.

b Imports in percent of apparent domestic consumption.

c ISIC (Rev. 3) sections 3410, 3420 and 3430. Correspondence between production data (ISIC Rev. 3) and import data (SITC Rev. 3) as follows: ISIC 3410 = SITC 781 + 782 + 783 + 784.1 + 713.2; ISIC 3420 = SITC 784.2 + 786.1; ISIC 3430 = SITC 784.3.

d Data prior to 1995 not strictly comparable due to the introduction of the revised classification (ISIC Rev. 3).

total imports of engines, of parts and accessories, and of electrical equipment. However, this share declined somewhat during the 1990s due to "voluntary" trade restrictions. Japanese automobile manufacturers under the 1992 "Global Partnership Program" stated that they expected to increase their purchases of US-made components. This included sharply increased purchases by Japanese auto companies based in the United States[11] of inputs produced in the United States, mainly from Japanese affiliates located in the United States (GATT, 1994).

Second, imports from Mexico have gained at the expense of European and Canadian exports. In the mid-1990s, Mexico's share in all three segments of the US automobile market was already bigger than the European share. It has to be noted that automobile parts are not only imported from Mexico but also exported from the United States to the export processing zones close to the border ("maquiladoras"). By contrast, other regions played virtually no role, with the exception of other Asian countries as suppliers of electrical equipment.

Regional trade arrangements have fostered this development (Hummels *et al.*, 1998):

- The 1965 Automobile Pact between the United States and Canada reshaped the industry, producing an integrated structure in which production by the major manufacturers was reorganized on a continental rather than a national basis. Canadian plants performed specific functions within the larger continental production system. The 1988 Canada–US Free Trade Agreement also contained important provisions for the automobile industry. In particular, it redefined the level of "North American content" necessary for a firm to claim duty-free movement within the North American market (Eden and Molot, 1993).
- The NAFTA (effective 1994) has even more far-reaching implications for the automobile industry because of the lower production costs of the Mexican

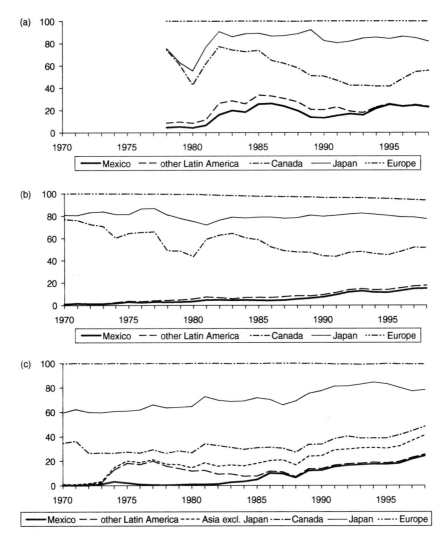

Figure 7.1 Geographical composition of US imports of automobile parts, 1970–1998:
(a) SITC 713.2 – engines; (b) SITC 784 – parts and accessories; (c) 778.3 –
electrical equipment.

Sources: OECD, ITCS; own calculations.

Note
Cumulative shares of total imports (percent).

automobile industry and the fact that it was already becoming increasingly
integrated into the North American market through the strategies of multinational producers. Tariffs are to be removed within NAFTA over ten years,
the same applies to Mexico's quotas on imports. Mexican import tariffs on

cars were immediately reduced by 50 percent. In addition, the US local content rule of origin was sharpened: the requirement was increased from 50 percent (under the US–Canada free trade agreement) to 62.5 percent. This may discourage trade in vehicles made in any NAFTA party with the use of non-NAFTA components (GATT, 1994).

In summary, international sourcing is relatively important in the United States, but the causes were different for parts from Japan and parts from Mexico. In the first case, increased imports are the consequence of increased Japanese production within the United States, that is, no outsourcing in the narrow sense. In the second case, production networks emerged between locations in Mexico and the United States.

The case of Japan

In the early 1980s, Japanese producers were clearly the least multinational of the major automobile producers, measured by the share of vehicles produced abroad. Japanese firms had established local assembly operations in a number of countries, but before 1982 there was not a single Japanese automobile production plant outside Japan. The spectacular increase of Japanese exports was achieved almost entirely without any overseas production. However, this has changed dramatically during the 1980s. Japanese companies changed their global strategy by locating major production plants in their major markets. The primary stimulus for this change was the increasing opposition in both North America and Western Europe towards the growth of Japanese imports, leading to protectionist measures such as VERs in both regions.

In 1980–1995, Japan was a large exporter of both finished vehicles and automobile parts (Table 7.10). The share of automobile parts in total exports of automobile products has more than doubled since 1980 and reached more than one-third in the 1990s. This clearly indicates the increasing role of Japanese production and assembly plants in North America, East Asia and, more recently, also in Western Europe. In addition, Japanese component manufactures followed the assemblers because of the use of just-in-time delivery systems (Sleigh, 1990). Since the first establishment of production facilities in the United States in the early 1980s, each of the major Japanese firms has made major investments in engine, transmission and components plants within the United States. Japanese automobile manufacturers are deeply involved in Asia through a network of assembly plants and joint ventures with domestic firms in Thailand, Malaysia, the Philippines, Indonesia, Taiwan, and China PR. In several of these countries Japanese firms dominate the automobile market (Legewie, 2000). In comparison, Japanese automobile manufacturers were slower to establish production facilities in Europe; meanwhile, major Japanese plants are located in the United Kingdom (see in the following section).

By contrast, imports of automobile parts are still tiny both compared to total imports of automobile products and to exports of automobile parts. However, imports of automobile parts have grown significantly faster than exports. Moreover, European producers recently entered the Japanese market through

Table 7.10 Japanese trade with motor vehicles and parts, 1980 and 1995

	Code (SITC, Rev. 2)	Exports (billion US$)		Change[a] (percent)	Imports (billion US$)		Change[a] (percent)
		1980	1995		1980	1995	
Cars	781	16.1	41.7	+6.5	0.5	10.0	+22.9
Trucks	782	6.4	9.6	+2.7	0.0	0.2	+13.5
Buses	783	0.6	1.2	+4.9	0.0	0.0	+15.7
Trailers	786	0.5	0.2	−7.3	0.0	0.2	+23.7
Engines	713.2	0.3	6.0	+22.0	0.0	0.1	+5.0
Parts thereof	713.9	0.9	4.6	+11.6	0.0	0.3	+16.9
Parts and accessories	784	2.2	19.7	+15.8	0.1	1.5	+19.5
Electrical equipment	778.3	0.5	2.6	+11.4	0.0	0.2	+13.1
Total		27.5	80.2	+7.4	0.6	12.5	+22.4
(thereof: parts[b]) (%)		14	38		29	16	

Source: OECD, ITCS; own calculations.

Notes
See Table 7.8.

mergers and acquisitions, for example, in the case of Renault/Nissan, Mercedes/Mitsubishi, and Bosch/Zexel, but there is no foreign car manufacturer producing in Japan.

The low level of imports is surprising, since the Japanese trade regime is fully liberalized. Japan applies no import tariffs on finished vehicles and on automobile parts. Moreover, it has not used anti-dumping or countervailing measures in the automobile sector (WTO, 1998). Allegedly, the low import penetration ratio is due to other regulations. For example, the United States and other countries repeatedly claimed that Japan's certification procedures have complicated the entry of foreign automobiles into the Japanese market (GATT, 1995). In recent years, the United States has claimed that close Japanese intercorporate relationships make it difficult for foreign automotive parts suppliers to compete with Japanese-owned suppliers for original equipment sales to Japanese automobile assemblers (WTO, 1998).

Within the automobile industry, the production of automobile parts was always relatively little export-oriented, both compared to other countries and to other subsectors of the Japanese automobile industry. This subsector recorded an export share of only about 10 percent of domestic production (Table 7.11). Likewise, the import market penetration for automobile parts is still negligible, and never reached the level of finished vehicles. The significant decline of export orientation of the production of finished vehicles from about two-thirds in 1980 to about one-third in 1995 again indicates the important role of Japanese transplants.

The regional structure of Japanese imports of automobile parts is hard to interpret, given the tiny volumes. However, there was a significant shift towards suppliers from other Asian countries, at the expense of Europe and the United States

Table 7.11 Export orientation[a] and import penetration[b] in the Japanese automobile industry[c]

	Export orientation			Import penetration		
	1985	*1990*	*1995*	*1985*	*1990*	*1995*
Automobiles and engines[d]	60.5	43.4	34.3	2.5	8.4	8.3
Automobile bodies and trailers[d]	3.3	1.1	1.3	0.0	0.3	0.3
Automobile parts and accessories[d]	9.6	8.7	10.2	0.4	0.7	0.9
Total automobile industry	33.3	24.2	20.3	1.0	3.5	3.7

Sources: OECD, ITCS; EUROSTAT, DAISIE; own calculations.

Note
See Table 7.9.

(Figure 7.2). This trend is most obvious in the case of electrical equipment, where imports from Asia accounted for 40 percent of total imports in the mid-1990s. Only in the case of engines, the share of Asian suppliers is still small since this market is dominated by imports from the United States. Compared to Western Europe and North America, East Asian imports of automobile parts account for a larger share of total automobile products, and are growing considerably faster. Hence, production sharing in East Asia is greater than is generally recognized (Ng and Yeats, 1999).

In summary, Japanese manufacturers participated in production networks largely in the form of supplying parts to foreign subsidiaries, later followed by local sourcing of parts. By contrast, imports of parts from low-income countries for plants located in Japan were still very low, although they grew much faster than imports from high-income countries. However, the economic crisis of the 1990s has forced Japanese manufacturers to reorganize their production networks, and that may soon change the picture (Park *et al.*, 1999).

The case of Germany

In the period under consideration, Germany was always a net exporter both of finished vehicles and of automobile parts. Automobile parts accounted for about one third both in total exports and in total imports of automobile products (Table 7.12). However, imports of automobile parts have grown considerably faster than exports, with the exception of electrical equipment. In the segment of vehicle engines, Germany has even become a net importer, albeit a small one.

The common trade policy of the EU was not as liberal as in the case of the United States or Japan. Import tariffs for automobile products in the EU ranged between 0 and 22 percent in 1997, with a simple average of 7 percent (WTO, 1997). Moreover, the tariff structure shows some escalation: rates were about 20 percent on buses and trucks and 10 percent on passenger cars, whereas the rates on parts were only 4.5 percent (EU-TARIC, 1995). In 1991, the European Commission negotiated an agreement with the Japanese government which phased out all national import restrictions but limited Japanese automobile imports to a given percentage of total EU vehicle sales for a transitional period of seven years

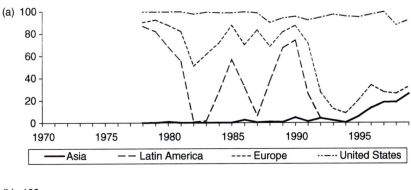

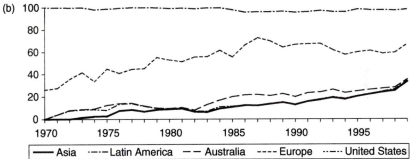

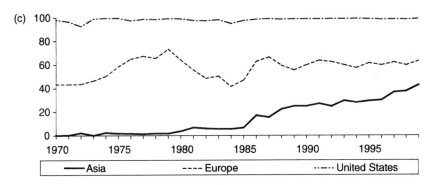

Figure 7.2 Geographical composition of Japanese imports of automobile parts, 1970–1999: (a) SITC 713.2 – engines; (b) SITC 784 – parts and accessories; (c) SITC 778.3 – electrical equipment.

Source: OECD, ITCS; own calculations.

Note
See Figure 7.1.

(1993–1999). Japan agreed to monitor its direct exports, whereas exports of vehicles from Japanese brand-name plants within the EU were explicitly excluded (GATT, 1993). This monitoring of export levels has been completely abolished as from January 1, 2000 (European Commission, 2000).

Table 7.12 German trade with motor vehicles and parts, 1980 and 1995

	Code (SITC, Rev. 2)	Exports (billion US$)		Change[a] (percent)	Imports (billion US$)		Change[a] (percent)
		1980	1995		1980	1995	
Cars	781	14.6	48.6	+8.4	4.8	23.3	+11.0
Trucks	782	3.9	6.1	+3.1	0.6	3.4	+12.9
Buses	783	1.1	4.2	+9.4	0.1	1.6	+23.4
Trailers	786	0.8	1.8	+5.1	0.2	0.7	+8.4
Engines	713.2	0.8	2.5	+7.3	0.4	2.7	+13.6
Parts thereof	713.9	1.2	3.6	+7.4	0.3	1.2	+11.0
Parts and	784	6.6	21.9	+8.3	2.1	12.9	+13.0
Electrical equipment	778.3	0.7	1.5	+8.8	0.3	1.0	+9.0
Total		29.7	90.2	+7.7	8.8	46.8	+11.8
(thereof: parts[b]) (%)		32	33		35	38	

Sources: OECD, ITCS; Statistisches Bundesamt, Foreign Trade according to SITC; own calculations.

Note
See Table 7.8.

Table 7.13 Export orientation[a] and import penetration[b] in the German automobile industry[c]

	Export orientation			Import penetration		
	1985	1990	1995	1985	1990	1995
Automobiles and engines[d]	53.6	49.6	48.1	21.9	30.1	31.8
Automobile bodies and trailers[d]	19.3	14.8	14.5	7.2	9.3	6.9
Automobile parts and accessories[d]	75.0	76.4	54.6	50.1	57.9	41.6
Total automobile industry	55.7	52.5	48.2	24.9	32.6	32.8

Sources: OECD, ITCS; Statistisches Bundesamt, Foreign Trade according to SITC; EUROSTAT, DAISIE; own calculations.

Note
See Table 7.9.

The production of automobile parts in Germany was always very trade-oriented, both in absolute levels and compared to the production of finished vehicles (Table 7.13). Export shares stood at about three quarters of domestic production, and import market penetration at about 50 percent.[12] This shows clearly the important role of parts produced in Germany for assembly plants in other countries, foremost in Western Europe. Two factors are behind this: first, international production sharing within multinational corporations (Ford, GM, and VW; cf. Sleigh, 1991), and second, technologically advanced, specialized suppliers (e.g. Bosch for electronic parts or ZF for transmissions; cf. Meissner *et al.*, 1994). The export orientation of the production of bodies and trailers is only moderate, but still significantly larger than in the United States.

German imports of automobile parts were always concentrated on Western Europe, accounting for 80 percent of total imports (Figure 7.3). However, two significant shifts were recorded: First, the share of suppliers at the European periphery[13] increased to almost 20 percent in the case of automobile parts and about one quarter in the case of electrical equipment. Second, the share of suppliers in

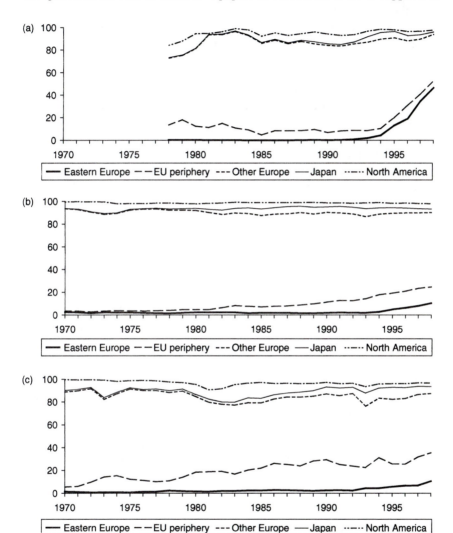

Figure 7.3 Geographical composition of German imports of automobile parts, 1970–1998: (a) SITC 713.2 – engines; (b) SITC 784 – parts and accessories; (c) SITC 778.3 – electrical equipment.

Source: OECD, ITCS; Statistisches Bundesamt; own calculations.

Note
See Figure 7.1.

Eastern Europe has increased since 1993, most notably in the case of vehicle engines where it stood at more than 40 percent in 1998.

Both shifts are clearly driven by labor-cost differentials and were facilitated by the European integration process and the opening-up of Eastern Europe to foreign direct investment.[14] This was at the expense of other Western European countries, since the share of other regions remained relatively small and almost constant over the whole period. Only in the case of electrical equipment, other regions[15] accounted for more than 10 percent of total German imports.

The intra-European production sharing can be illustrated with the case of Volkswagen (VW).[16]

Prior to the opening up of Eastern Europe, VW concentrated its production in two countries in a clear strategy of spatial segmentation. High-value cars were produced in the former West Germany, low-cost, small cars were produced in Spain where VW undertook a massive investment program in the former SEAT company. During 1990, VW moved very rapidly to establish production of small cars in Eastern Germany and to take a majority stake in the Czech firm Skoda. VW has embarked on a major restructuring program which involves reducing the number of vehicle "platforms" used by the four companies forming the VW group (VW, Audi, SEAT, Skoda) to ensure the maximum sharing of basic structures on which differentiated vehicles can be based. VW is also introducing radically new sourcing arrangements with its key suppliers. Outside Europe, VW has major production plants (not only for local markets) in Brazil, China, and in Mexico. The latter has effectively replaced much of the production formerly located at VW's Pennsylvania plant, which was closed in 1988 (Dicken, 1998: 347).

The case of the United Kingdom

In the 1970s and 1980s, the UK automobile industry went through a long period of absolute decline, which first affected the production of finished vehicles and subsequently also that of automobile parts. However, the establishment of new assembly plants in the 1980s and early 1990s brought a dramatic change in the automobile production within the United Kingdom.

In the early 1980s, the United Kingdom was net exporter of automobile parts and net importer of finished vehicles, but this pattern has been reversed completely. In 1995, automobile parts accounted for only about 40 percent of total exports after almost 60 percent in 1980, and for about 40 percent of total imports after only one quarter in 1980 (Table 7.14). Imports of automobile parts have grown considerably faster than exports in all segments, in particular in the segment of parts and accessories. Only in the segment of vehicle engines the United Kingdom still is a net exporter, albeit a small one, whereas it has become a strong net importer of all other automobile products. Moreover, the United Kingdom is still a net importer of finished vehicles, although exports have increased significantly due to the large foreign investments in the UK automobile industry.

Even though the production of automobile parts in the United Kingdom has become less export-oriented, this segment is still very trade-oriented, both in

Table 7.14 UK trade with motor vehicles and parts, 1980 and 1995

	Code (SITC, Rev. 2)	Exports (billion US$)		Change[a] (percent)	Imports (billion US$)		Change[a] (percent)
		1980	1995		1980	1995	
Cars	781	1.9	11.0	+12.2	4.9	15.6	+8.0
Trucks	782	1.3	1.3	−0.0	0.6	2.2	+8.9
Buses	783	0.1	0.2	+3.5	0.2	0.4	+3.7
Trailers	786	0.2	0.5	+5.1	0.1	0.3	+8.3
Engines	713.2	0.5	1.8	+8.7	0.1	0.9	+12.5
Parts thereof	713.9	0.8	1.0	+1.6	0.3	1.3	+9.7
Parts and accessories	784	3.6	5.2	+2.5	1.5	9.3	+13.9
Electrical equipment	778.3	0.2	0.5	+7.9	0.2	0.7	+10.4
Total		8.6	21.5	+6.3	7.9	30.7	+9.5
(thereof: parts[b]) (%)		59	40		27	40	

Sources: OECD, ITCS; own calculations.

Note
See Table 7.8.

Table 7.15 Export orientation[a] and import penetration[b] in the UK automobile industry[c]

	Export orientation			Import penetration		
	1985	1990	1995	1985	1990	1995
Automobiles and engines[d]	21.7	28.6	46.6	41.0	42.2	53.0
Automobile bodies and trailers[d]	5.5	9.1	12.4	7.5	7.1	5.7
Automobile parts and accessories[d]	74.5	71.3	49.7	71.0	76.7	64.4
Total automobile industry	31.2	34.9	45.0	43.4	46.4	53.6

Sources: OECD, ITCS; EUROSTAT, DAISIE; own calculations.

Note
See Table 7.9.

absolute levels and compared to the production of finished vehicles (Table 7.15). Export shares and import market penetration were higher than 70 percent of domestic production in the 1980s, but both ratios decreased during the 1990s. The import market penetration in finished vehicles has always been relatively high in the United Kingdom, and reached a level of more than 50 percent during the 1990s. Finally, the export orientation of the production of bodies and trailers increased and, in 1995, it reached a level close to that in Germany.

Two factors were responsible for the surge of foreign direct investment: first, a combination of average labor productivity and relatively low wages made the United Kingdom an attractive location within Western Europe; second, the Thatcher government guaranteed a liberal trade[17] and investment regime and offered financial incentives. Hence, the United Kingdom provided a production base for the (then still coming) Single European Market (Hudson, 1995). In the

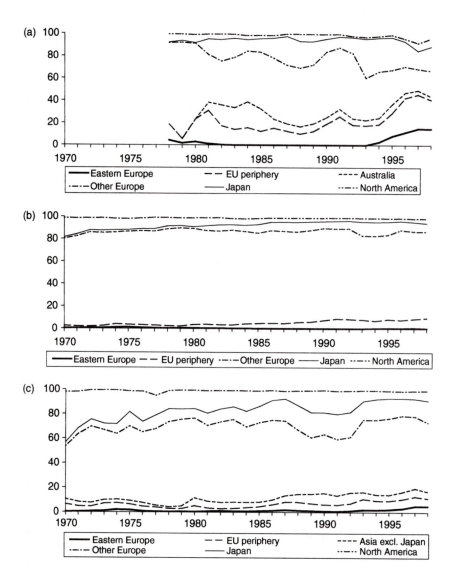

Figure 7.4 Geographical composition[a] of UK imports of automobile parts, 1970–1998:
(a) SITC 713.2 – engines; (b) SITC 784 – parts and accessories; (c) SITC 778.3 –
electrical equipment.

Sources: OECD, ITCS; own calculations.

Note
See Figure 7.1.

negotiation process for the 1991 "Consensus" between the EC and Japan, the biggest controversy was over the treatment to be accorded to Japanese vehicles manufactured within Europe itself. In this respect, the European Commission insisted on specific levels of local content in vehicle manufacture of foreign producers. As far as Japanese firms in Europe are concerned, a level of 80 percent local content was regarded acceptable (Dicken, 1998: 331).

The structure of UK imports of automobile parts differs significantly across segments (Figure 7.4). Whereas imports from Western Europe dominated in the parts and accessories segment with more than 70 percent of total imports over the whole period, non-European suppliers accounted for about 50 percent of total imports of engines and electrical equipment. Among them, Japanese suppliers held the largest share with more than 20 percent in both segments, whereas suppliers in the EU periphery held a significant (and increasing) share of total UK imports only in the segment of vehicle engines. Suppliers in Eastern Europe have gained a sizable market share in UK imports of vehicle engines since the early 1990s, which was at the expense of suppliers from Western Europe. The share of other regions remained relatively small over the whole period.

The intra-European production sharing of the United Kingdom can be illustrated with two examples: GM's operations in Europe had long been based upon two separate national subsidiaries: Vauxhall (United Kingdom) and Opel (Germany). When Vauxhall's performance became progressively weaker during the 1970s, Vauxhall was relegated to serving the UK market only and much of its production was simple assembly of imported subassemblies from Opel (Dicken, 1998: 346).

In the 1990s, Toyota and Honda established plants for the production of cars and engines in the United Kingdom. They started at relatively low levels of local content and progressively increased them when local supplier networks were built up and Japanese component suppliers have joined end producers as foreign investors in the United Kingdom (Vickery, 1996: 195). In contrast to the United States, Japanese subsidiaries purchase components mainly from the established Western European suppliers (Hudson, 1995).

In summary, the United Kingdom is highly involved in regional production networks, mainly as importer of automobile parts. However, information about the specific skill requirements of the production process within the United Kingdom is needed to conclude about labor market consequences.

Distributional effects of globalization

Trade models predict that the gains and costs of globalization should be unevenly distributed among the various employment groups and the various subsectors of the automobile industry. Accordingly, low-skilled workers and labor intensive segments of the sectoral value-added chain should be vulnerable to competitive pressure from low-wage countries and face declining wages and employment. Such distributional effects can emerge in two dimensions: the vertical dimension of income inequality, that is, wage differentials between workers of different skill levels, and the horizontal dimension of income inequality, that is, wage differentials between workers of the same skill level in different sectors.

Nunnenkamp and Spatz (2002) assessed both dimensions of distributional effects. The authors traced the wage and employment trends in the German, Japanese and United States automobile industry since the late 1970s and linked these trends to the globalization-induced competitive pressure. Compared to total manufacturing, automobile workers received a significant wage premium and enjoyed a rising or at least stable employment level in all three countries. They were, thus, among the winners of globalization.

However, the favorable wage and employment trends mask substantial differences between the various subsectors of the automobile industry. For instance, the average wage level in Japan and the United States rose far more steeply in the relatively human-capital-intensive automobile assembly than in the relatively labor-intensive production of automotive parts and components.

Moreover, the human capital intensity (i.e. the employment share of low-skilled workers) increased steadily over the last two decades in the German assembly sub-sector, while it remained basically unchanged in the German production of parts and components where it began to increase only in the mid-1990s. The different time pattern may be attributed to high transportation costs for automotive parts and components and their use in just-in-time production. Only the opening-up of the geographically close Central European transition economies triggered a comprehensive restructuring process in this subsector. Human capital intensity increased sharply while the total workforce even increased. By contrast, human capital intensity remained almost constant in the US production of parts and components and decreased in automobile assembly since the mid-1980s. High unionization and militant labor disputes may have prevented a successful restructuring in the latter subsector.

Nunnenkamp and Spatz (2002) also found evidence that the labor market situation of low-skilled automobile workers deteriorated in the traditional producer countries over the last two decades. In Germany, the sectoral human capital intensity rose and the sectoral relative wage of low-skilled workers fell. In the Japanese automobile industry, the employment prospects of low-skilled workers deteriorated while their relative wages remained fairly stable. Only in the United States the sectoral human capital intensity did not reveal a clear trend. Even more surprisingly, the relative wage of low-skilled automobile workers in the United States remained above its 1978 level throughout the entire observation period.[18]

Finally, the authors correlated the intrasectoral wage and employment ratios with a number of indicators reflecting the sector-specific intensity of international competition (e.g. the ratio of imports to domestic production and the share of low-income countries in total imports). Apart from the US automobile industry, they found Stolper–Samuelson type adjustment to growing competitive pressure from low-wage countries:

- Correlation coefficients are high for the German automobile industry and its two subsectors both for the wage ratio and the employment ratio. This implies that the entire sector adjusted to globalization by specializing in human-capital-intensive products and by outsourcing labor-intensive segments to low-income countries, in particular in the production of automotive parts and components.

- Japan resembles Germany only with respect to the effects on human capital intensity but not with respect to the wage ratio. This suggests that the intrasectoral wage effects were blurred by other factors. For instance, the seniority principle in wage setting and the high job tenure even of low-skilled workers counteracted a rise in the skill premium.
- In the United States, the two subsectors responded differently to globalization. Growing international competition went along with falling human capital intensity and a rising relative wage of low-skilled workers in automobile assembly, but not in the production of automotive parts and components.

In summary, Nunnenkamp and Spatz (2002) have shown how the development of wages and employment in the automobile industry in Japan, the United States and Germany can be linked to the respective adjustment strategies.

Conclusions

Since 1970, some important new locations for automobile production have emerged outside the triad (Japan, the United States, and Western Europe). However, not only the import market penetration in the major producer countries has steadily increased during the last three decades, but also their export orientation. A priori, there are two possible explanations: increasing intra-industry trade in finished vehicles or expanding international production networks.

From the analysis of international trade statistics it emerged that trade in automobile parts accounted for a relatively stable fraction of total world trade in automobile products. However, this is not to say that global production networks have not expanded. For example, automobile parts are to some extent delivered to assembly plants abroad which were established for re-export rather than for the respective local market. In that case, imports of finished automobiles and exports of parts increase at the same pace.

The analysis of the geographical pattern of world production and trade in automobile parts showed that the share of imported parts in total production costs has increased significantly. Moreover, some low-income countries (e.g. Mexico and Spain) have become strong net exporters of automobile parts. This fits the anecdotal evidence on international production networks, for example, the United States within NAFTA or high-income EU countries with Southern and Eastern Europe. However, exports of automobile parts from low-income countries in Asia, Latin America and Eastern Europe are still relatively small compared to the total imports of high-income countries. Some high-income countries (e.g. Japan and Germany) have been large net exporters of parts during the last two decades. Again, this shows that international production networks are relevant since these exports are servicing large-scale assembling activities of subsidiaries in third countries.

These general findings are corroborated in case studies on four major producers (the United States, Japan, Germany, and the United Kingdom). Considerable differences were found with respect to the export orientation and import market penetration of the automobile industry in these countries, and in changes of the regional structure of imports of automobile parts. The main conclusion is that international production networks matter but mainly on a regional level.

The assessment of the distributional effects of globalization has shown how the development of wages and employment in the automobile industry in Japan, the United States, and Germany can be linked to the respective adjustment strategies.

Appendix

Table 7A.16 Classification of motor vehicles and parts thereof before 1995

ISIC (Rev. 2)	Product description	NACE 1970	SITC (Rev. 1)	SITC (Rev. 2)
3843	Passenger motor cars	ex351	732.1	781
	Buses	ex351	ex732.2	ex783.1
	Lorries and trucks	ex351	732.3	782.1
	Road tractors	ex351	732.5	783.2
	Combustion engines	ex351	*ex711.5*	*ex713.2*
	Chassis with engines	ex351	732.6, 732.7	784.1
	Chassis, frames and other parts (excluding plastic, windscreens)	ex351, ex352, ex353	732.8 (excluding ex732.89)	784.2, ex784.9
	Pumps and filters,[a] crankshafts etc.	ex353	*ex719.2, ex719.64, ex719.93*	*ex742, ex743.6, ex745.27, ex749.3*
	Motorized invalid carriages[b]	*ex365*	ex733.4	ex785.3
	Non-industrial trailers	ex352	ex733.3	786.11, ex786.8
ex3829	Industrial trailers,[c] transport containers[c]	*ex315.2,* ex352	ex733.3, 731.63	786.12, 786.13, ex786.8
ex382x/383x	Special purpose vans	ex351	732.4	782.2
ex3551	Rubber tires and tubes	*ex481.1*	*ex629.1*	*ex625*
ex3560	Plastic parts	ex353	ex732.89	ex784.9
ex3620	Windscreens and framed windows	*ex247, ex353*	ex732.89	ex784.9
ex3811/3812	Locks, metal chairs	*ex316*	*ex698.1, ex821.01*	*ex699.1, ex821.1*
ex3831/3839	Batteries, electric lamps, other electrical equipment	*ex343.1, ex343.2, ex347.1*	*ex729.1, ex729.2,* 729.4	*ex778.1, ex778.2,* 778.3
ex3851	Measuring and control equipment	*ex344, ex371*	*ex729.52, ex861.8, ex861.97*	*ex873.2, ex874.3, ex874.8*
ex3853	Clocks	*ex374*	*ex864.2*	*ex885.2*
9513	Repair of motor Vehicles	*ex671*	n.a.	n.a.

Source: UN Statistical Office.

Notes
Codes in italics refer to items that are not classified in manufacturing of motor vehicles in the respective classification system.

a In ISIC (Rev. 3) and NACE (Rev. 1) included in "non-electrical machinery."
b In ISIC (Rev. 3) and NACE (Rev. 1) included in "other transport equipment."
c In ISIC (Rev. 3) and NACE (Rev. 1) included in "motor vehicles."

Table 7A.17 Classification of motor vehicles and parts thereof since 1995

ISIC (Rev.3)	Product description	NACE Rev.	SITC (Rev. 3)	CN 1991
3410	Passenger motor cars	3410	781.2	8703 (excl. 8703.1)
	Other passenger motor vehicles		781.1	8703.1
	Public-transport passenger motor vehicles		783.1	8702
	Motor vehicles for the transport of goods		782.1	8704
	Special purpose motor vehicles		782.2	8705
	Road tractors for semi-trailers		783.2	8701.2
	Chassis fitted with engines for motor v.		784.1	8706
	Engines for motor vehicles; parts		*713.2, ex713.9*	*8407.3, 8408.20, ex8409.9*
3420	Bodies (incl. cabs) for motor vehicles	3420	784.2	8707
	Trailers of the caravan type		786.1	8716.1
	Trailers for the transport of goods		786.22	8716.3
	Parts of trailers		ex786.89	ex8716.9
	Transport containers		*786.3*	*8609*
3430	Parts and accessories of motor vehicles	3430	784.3	8708
ex2912	Pumps and filters for motor vehicles; parts	*ex2912*	*742.2, ex742.91, 743.63, 743.64, ex743.95*	*8413.30, ex8413.91, 8421.23, 8421.31, ex8421.99*
ex2921	Agricultural tractors and trailers	*2931, 2932*	*ex722.41, 786.21*	*ex8701.1, 8716.2*
ex3140	Batteries	*ex3140*	*ex778.1*	ex8507
ex3190	Electrical equipment for motor vehicles	*3161*	*778.3*	8511, 8512
5020	Maintenance and repair of motor vehicles	*5020*	n.a.	n.a.

Source: UN Statistical Office.

Note
Codes in italics refer to items that are not classified in manufacturing of motor vehicles in the respective classification system.

Statistical sources

EUROSTAT, DAISIE: Industrial Survey Data in *New CRONOS* (CD-ROM).

OECD-DSTI: *The OECD Input–Output Database, Edition 1995*, derived from National Input–Output-Tables by the OECD Directorate for Science, Technology and Industry. Online, download at http://www1.oecd.org/dsti/sti/stat-ana/stats/eas_io.htm (accessed September 20, 2001).

OECD, ISIS: *Industrial Structure Statistics* (CD-ROM).

OECD, ITCS: *International Trade by Commodities Statistics* (CD-ROM).

OECD, STAN: *Structural Analysis Industrial Database* (CD-ROM).

Statistical Handbook of the Republic of China (Taiwan) 1998. Taipei, 1998.
Statistisches Bundesamt: *Foreign Trade according to the SITC* (various issues).
Statistisches Bundesamt: *Input-Output-Tabellen 1970 und 1974.* Wiesbaden, 1981.
UN: *International Trade Statistics Yearbook.* New York (various issues).
UNIDO: *Industrial Statistics* (CD-ROM).
Verband der Automobilindustrie (VDA): *International Auto Statistics.* Frankfurt/Main.
Ward's 1964 Automotive Yearbook. Powers and Company: Detroit.

Acknowledgment

This research has been performed as part of the TSER project on "Globalisation and Social Exclusion." Financial support from the European Commission is gratefully acknowledged.

Notes

1 At the time of writing, Markus Diehl was a research fellow at the Institute of World Economics in Kiel. The views expressed are those of the author and should not be attributed to the WestLB AG. This chapter has benefited from discussions with participants in the TSER-funded research project on "Globalization and Social Exclusion," and Peter Nunnenkamp (Kiel Institute of World Economics).

2 Campa and Goldberg (1997) and Hummels *et al.* (1998) described the facts. Feenstra and Hanson (1996a,b), Jones (1996), Deardorff (1998) and Venables (1999) provided different theoretical insights.

3 Outsourcing ("*out*side re*source* us*ing*") refers to the fragmentation of a production process in sequential stages (i.e. the opposite of vertical integration) and the development of new input–output relations; moreover, the stage outsourced could be either a service activity (e.g. maintenance, logistics) or a production activity (e.g. the supply of intermediate inputs). In contrast, "relocation of production" usually refers to the deployment of a complete production process, that is, it disregards international trade in inputs.

4 Japan's share was about one quarter of the world total in the 1980s. Since then, Japan's domestic automobile production has fallen back, but this largely reflected the fact that an increasing proportion of Japanese vehicle production is now carried out in overseas Japanese plants. The temporarily strong Yen may have contributed to the accelerated relocation activities.

5 For an analysis of German intra-industry trade in automobile products see Heitger *et al.* (1999: 117–123).

6 It has to be noted that CKD vehicles are often recorded as finished vehicles in international trade statistics.

7 However, this indicator seems to be less reliable. One would expect that the share of apparent consumption (i.e. domestic production plus imports minus exports) of parts in total output of the automobile industry is in the same order of magnitude in all countries. Given the large variance of this share, it is doubtful whether the output values recorded in industrial surveys for the production of parts fully include intra-firm supplies. If that presumption holds, a low share would simply reflect the fact that the industry of the respective country is highly vertically integrated.

8 In the following, this group consists of Greece, Ireland, Portugal, Spain, and Turkey. Usually, the term "EU periphery" refers only to low-income countries which are members of the EU. However, Turkey was included because it signed an Association Agreement with the EU in 1973.

9 Note that the most recent input–output tables in the OECD database are for 1990. Meanwhile, input–output tables for 1995 are available but have not been used since the internationally agreed method for the compilation of input–output tables has changed significantly in the early 1990s (cf. Bleses and Stahmer, 2000).

10 Härtel and Jungnickel (1996: 279) objected that international trade in automobile parts includes spare parts for previously sold vehicles. However, the share of spare parts is estimated to be below 15 percent.

11 In the mid-1990s, about one-sixth of all vehicles produced in the United States were manufactured in Japanese plants.

12 No explanation could be found for the significant decline in both ratios from 1990 to 1995. The previously mentioned change of the industrial classification system in the early 1990s may be the reason.

13 Greece, Ireland, Portugal, Spain, and Turkey.

14 Meanwhile, Asian automobile manufacturers (most notably Daewoo) are strongly engaged in Eastern Europe, and may use their subsidiaries to serve the Western European car market (Tutak, 1999).

15 Countries like China, Brazil, and Mexico with long-standing relations to German automobile manufacturers were major importers of German automobile parts but were not relevant as suppliers of parts for assembly in Germany (Nunnenkamp, 1998).

16 In the mid-1990s, about 40 percent of all vehicles produced in Germany were made by the VW group, about 20 percent were produced by Opel (subsidiary of GM) and about 10 percent by Ford.

17 Note that Italy and France (but not the United Kingdom) applied import quotas for automobile products in the 1980s. The Japanese plans to establish production plants in the United Kingdom were probably the main reason for the negotiation of the 1991 "Consensus" on car imports from Japan (see previous section).

18 The employment situation in the US automobile industry was dominated by the severe crisis in the 1980s, in which low-skilled workers were more severely affected by layoffs than high-skilled workers. However, they regained their initial employment share during the 1990s, in contrast to other countries.

8   Outsourcing, outward processing and output quality

A case-study from the ceramic tableware industry

Valerie Jarvis

Introduction

Much is written on the increasing tendency of outsourcing in the production capabilities of industrialised states; but the phenomenon remains ill-understood, with little detailed analysis of the relative importance or cost-effectiveness of this widespread practice.[1] This chapter seeks to inform the debate on outsourcing by presenting brief but detailed empirical evidence on the mechanics of outsourcing activity of British and German producers in one narrowly defined branch of manufacturing: the ceramic tableware industry. In reporting on differences in outsourcing strategies taken in the two countries, this chapter examines in particular:

- differences in the extent and methods of outsourcing typically undertaken in the two countries;
- differences in relative costs of quality-equivalent output produced in a selection of lower-cost producers;
- differences in the responses of the manufacturers in Britain and Germany to the growing competition from lower-cost economies;
- the implications for lower-skilled employees in industrialised economies, and the policy implications of these results.

A semantic digression: defining outsourcing

Many companies now outsource, although to greatly varying degrees. The term remains ill-defined among economists – covering a range of activities, from the simple 'sub-contracting' of both core production activities (direct production by smaller or more specialised companies) and/or peripheral services (such as cleaning or security activities), through 'contracting out' of non-production activities (for instance, the maintenance or design functions), through to full-scale 'outward processing' ('off-shore' production) of core production activities. One point which seems worth making is that, as economists, we might be somewhat tighter in our use of language – in particular, distinguishing more carefully between that which is outsourced to other *domestic* suppliers (though the use of sub-contracting or contracting out); and that which is entrusted – and under what circumstances and methods – to overseas facilities. As we shall show in what follows, even between industrialised countries, there remain significant differences in the methods and mechanisms used to outsource those parts of manufacturing sequence deemed too costly, too inefficient, or too labour-intensive for in-house production.

In practice, manufacturers rely on a range of outsourcing activities, which might better be defined, *faute de mieux*, along the lines of:

- *contracting out*: used to indicate the buying in of external *services* (e.g. maintenance, security, marketing, design, etc.) for non-production activities;
- *subcontracting*: defined here as the full- or partial processing of core *production* activities by other firms;
- *outward processing*: defined as the *non-domestic production* of output. Within this wider category, it may be useful to further distinguish between that part of production sourced from the originating company's wholly owned overseas subsidiary, or with own production overseen and quality-controlled by on-site company staff; to that simply produced and 'bought in' from foreign-owned and controlled potential competitors.

Differences in methods and usage of outsourcing: evidence from case studies

This chapter draws heavily on the results of a wider investigation of competitiveness issues in the British and German tableware manufacturing industries.[2] That study included visits and interviews to a total of 23 tableware manufacturing firms across the two countries (12 in the United Kingdom, 11 in Germany), involving discussions with factory owners, production managers, and directors, whose firms between them represent over 20,000 employees – equivalent to roughly half of total industry employment – across the two countries.[3] Our observations were further informed through extensive conversations with representatives of the relevant trade associations in the two countries, as well as participants at the two major European trade fairs for tableware, held in Frankfurt in February and August 2000.

As an industry for study, the tableware sector offers a potentially interesting example of a mature industry, where production technologies and processes are largely known, and in which the division of labour is well established. Moreover, in keeping with many mature industries, the sector in both countries is charac-terised, on the one hand, by state-of-the-art 'high-tech' production facilities *alongside* large numbers of relatively low-skilled employees working with rela-tively low capital–labour ratios. The important point to understand is that these two extremes can and do co-exist in the real world because of the highly hetero-geneous nature of the individual items that make up each firm's full range of production – a detail often lost on economists in their acceptance of too general a definition of 'output'. This one-size-fits-all definition consequently misses many of the important details of manufacturing trends in the real world. In the sector under investigation, for instance, state-of-the-art production technologies tend to be concentrated only among the largest firms in the industry in both countries, and tend to be used only for the manufacture of the easier-to-produce 'flatware' components (e.g. plates) of total output, while the large proportion of output accounted for by the technically more demanding cast- and hollowware items (e.g. bowls, jugs, coffee pots), and much of the important decoration activity, still require a numerically large, though relatively unskilled, human input.

Finally, to set this chapter in context, the two countries selected for comparison comprise the two largest tableware-producing industries in Europe. The sector is one in which Britain continues to fare relatively well in comparison to Germany – both in terms of employment and trade performance, with official figures for 1998 suggesting total output and employment in the household ceramics industry to be around 25 per cent higher in Britain than in Germany (at PPP exchange rates), and net exports of the order of around £120 million, compared to a slight trade deficit (*c.*−£17 million) for Germany.[4] Both countries in recent years have seen dramatic increases in import activity – particularly from lower cost producers (albeit of different origins) – though, as we shall demonstrate later in this chapter, the response of domestic manufacturers to this increased activity from low(er)-wage country (LWCs) producers has been very different in Britain and Germany.

Technological considerations

Much investment has taken place in both countries in recent years in an effort to reduce labour input (or rather, labour costs). The labour savings from these investments are clearly illustrated by the relative output levels of the various generations of technology: for flatware, for example, a state-of-the-art isostatic dust pressing machine typically produces around 4,000–5,000 items per shift (roughly 500 per hour), and can be operated by one man. Moulds last an average of 50,000 impressions. Using the intermediate technology of a six-headed semi-automatic plate press can produce around 400 plates an hour, but the moulds will need changing after every 50–60 impressions; this may involve a member of the maintenance crew and will last around 30 minutes after every $1\frac{1}{2}$–2 hours' production.

From a policy perspective, however, a distinction needs to be drawn clearly between the requirements of the very large manufacturer in each country, capable of routinely operating at a volume suitable to justify the considerable investments in such state-of-the-art technologies, and the operational needs of the more typical producer, where smaller batches effectively prohibit efficient scales of production. Thus, for example, while *in addition to* its higher hourly yield, the dust presser typically replaces a further 3–4 workers in automating a wide range of *associated* functions (clay-mixing, trimming and smoothing of the castware, etc.), the heavy retooling costs (often involving the services of highly qualified electro-mechanical engineers) and the high costs of the moulds for these high-tech presses render them inappropriate for batches of less than 10,000–15,000. For many smaller companies (say, less than 250 employees) – or those for which the necessary raw materials (e.g. granulates and 'slips') are commercially unviable (due to the 'small' nature of their orders) – investments in such machines are then clearly unsuitable. For these companies, the £250,000–£300,000 required to buy a single dust press is often better spent on (several) automatic or semi-automatic presses, which are less fast, but easier to retool.

In their pursuit of greater cost-effectiveness, manufacturers face the theoretical trade-offs of seeking to substitute capital for labour, to seeking to outsource the labour-intensive activities to lower-cost employees. In practice, however, the choice is less clear cut, since it depends heavily on the availability, location and quality of that cheaper labour, and it is to this question that we now turn.

Differences in outsourcing activity

One of the most striking differences we found in the organisation of production between the two countries' production related to the use and location of that part of manufacturing carried out outside the physical limits of the companies themselves. In both countries, only the very largest domestic producers tended to make use of external manufacturers far away ('outward processing') to supplement their domestically produced ranges. But there were important distinctions also in the ways in which total *domestic* output was shared among domestic producers. Indeed, we were struck in our factory visits in Germany by the high degree of *Zulieferung* (literally: subcontracting) taking place there, whereby lesser-known producers contract to supply the better-known manufacturers with finished items (often including the 'brand' back-stamping and packaging functions). This 'internal' aspect of intra-firm trade, we were told, has the advantage that the brand-owner can still stamp this output as 'Made in Germany' and thus maintain the 'quality hallmark' in the consumer's mind.

The British approach to domestic outsourcing – while developed to a similar degree – appeared to us quite different in nature: Many British manufacturers appeared happy to supplement their own in-house production by simply 'buying in' unfinished low-cost 'blanks' from other domestic producers for decoration, packaging and dispatch; put conversely, many of the smaller suppliers are content to act as 'component suppliers' to the larger concerns, who then perhaps decorate, glaze and brand the items for sale alongside the rest of their domestic production. The strategy again offers the advantage that production can be categorised as wholly UK-produced, but differs from that typically employed in Germany in an important respect – namely, that most of the profitable, high value-added, decorating operations are carried out in the buying-in firm. From the German perspective, the British strategy is perhaps damaging in that very little of the manufacturing profit 'trickles down' to the blanks supplier, rendering his long-term prospects for survival (and the long-term prospects of the buying company to continue this method of meeting fluctuations in demand) in doubt.

Outward processing

In both countries, the direct use of off-shore operations to supplement domestically produced output is almost exclusively the preserve of only the largest companies, though here too, there appear to be significant differences between the countries in the methods and frequency of these operations. Among British manufacturers, it seems, an increasing proportion of total output is composed of *bought-in* finished wares from any of a wide (and often changing) range of lower-cost overseas producers, often simply to be repackaged (and perhaps 'back-stamped') for sale alongside a 'virtually indistinguishable' range (according to the representative of one large British producer with a long history of such production) from domestically produced items.[5] (A considerable profit is, it seems, still to be made from the provision of the original design and decoration.) Among the larger German manufacturers we visited, by contrast, it seems that substantial 'outward processing' of full ranges beyond the German borders is reserved merely for those long runs of standard-ware used to *supplement* higher-grade domestic ranges. Such production is typically undertaken in a limited number of the home company's wholly or jointly owned overseas factories, or at least with overseas production in foreign-owned factories overseen by the home company's own in-house supervisory personnel. Interestingly, while the phenomenon of overseas production appears to be growing among British tableware firms, several of the German companies we interviewed are apparently scaling down their overseas operations, since the additional shipping and supervision costs, as well as the time involved in shipping production from say, the Far East, reduces much of the apparent cost-saving to the extent that further investment in labour-saving technologies for domestic production can actually reduce domestic unit costs of production to below those of Far Eastern suppliers.

Different strategies

By far the most labour-intensive aspect in standard tableware production comes at the decoration stage. The typical method of decoration throughout the industry remains the manual application of lithographed transfers ('decals') to glost-fired whitewares by large numbers of semi-skilled operatives. Few come with any formal decoration qualifications in either country; most learn on the job. Although largely unskilled, it may take many months for operatives to reach efficient performance levels – around six months, according to manufacturers in both countries, for the simpler patterns on flatware; several years to become fully efficient at applying more complex decorations to hollowware. But cost-containment pressures – as well as the difficulties of 'holding on' to good decorators in an industry where prospects seem, at best, limited – have led manufacturers in both countries to look to reduce their reliance on in-house decorating personnel through a range of approaches.

For simpler shapes, a variety of levels of automation are available: for flatware, for instance, direct printing equipment can be used to print up to eight colours at a time (the illusion of even more, if the engraved 'plates' can be carefully aligned); 'heat release' machines can be used to apply transfers to flat-sided mugs and cups; simple 'stripe' and 'banded' designs can be fairly easily automated for most wares through the use of jigs and rollers. But investment in the plates and jigs required for automation, and the considerable re-tooling costs involved, may render automation less efficient for all but the larger (say, 10,000 plus) batch sizes. Moreover, for many of the items which make up the standard dinner service, automation of the decoration function is less feasible, due to the three-dimensional – and asymmetric – nature of the items involved.

Faced with higher wage costs, the response of many German firms is to seek to 'outsource' where possible the less urgent (and usually simpler) decorating activities to the specialist decorating units (often located close to the German borders) of the Czech Republic and Poland.[6] The practice is relatively widespread in Germany, and accounts for the equivalent of roughly 20 per cent of total output volume. Quality is typically maintained through supervision of the off-site work by the German manufacturer's own foremen. The net saving in labour costs – that is, net of supervisory personnel, transport costs and breakages in transit – amounts to roughly 30 per cent in comparison to German decorators.

Greater savings still – around 50 per cent less in comparison to the costs of manual decorating in Germany – can be achieved through the use of direct printing technology, but for the reasons set out earlier (small batches, asymmetrical objects), they are often less appropriate for the task in hand than the flexibility afforded by manual operatives. Such machines appeared to us rather more common in the United Kingdom than in Germany for the processing of flatware – where the larger batch sizes typically decorated in the United Kingdom (for plates, around 14,400 in the United Kingdom, compared to less than 9,000 in Germany), and the somewhat higher proportion of flatware in total output volume, warrant the £1,000+ investment per colour for each engraving plate used and help to minimise the considerable re-tooling costs involved in each changeover. While many in both countries recognise, even for the simpler, flatware shapes, a qualitative advantage of the traditional labour-intensive application of 'decals' over more high-tech methods – that is, for reasons of greater refinement (better colours and higher resolution) possible with decoration by transfer – the lower average wage costs typically faced by British manufacturers, and the less convenient location of LWC-labour, make the incentive to find an alternative source of labour for part-finishing, as yet, less pressing.

Relative prices and qualities of production

So far, we have outlined the various means and methods at the disposal of firms in the two countries for outsourcing, and offered insights into the incidence with which such practices typically occur. And we have suggested also one of the choices faced by firms in seeking to decide whether to innovate or outsource by describing the typical considerations of managers in deciding between capital and labour substitution in this industry. But it is not simply the manufacturers themselves who look for cheaper sources of production, but also – and perhaps increasingly – retailers (and intermediaries). So far, we have said little about a key element behind the rationale to source externally – namely, the lower costs of producing compared to domestic production. Perhaps unsurprisingly, the companies taking part in our inquiry tended to be somewhat guarded about the relative levels of production costs, so an alternative means of estimating relative costs was required. Our inquiry thus included visits to the two major biannual trade fairs held in Europe – the *Ambiente* and *Tendence* – for tableware producers. Exhibitors at these trade fairs are not limited to European producers, but – as a cursory glance at the trade catalogues demonstrates – encompass producers and suppliers from some 80 countries from Argentina to Vietnam. Many of the large European producers (for instance, Britain, Germany, France, Italy, Portugal, etc.) are heavily represented, but so too are traditional East European and Far Eastern suppliers (the Czech Republic, Poland, Thailand and the Philippines), as well as less traditional suppliers, such as Bangladesh, India and Sri Lanka. Our aim in visiting these trade fairs was to provide a first systematic breakdown of the relative producer prices of the output of a sub-sample of non-European producers, and to compare these with producer prices for *output of a similar quality* with the two countries studied in detail in our earlier work. To keep our investigations manageable, we concentrated on collecting price data for a single sample product matched across the various manufacturers: that of a standard dinner plate. These results are shown in Table 8.1, but before we turn to that table in detail, a word needs first to be said on the breakdowns given in this table, as well as on the quality gradings used.

Firstly, it should be emphasised, that the results presented in Table 8.1 for 'third country' producers (that is, outside the United Kingdom or Germany) cannot at this stage be treated as representative of all producers in the listed countries, since our limited time and resources whilst visiting the trade fairs meant that only a small sample of producers from a handful of countries could be visited. Moreover, our ability to obtain indicative prices from the various producers depended crucially on their ability and willingness to divert their attention from the important business of selling to the buyers and suppliers attending the trade fair, to speak frankly and accurately about the prices, minimum order sizes and technical attributes (form of decoration – in-glaze, on-glaze, etc.; likely manufacturing lead times, etc.) to us as non-purchasing researchers. Without wishing to push too far the possible implications of this potential (in statistical terms, selectivity) bias in our method, it is perhaps worth stating that for two of the lower-cost producers for which we should have liked to have obtained observations – notably, the Czech Republic and Portugal – the very high degree of commercial interest shown at the trade fair rendered effective data collection unfeasible.

To turn to the important issue of quality assessment, one does not need to be a very sophisticated consumer to recognise that tableware qualities vary greatly even within countries; and manufacturers themselves often produce a range of qualities designed to appeal to different segments of the market. Since the current team believes the issue of product quality of major importance in explaining patterns of inter- and intra-country trade, it would be curious, at least, were we not to attempt to distinguish our price-relatives by quality bands.

In keeping with our earlier detailed comparisons of output-quality for a large sample of British and German plates, each of the sample 'foreign'-produced

Table 8.1 Relative prices, adjusted prices and convenience factors for a sub-sample of tableware-producing countries by quality-grade of tableware output, 2000

Producing country by quality-grade	(1) Producer price[a]	(2) Adjusted producer price[b]	(3) Typical delivery times (weeks)[c]
Basic quality			
People's Republic China – earthenware	34	43 ⎫	12–14
People's Republic China – porcelain	44	55 ⎭	
Indonesia	54	—	8–12
India	77	80	8
Germany	100	100	n.a
UK	106	106	n.a
Standard quality			
Thailand	30	—	
Poland	30	30	3–4
Vietnam	33	—	6–9
Bangladesh	39	41	6–8
Germany	100	100	n.a
UK	144	144	n.a
Superior quality			
Poland	24	24	3–4
India	42	43	8–10
Bangladesh	44	45	6–8
Germany	100	100	n.a
UK	153	153	n.a

Notes

— No data available; n.a. not applicable.

a Unadjusted unit price per standard decorated dinner plate. For each grade, German producer price equals 100.

b Unit price adjusted by shipping cost and, for China, by an additional 12 per cent, to reflect the costs of the necessary 'quota' required for importation into Europe.

c Sum of typical manufacturing plus shipping time by sea.

plates for which price information was collected was assessed and allocated to one of four 'rule of thumb' quality grades. These quality-gradings were carried out by the researchers, on the basis of their considerable experience in the earlier United Kingdom–German comparisons. Allocations across the quality bands were made on the basis of the *overall combination* of each plate's physical (for instance: the 'embodied' attributes of body paste; form – for example, on-glaze or in-glaze – of decoration; glazing, etc.) and aesthetic characteristics (design and decoration, form and feel) only – *not* its price.[7] Thus a plate from Poland or Vietnam categorised to the standard-quality grade can and should be viewed as every bit as good in overall quality terms as a standard-quality British- or German-produced plate, *despite* the large price differentials between the various producers.[8]

To avoid misunderstanding, it should be emphasised that while the researchers involved were careful in their quality-gradings of the plates for which prices were collated, they are *not* an attempt at this stage to try to categorise the overall quality-specialisation of the 'third' countries referred to; put conversely, the rankings shown refer only to *plates for which price quotations were obtained*, and it is therefore entirely plausible that all countries might reasonably be represented in all quality-grades (though, it might be expected, to notably varying degrees), were a broader inquiry carried out. While such a study would undoubtedly be of great use and interest to those involved in empirical questions of the competitive advantages of the various economies, that aspect of our investigations was carefully undertaken only for the two countries in the broader study by Jarvis, O'Mahony and Wessels (2002).[9]

Caveats aside, Column (1) of Table 8.1 shows the dramatic raw price differentials between industrialised Western European producers and the lower cost producers of Southeast Asia, the Indian Sub-continent and, as an example of Eastern European porcelain producers, Poland. The prices quoted in this table, although small in number, represent a considerable improvement on traditional sources available to researchers in a number of ways: First, the level of disaggregation of the data is considerably greater than that typically available from more statistical sources, such as trade data and production censuses, where comparisons of unit values are frequently limited to comparisons of weight (tonnes of output) or volumes of broad categories (e.g. *'units'* made of porcelain or china) of output. Moreover, by collecting data directly from LWC-based producers, we avoid the contamination problems often inherent in these data due, for instance, to the inclusion in such sources of the prices of re-exports of foreign-produced wares, as well as artificial constructs such as transfer pricing, etc. But perhaps the major advantage of this form of price presentation is that it allows for the important distinction of relative prices *by quality*-grading of the specimen products, thus enabling greater insight into the real magnitude and nature of the comparative advantages of the countries under consideration. A broader data set – of a greater number of observations, and for a greater number of products – would undoubtedly prove helpful. At its most useful, such a study might seek to report also on the degree of representativeness of the various quality-grades in each country's production.

In each group, the unadjusted producer price for a given quality of tableware ranges between 24 and 77 per cent of the German price.[10] It is interesting to note that we find a somewhat lower cost advantage among LWC producers in the lowest quality grades, but a far greater advantage at higher qualities. Perhaps the most plausible explanation for this (at first blush, perverse) observation is that it is the result of a greater downward pressure on European prices in the lower quality grades due to a proportionately greater competition from LWCs in product markets at this quality level. The result is consistent with the views expressed by manufacturers in the two countries, who claimed that price competition was particularly fierce at this end of the market.[11]

In terms of direct price competition – in Western European markets, at least, there is an important addendum to these prices – namely, the significant shipping costs which also apply. None of the exporting companies (at least, from the Far East) that we spoke to were willing to supply less than a single 20-foot container-load.[12] The standard 20-foot container has an approximate capacity of 26 cubic metres. Used exclusively for dinner plates, such a container can transport approximately 14,400 items.[13] Thus the unit prices of these off-shore producers were adjusted to take account of the average shipping costs, and, in the case of Chinese exports, by an additional 12 per cent to take account of the tariff then in force on Chinese tableware imports into Europe.[14] These modifications are shown in Column (2).

As can be seen, adjustment for freight (and tariff) costs makes little difference to the overall result of a considerable cost advantage of the overseas producers, other than to further raise the apparent advantage of Poland as a major source of low-cost production – and competition – at least in European markets.[15] But the Polish producers we spoke to had a further important *qualitative* advantage in supplying the European market – namely, in the significantly reduced lead times required to supply the European mainland (see Column 3). While production times for Polish and Far Eastern suppliers remain comparable – at around 3–4 weeks from placement of order, on average, – the geographical proximity of Poland to its major markets significantly reduces the time in which orders can be delivered: simply stated, processed orders can be transported by road in a matter of days, compared to the 4–6 week shipping requirements for Asian producers.

The ability to respond quickly and flexibly has long been seen as a major source of potential advantage for European producers. The Polish producers – alongside, we understand, their Czech and Portuguese equivalents – have to some extent succeeded in capitalising on their lower cost-base and proximity to their major markets by operating their own concerns, though to date the ranges offered remain, on average, less extensive in the assortment of items produced and perhaps (or, at least, so we were told by many of the British and German manufacturers we visited) somewhat less fashion-conscious than their Western European counterparts.

The responses of industrialised countries: implications for employment

In global terms, European producers have something of an advantage over their far-off LWC competitors in that the quality of European clays are particularly fine.[16] Moreover, the inherent 'bulk' of ceramics, and the consequent need to ship (as opposed to the ability to use air freight) minimum container cargoes over large distances offers a potential advantage to geographically well-placed suppliers. Even within domestic markets, the (relatively) delicate nature of the output means that packaging and transport costs may add some 3–5 per cent to factory prices, further improving the comparative advantage of local suppliers willing and able to offer the consumer the product he wants *when he wants it.*

The response of the average German producer to this perceived 'window of opportunity' has been to deliberately seek to increase the *quality* of his output by means of a finer, whiter body; a higher degree of differentiation of output, through the introduction of new forms and more refined designs; and smaller batches of more deliberately finite (and 'fashion-conscious') tableware ranges. Spare productive capacity in the smaller firms is 'soaked up' through the processing of small batch orders from the larger German suppliers – a relationship of mutual advantage, since the high degree of flexibility of these smaller domestic suppliers acts as an important means of supplementing the larger runs produced on the international names' state-of-the-art technologies.

In terms of employment considerations, while many of those employed in the industry remain in relatively low-skill and routine operations, the success of this strategy depends crucially on ensuring adequate technical support – for instance, the engineering crews, vital for the frequent re-setting and re-tooling of automatic and semi-automatic machinery required for non-standard production, and for the in-house customisation of standardised machinery to best exploit the company's product-mix; tool-cutters, capable of reliably producing and replacing the new moulds required for new structural forms; and designers, capable of providing the 'fresh ideas' with the company's technical capabilities in mind – for smooth production. From our comparisons of similarly sized plants in Britain and Germany, it seemed that these skills were considerably more in evidence in the German plants than in the UK firms we visited.[17]

In Britain, by contrast, the response to increased LWC competition seems to remain one of seeking new ways of further reducing costs. With cost-containment often the uppermost consideration, many companies have invested heavily in recent years in a deliberate effort to substitute capital for labour, but have found it difficult fully to exploit the benefits of such investments since typical order sizes render efficient use of such technologies less than optimal. (Small wonder then, that so many of the British companies we visited were willing to seek to survive by supplying their excess production as low-cost blanks to their more renowned domestic competitors.)

From an empirical perspective, the strategy appears flawed on two counts: First, the heavy reliance on mass-production technology actually reduces the prospects for increased flexibility, since its efficient use typically *requires* large batch sizes to justify the re-setting costs, specialised jigs and moulds, etc. Attempts to increase flexibility of supply – though reduced delivery times and smaller orders accepted – must consequently be accommodated through increased inventories. Second, and an important issue for industrialists and policy-makers to bear in mind, these advanced technologies are equally available to – and used by – lower-cost producers. Thus the wage-cost advantages of these countries are further enhanced by these advanced technologies, where the standardised nature of the production of these LWCs provides the optimal conditions for their successful implementation. Moreover, through co-operative working arrangements with the firms of industrialised countries, lower-cost suppliers have learnt not simply how best to apply such technologies, but – by dint of their continuing relationships with firms from the industrially advanced economies – are perhaps better able to exploit more fully these advanced mass-production technologies since the outsourced contracts of standardised runs help both to justify the initial investments and to 'soak up' any excess capacity.

As is by now clear, for both countries, it is typically only the largest producers which engage in outward processing. But this strategy involves considerable search and investment costs, which are often prohibitive to average-sized producers, and their strategies thus differ by necessity. Faced with significant price competition from geographically adjacent countries (in particular, Poland and the Czech Republic), the average German producer has thus sought to incorporate the benefits of this lower cost base into his own production, by subcontracting a sizeable proportion of the labour-intensive decoration activities to these lower-cost countries. This option is less viable (due to geographical constraints) for British producers, who have thus instead invested more heavily in automated decorating equipment.

Since automated decorating equipment cannot yet replicate the degree of refinement in surface decoration afforded by manual decoration (and is not yet available for many of the items which make up a standard dinner service – think, for example, of the difficulties in trying to decorate asymmetric hollowware shapes such as jugs, coffee pots, and the like), British manufacturers are thus forced into an unhappy dilemma – higher costs or lower quality. To date, it seems the strategy has been one of reduced emphasis on output quality, in stark contrast to that of their German equivalents.

Summary and implications

This chapter reports in detail on differences between two industrialised countries – Britain and Germany – in the extent and forms of outsourcing activity in one narrowly defined branch of manufacturing: the ceramic tableware industry. On a semantic point, the term 'out-sourcing' is broad and ill-defined. At an academic level, we need to be more careful in our use of terminology – for example, outsourcing to other domestic firms, to domestically owned or domestically controlled overseas firms, or foreign-owned overseas firms – so as to be clearer about what we are actually observing and the full implications of 'outsourcing' activity for employment and living standards in industrialised countries. Moreover, we need to be more careful in our interpretation of, for instance, trade data so as to be clearer as to what exactly is being captured – that is, *increased competition* for domestic companies from foreign-based suppliers or *increasing reliance on foreign-based labour* by domestic-based producers.

Significant cross-country differences were found in the ways in which firms typically use both domestic and foreign suppliers to supplement their in-house production, in particular:

• only the largest firms in both countries tended to engage in overseas outsourcing to supplement domestically produced items. Among the larger

German firms, the preferred method tended to be 'outward processing' – that is, full overseas production of finished products in German-owned (or part-owned) and technician-supervised overseas factories. Among the larger British firms, the tendency was to buy in finished items from overseas-owned suppliers, to be simply repackaged and marketed alongside domestic output;

- within Germany, much outsourcing activity frequently involved the subcontracting by the larger firms of smaller batches to smaller and medium-sized domestic competitors;
- for many German firms, outsourcing beyond the German border involved subcontracting the less-skilled labour-intensive elements of decoration activities to specialist lower-cost facilities of the nearby Czech Republic and Poland;
- in Britain, domestic subcontracting activities tended to involve only partial production activities – such as the buying-in of low-cost blanks by larger manufacturers from smaller domestic suppliers;
- for British firms, the lack of availability of a conveniently located supply of lower-cost labour for partial processing has led to an increased reliance on technological innovation, where applicable, as a means of reducing labour costs in the labour-intensive activities.

An additional dimension to this chapter is that it provides original data on relative producer prices of quality-matched specimen products from a small sample of tableware producers from Western Europe and LWCs. In providing illustrative producer prices for sample matched items, these data improve on existing sources available to researchers in three ways:

- the level of disaggregation of the data is considerably greater than that typically available from more statistical sources (trade data, production censuses, etc.) in that it offers an illustration of *matched individual products* (as opposed to tonnes of output, nos of ceramic goods, etc.);
- by collecting data directly from LWC-based producers, we avoid contamination problems due to artificial constructs such as transfer pricing, or by the inclusion of re-exports of third-country-produced output;
- the individual products were further *disaggregated by quality-equivalence* of the output on offer, thus enabling greater insight into the scope and nature of the comparative advantages – in terms of quality-specialisation – of the countries under consideration.

We find a somewhat lower price advantage among LWC producers in the lower-quality grades of production, suggestive of a greater impact of competition from LWCs in these product markets. Our sample of prices is, however, small. A broader study of quality-differentiated producer prices for a wider range of products would undoubtedly be a worthwhile exercise.

Increased competition in product markets from LWCs is an important and growing trend, and has undoubtedly led to increased cost-containment considerations among industrialised producers. But the responses of firms operating in Britain and Germany to this increased competition have been notably different – and perhaps of differing long-term viability. In Britain, the response has been largely one of seeking to *confront head-on* the impact of greater price competition, either through removal of many of the costly labour-intensive processes by means of increased investment in new technologies or – among the very largest companies, at least – through direct importation of LWC-produced output for marketing alongside domestically manufactured ranges. The response of the average German producer in this industry has been to seek to *move away* from direct price competition by seeking to produce a higher-quality product, and to accentuate the quality differences of German-made output in the eyes of the consumer. Both tendencies imply a considerable – and continuing – decline in demand for lower-skilled labour: in Germany, the response requires a *shift* to higher-quality technical and engineering skills capable of ensuring smooth operation of smaller batch sizes. In Britain, the strategy might best be characterised rather by a *substitution* into capital where possible.

This chapter has considered differences in British and German firms' use of outsourcing in the face of ever-growing competition from LWCs. The price comparisons in Table 8.1 demonstrate the advantages of combining lower production costs with the premia typically commanded through sophisticated marketing and branding techniques. But this strategy involves considerable search and investment costs, which are often prohibitive to average-sized producers, and their strategies thus differ by necessity. Faced with significant price competition from geographically adjacent countries, the average German producer has thus sought to *incorporate* the benefits of this lower cost base into their own production, through the use of subcontracting. This option is less viable (due to geographical constraints) for British producers.

There remains considerable academic interest and debate as to whether it is increased reliance on new technology or competition from lower-wage countries which has brought about a large decline in demand for unskilled labour within industrialised countries. In light of the observations set out earlier, however, it seems to the present author that much more is to be gained – from a policy perspective – from studying the extent to which differences in quality-specialisation across countries help to explain the reduction in demand for higher-cost lower-skilled workers. Such research would undoubtedly offer insights into the ways in which previously unskilled workers might be better endowed with the higher skills required to operate in less price-competitive product markets. To date, very limited research of this type has been carried out: much more is required if we are to reach a clearer understanding as to the *optimal mix* of production, technical and engineering skills required for high quality production.

Acknowledgement

This research has been performed as part of the TSER project on 'Globalisation and Social Exclusion'. Financial support from the European Commission is gratefully acknowledged.

Notes

1 See, for instance: Feenstra and Hanson (1996a,b, 1999); Anderton and Brenton (1999c).
2 See Jarvis *et al.* (2002).
3 These figures exclude group employment accounted for by other branches of ceramic manufacturing (e.g. sanitaryware, technical ceramics, sales activities) as well as by directly owned 'overseas' operations.
4 On crude measures of output per employee, therefore, there appears little difference in the average productivity of labour in the two countries. Clearly there are major caveats to be borne in mind in making such comparisons – not least, potential differences in hours typically worked in the two countries; in differences in the composition of output – bone china, porcelain, earthenware, etc. – and corresponding differences in the costs of the raw materials involved, etc. In terms of value-added per employee, aggregate data suggest a German productivity advantage of around 21 per cent. Sources: for United Kingdom: ONS, *PRA 27 Household and Miscellaneous Ceramics*, 1998; unpublished data from Annual Employment Survey, 1998; ONS, *Annual Census of Production, 1998*; for Germany: Statistisches Bundesamt, *Produzierendes Gewerbe Fachserie 4 Reihe 4.1.1 Beschäftigung, Umsatz und Energieversorgung der Unternehmen und Betriebe im Bergbau und im verarbeitenden Gewerbe, 1998*; Ibid., *Produzierendes Gewerbe Fachserie 4 Reihe 4.3 Kostenstruktur der Unternehmen des Verarbeitenden Gewerbes sowie des Bergbaus und der Gewinnung von Steinen und Erden, 1998*; international trade: OECD, *International Trade by Commodities Statistics, Revision 2, 1990–1999*. Our own comparisons of productivity differentials for plants *matched for size and output mix*, however, suggest a rather larger differential – of the order of 65 per cent – in Germany's favour.
5 The result mirrors that found in a comparison of medical equipment manufacturers in the same countries by Anderton and Schultz (1999).
6 The growth in this practice over the 1990s shows up also in the trade statistics. (Data 1990–1995–1999: Germany – Czech Republic and Poland; United Kingdom – Portugal, Thailand, Bangladesh.)
7 In the detailed background study on which this chapter builds, four quality-grades were distinguished: *Top-quality* plates invariably denoted the highest grade formalware, made of bone china or very fine grade porcelain, decorated with an elegant surface design or embossed pattern, and perhaps with a degree of gilding. *Superior* quality plates shared many of these characteristics, though to a lesser degree overall. The plates assessed here included both what might be categorised as high-grade everydayware, as well as more traditional wedding-list items. A major distinction between this and the above and lower categories had much to do with the body paste of the plates in question (generally finest quality porcelain or bone china); exceptions were made for items deemed of such high quality in other aspects – perhaps due to an innovative design or shape – that their overall composition warranted inclusion in this 'superior quality' category. *Standard* quality plates included plates of porcelain, earthenware and stoneware, generally intended for everyday use, but lacking the refinements or originality of the higher grades. *Basic* quality plates were clearly lacking in at least one dimension. This included plate samples with poor coverage or 'crazing' of the glaze; pitted – 'orange peel' – surfaces; firing chips not ground down; or poor-quality copies of original designs. Functionally, the plates were usable; but their durability was questionable. For a more detailed description of the ways in which these quality grades were arrived at, see Jarvis *et al.* (2002), op. cit. For the purposes of this chapter, the highest – 'top' – quality grade is excluded here, since no observations for this category were collected. To avoid misunderstanding, that is *not* to say that the countries cited in Table 8.1 did not produce in this highest quality-grade – indeed, the present author would recognise that most countries are capable of producing all quality-grades; the point of interest is in the tendency for one country to produce on average a higher

quality product than another; but rather that the price-quotations collated by these researchers did not include production at that level.

8 To avoid misunderstanding, it should perhaps also be noted that, while the plates categorised here can be deemed of equivalent quality in terms of their embodied characteristics, there may be additional quality elements – for instance, how those plates fit in to the overall tableware ranges typically produced in the various countries (availability and number of complementary elements, etc.), how well new designs keep abreast of changes in consumer trends and fashion in different countries, after-sales guarantees regarding replacements, etc. – which were *not* taken into account in these quality gradings. This point is important, since it is viewed by many Western European producers as a major means of staying ahead of the lower-cost competition from Eastern Europe.

9 That study – limited to Britain and Germany – found a significantly higher average quality specialisation in Germany, to the extent, as valued by the market at common (United Kingdom/German) prices, that the average German-produced plate typically attracts a premium of around 44 per cent in comparison with the typical unit manufactured in the United Kingdom. The result is consistent in direction and magnitude with the results of the earlier work of the team, which found an average quality-differential between the typical output produced in Germany and Britain in three very different sectors of around 65 per cent (see Jarvis and Prais, 1997).

10 The higher average prices quoted for Britain compared to Germany perhaps require explanation: as in other sectors studied by the NIESR team, the broader study of tableware prices in Jarvis *et al.* (2002) found a significant price differential for matched quality grades between Britain and Germany – to the extent that a common basket of qualities typically consumed in the two countries costs around 50 per cent more in Britain than in Germany.

11 The logic is clear: many more LWCs are able to produce at the lower quality levels than at higher levels. (Newly Industrialising Countries begin with making the lower quality grades before they develop expertise to produce higher grades.) The result suggests an interesting empirical test of the Stolper–Samuelson theorem at a highly disaggregated level. For a concise elaboration of the assumptions and implications of that theorem, see: Sachs and Schatz (1996).

12 Although companies differed significantly in the numbers of patterns and styles that might be combined per container – from a single, or perhaps two, stock patterns from most Chinese producers, to up to four distinct stock patterns and forms from a large Vietnamese supplier. From our small sample of exhibitors, it seemed that producers from the Indian sub-continent were highly flexible in their willingness to combine patterns and forms, with companies from India and Bangladesh quoting minimum orders of 250–500 pieces per design – an aspect which they (and their purchasers) viewed as a major benefit in getting orders to these non-traditional suppliers.

13 We are grateful for the patience and careful consideration of the various exhibitors in helping us to devise this 'rule-of-thumb' calculation. We were told that each 20 foot container might typically be expected to convey around 800 'master cartons' (each equivalent to some 0.324 m^3 including packing materials), each packed with 18 dinner plates.

14 Importantly, however, for traditional suppliers to the US market, similar quotas and the associated *ad valorem* tariffs do not apply to North American markets.

15 A word perhaps needs to be said regarding the apparent anomaly in Table 8.1 regarding the relative producer prices of Poland and other lower-cost suppliers, such as India and Bangladesh – particularly the large differential in the superior quality grade: The Indian and Bangladeshi production classified to this and the higher – 'top quality' – category was made exclusively from the high-cost 'bone china' greatly admired in the United Kingdom and United States, but less revered in Continental European markets; the body paste of the Polish production classified to the superior quality grade was of the higher-grade 'fine porcelain' more commonly selected by European purchasers.

16 Indeed, for many of the finer quality articles produced by the lower-cost economies, clays and other high quality inputs (glazes, ceramic colours) are actually shipped out from Europe.

17 The extent of the difference is perhaps best illustrated by the figures on technically qualified personnel in the matched plants we visited in the two countries: around 1 in every 10 shopfloor workers in Germany held a recognised technical qualification at the industry standard – 'craft' – level, compared to 1 in every 25 in Britain. Maintenance crews (as a proportion of total employment) were also notably larger in the German plants than in the British producing units we visited – equivalent to roughly 1 maintenance engineer per 26 production workers in Germany, 1 in 55 shopfloor workers in Britain.

9 Adjusting to globalisation

Policy responses in Europe and the US

Paul Brenton

Introduction

Everyday experience suggests that globalisation, as reflected in the increasing availability of cheap imports from low-wage countries, could lie at the heart of the recent adverse developments in European and North American markets for relatively unskilled workers. This has led to the popular impression that trade liberalisation and increasing flows of foreign direct investment to developing countries, together with improvements in transport and communications, have resulted in products formerly produced by unskilled workers in industrial countries being increasingly purchased from low-wage countries. Economic theory supports these notions. Economists strongly believe that trade and investment liberalisation bring overall gains to an economy. However, the theory demonstrates that there are distributional consequences of globalisation, such that in industrial countries unskilled workers may suffer temporary or permanent losses of employment and income. But globalisation is only one of a range of factors and shocks that can adversely affect the situation of less-skilled workers in industrial countries.

This chapter discusses policy responses in Europe and the US to the challenges posed by globalisation. These include how to ensure that whilst society overall gains from freer trade in goods and services, specific groups within that society are not overly disadvantaged. This is important so as to avoid problems arising from social exclusion and also to maintain broad-based support for liberal trade and investment policies. This not only allows countries themselves to benefit from the gains from trade but also supports the use of liberal trade policies as a means to achieve development objectives for the poorest countries in the world economy, and in particular to stimulate trade through liberal access for those countries' exports to industrial country markets.

The chapter concentrates on policy responses in the EU and the US to the problems of adjusting to globalisation and the arguments which favour policies to assist those displaced by trade and investment. First it assesses whether trade restrictions are appropriate and argues that there will always be better policies which can redistribute income towards displaced workers whilst maintaining the gains from trade. An important issue, particularly in the context of the different policy responses adopted in Europe and the US, is if, and why, trade displaced workers should receive special assistance compared to other workers displaced by, for example, new technologies. The argument centres around the characteristics of trade displaced workers and the particular difficulties that they may face in retraining and finding new employment.

The chapter then briefly considers arguments which suggest that the process of globalisation and the increasing mobility of skilled workers and capital will act to compromise the revenues of governments who wish to intervene to assist displaced workers. This in turn may lead to a decline in broad-based support for open trade and capital movements. This will clearly become an important issue for governments who will have to look carefully at sources of revenue. Nevertheless, European experience suggests that there may be limits to the extent of integration and to the degree to which traditional revenue sources disappear. Finally, the chapter looks at arguments for trade restrictions to support jobs lost due to perceived 'unfair trade' emanating from lack of basic labour rights in developing countries and to force those countries to adopt rules on child labour and other basic labour rights. Again we show that trade restrictions are not the best mechanism for tackling this issue and in assisting developing countries to raise their labour standards.

Appropriate policy responses to the impact of globalisation

Unemployment is generally seen as the major factor leading to social exclusion, particularly long-term unemployment. However, in the EU it has been recognised that 'the very fact of holding a job at a particular time does not necessarily protect people from the risk of social exclusion... between 20 and 40 per cent of the population live on the margins of the poverty line and experience spells of low income over a period of 3–6 years, particularly as a result of repeated periods of unemployment'.[1] In the US the refrain 'the working poor' is often heard and surveys show that a proportion of displaced workers earn significantly less in subsequent employment. Job loss can lead to substantial costs to the individual both during spells of unemployment but also afterwards if they are forced to take a lower paying new job. Therefore, from the perspective of social exclusion, the quality of work, in terms of its duration, stability and income, is crucially important. Trade liberalisation can be important in affecting all of these dimensions of economic and social welfare.

A key factor underlying social exclusion in Europe and in North America has been the increasing inequality between unskilled and skilled workers in terms of incomes and/or employment opportunities. These developments entail that significant groups of society are unable to fully participate in the basic social structures and activities enjoyed by the rest of the population. Wage and income inequality is often linked to exclusion from suitable housing, transport, health, education and training. At the root of these changes appears to be a substantial fall in the relative demand for unskilled workers during the 1980s and 1990s.

What are contentious, however, are the reasons for this slackening of the demand for unskilled workers. Globalisation is one of a range of factors or shocks which displace workers. Technological progress may have led to the automation of many of the tasks previously undertaken by unskilled workers in the industrial countries. The main issue which has concentrated the minds of analysts has been the relative extent to which globalisation and technological change are to blame for increasing social exclusion of groups of unskilled workers in industrial countries.

Regardless of whether globalisation has been the *main* cause of the decline in the relative wage and employment prospects of low-skilled workers it is apparent that particular groups of workers have been adversely affected, as reflected in some of the chapters in this volume. In the US, Lewis and Richardson (2001) show that whilst freer trade has brought overall gains to the US economy there are groups who have suffered; in particular, those 'that cannot or will not engage the global economy lose heavily over time'.

If increased imports from, and capital flows to, developing countries are important factors affecting the employment and income outcomes of less-skilled workers in industrial countries what is the appropriate policy response? An impulsive reaction might entail stopping those factors which are perceived as contributing to the worsening of economic and social conditions for the less-skilled with restrictions on imports and outflows of capital. However, given the array of domestic policies available in modern industrial countries, intervention that constrains trade will be one of the least effective mechanisms. In essence, trade brings benefits as well as difficulties and those benefits are strongly expected to significantly exceed the costs that arise. Thus, more effective policies will be those which tackle the problems of income loss and temporary adjustment problems without removing the gains from trade. In other words, policy should seek to address as directly as possible the problems facing less-skilled workers without making matters worse elsewhere, as trade barriers would do (Deardorff, 1998).

It is useful to distinguish between the permanent effects on the distribution of income and the short-term costs that arise from constraints on the adjustment process. With regard to the former, the EU and US could introduce trade barriers on imports from developing countries to try and reverse the increase in wage inequality. The extent to which such a policy would be successful in raising the relative returns to unskilled labour is unclear given the lack of certainty concerning the precise role of trade, relative to technology, in generating inequality. Nevertheless, there will always be other policies which could achieve the same reversal of inequality but at a lower cost elsewhere in the economy. For example, the government could tax the wages of skilled labour and redistribute to low income households and/or it could levy a tax on the production of products which use skilled labour intensively. So, even if trade was the root cause of rising inequality and social exclusion, then trade restrictions are not the appropriate response because better policies for redistribution are available.

Along similar lines, if it were convincingly demonstrated that technological advancement was the main factor behind rising wage and employment inequality in Europe and the US, would it really be sensible to restrict the development and application of new technologies? Most people would accept that even if new technology does cause inequality it brings other substantial benefits that are not worth losing. Again, better policies for redistribution exist than curtailing technical progress. Those who advocate restricting trade but are unwilling to contemplate constraining technology are unlikely to be taking account of the full benefits of trade. Deardorff (1998) argues that from the point of view of policy response it does not matter whether the main source of rising wage and unemployment inequality is trade or technology. The appropriate intervention, in the form of policies for redistribution via taxes on skilled labour or on skilled labour intensive products, will be the same whichever is the primary cause.

An important issue is whether trade displaced workers should be targeted for specific additional assistance relative to other groups of displaced workers. Such a case can be made if the typical trade displaced worker possesses characteristics which entail greater adjustment costs than those faced by the typical technology displaced workers. As we shall see there is some evidence to suggest that trade displaced workers do face higher costs of adjustment in the US. Although it should be stressed again that optimum intervention would never be in the form of trade restrictions.

Policy responses to the impact of globalisation on low-skilled workers in the EU and the US

There are extensive policies of redistribution in all EU countries to assist displaced workers which are applied regardless of the cause of dislocation. In the US in contrast there are policies specifically targeted at trade displaced workers. In this section we briefly discuss these approaches and consider why there is a divergence across the Atlantic.

In many ways there appears to be greater sensitivity to the issue of globalisation in the US than in the EU. At a general level, concerns over globalisation in the US are difficult to comprehend since the US economy experienced a period of unprecedented economic growth and rising living standards over the past two decades. During the 1980s and 1990s for every job lost in US manufacturing more than two jobs were created in the US economy (Rosen, 2002). The unemployment rate in the US remains historically low. In Europe in contrast growth has tended to be sluggish, job creation slow and unemployment rates have remained high, particularly relative to that of the US.

An important difference between the EU and the US is that the rate of job turnover in the US is much higher (Kletzer and Litan, 2001). On the one hand such flexibility in the labour market has benefits in terms of facilitating redeployment of labour from declining to expanding firms and sectors and providing better matches between workers and employers. This contributes to higher rates of productivity. On the other hand, substantial job loss can lead to uncertainty and insecurity which can have implications for worker morale and for general support for liberal trade policies. Further, job creation does not necessarily take place in the same location as job destruction. New jobs can be in different industries to those where jobs are lost. The new jobs may pay lower wages and provide fewer benefits than the old jobs. These factors may be particularly relevant in trade-related dislocations which tend to be sector and often location specific. Trade-related job losses have been concentrated in older traditional manufacturing sectors whilst most of the new jobs have been in services. The skills required in the newly created jobs can be quite different to those utilised in the old jobs. Evidence from the US suggests that it is older, less-skilled workers who had relatively long periods of tenure in their previous job who are typically displaced by trade. This group of workers appear to face particular difficulties and incur higher costs in adjusting to displacement than workers displaced from non-traditional manufacturing sectors.

This higher profile of globalisation in the US also reflects in part that trade penetration, and in particular imports from low-wage countries, increased at a much faster rate in the 1970s and 1980s in the US, although from a much lower base than in Europe. It also reflects that political decisions concerning trade policy are much more sensitive to specific groups, industries and regions in the US. A feature of the negotiations surrounding the passing of the Trade Act of 2002 which granted the US President trade promotion authority to negotiate additional trade deals including that under discussion at the WTO, was the enhancement of trade assistance measures, which will be discussed in more detail later, and specific policy changes to engender support from representatives from states with trade sensitive sectors. For example, changes were made to the rules of origin governing the preferential access of textiles and clothing products from Caribbean Basin countries such that the processes of dyeing, printing and finishing of fabrics must now be performed in the US before the fabric can be cut and made-up into clothing in the Caribbean countries. This reduces the value of these trade preferences since previously such activities could be undertaken in the Caribbean countries.

Trade policy (for goods and certain services) is in the unique competence of the EU whilst the principal means of redistribution between different social groups remain in the hands of national authorities. Hence, the impact of sectoral interest groups organised at the national level on trade policy making in the EU is much weaker (with the notable exception of agriculture) than in the US. The more extensive social protection systems in Europe have also shielded the most vulnerable and have therefore limited sensitivities to the perceived impact of globalisation on the employment and wage prospects of less-skilled workers. Moreover, less flexible labour markets in Europe, whilst contributing to the relatively higher stock of unemployed compared to the US, have insulated European workers from some of the uncertainty and insecurity engendered by globalisation.

To date neither the US nor the EU has resorted to widespread trade protection in the face of globalisation, although this abstinence from trade measures is far from guaranteed. However, anxiety towards the impact of more open trade in the US has been reflected in difficulties in achieving broad support for further trade liberalisation. Social policies and the safety net provided by the welfare state are clearly a fundamental foundation in all European countries and play an integral role in cushioning the impact of economic changes resulting from globalisation as well as rapid technological change.

There is little scope for the EU to intervene to compensate those who suffer permanent income loss due to globalisation and technological progress. As we shall discuss later, EU social policy is almost entirely dedicated to employment and adjustment issues, based on the perception that unemployment is the principal factor underlying social exclusion. EU policy does not seek to directly address problems arising from increased wage inequality for those in employment. This remains entirely in the domain of national authorities.

There are also no policies in the EU which are *specifically* targeted at trade affected sectors or trade displaced workers. This differs from the situation in the US where there is a dedicated program for trade affected workers. The Trade Adjustment Assistance (TAA) programme, established in the early 1960s, initially offered unemployment compensation and re-employment adjustment services to workers who had lost their jobs due to increased import competition. In the 1980s the programme rules were changed to shift the emphasis from compensation to training. As we will discuss further, this reflects a general desire in OECD countries to move from passive to active labour market policies. In the 1990s an additional programme was added (NAFTA–TAA) to provide assistance to those negatively affected by imports from Canada or Mexico, or total or partial plant relocation to these countries, following the implementation of the North American Free Trade Agreement. The current US Department of Labour fact sheet on TAA states that 'If Imports Cost You Your Job... Apply for Trade Adjustment Assistance'.

These trade adjustment assistance programmes in the US in the 1980s and 1990s were relatively small scale. Sapir (2000) reports that on average less than 4,000 workers per month were receiving assistance under the two schemes compared with a total number of long-term unemployed of 175,000 per month. So less than 2.5 per cent of unemployed workers were receiving trade adjustment assistance. Rosen (2002) suggests that in 1999 less than 10 per cent of workers who lost their jobs from industries facing heavy import competition received assistance under the TAA programme. Samuel *et al.* (2000) report that in 1997 the cost of the two schemes was $300 million, of which $120 million was dedicated to training with the rest for income support. The latter was typically available for one year after unemployment benefit, which is usually provided for 26 weeks, ceases. Thus, trade adjustment assistance in the US amounted to a tiny fraction of GDP, less than 0.01 per cent.

Despite these trade adjustment schemes considerable resistance amongst organised labour in the US to further trade liberalisation remains, apparently much more so than in EU countries. Sapir (2000) suggests that this is because the increase in trade with low-wage countries in the 1980s and 1990s has led to permanent income losses as well as temporary adjustment costs for groups of US workers. Kletzer and Litan (2001) report that the average worker displaced from an import competing industry in the US experienced a 13 per cent decline in average weekly earnings in subsequent employment. Further, for some 25 per cent of workers who lost their jobs in import-competing industries the loss of earnings in subsequent employment amounted to 30 per cent or more.

Surveys in the US consistently report support for trade liberalisation but conditional on assistance being provided to workers adversely affected. Discussions concerning trade adjustment assistance were at the centre of the recent debate and negotiations over the Trade Act 2002 which granted trade promotion authority to the President to pursue further trade liberalisation at the WTO and in regional and bilateral agreements. Three issues with regard to adjustment assistance came to the fore in discussions concerning this Act; the coverage of the scheme, the case for a wage insurance scheme whereby displaced workers would be compensated for a proportion of the loss of earnings between previous and new jobs for a certain period, and assistance to trade displaced workers in covering health insurance premiums. Rosen (2002) highlights that after mortgage payments, health insurance is the largest financial burden on unemployed workers. Rosen notes that in the US, the average family premium for health insurance can amount to a half of the average unemployment insurance payment. This issue is less prevalent in Europe where unemployment rarely affects access to health services.

The final outcome of the negotiations surrounding the Act led to some significant changes to the TAA programme. Specifically, the scheme, which now integrates the NAFTA programme:[2]

- extends benefits to secondary workers, displaced from companies supplying parts to a trade affected firm,
- includes farmers and ranchers in the scheme for the first time,
- expands eligibility to cover workers affected by a shift of production to another country (previously only workers affected by a shift of production to a NAFTA country were covered).
- provides a 65 per cent tax credit for health insurance for trade displaced workers,
- doubles the funding for training,
- provides a limited wage insurance scheme for older workers only, which can pay up to half of the difference in wages.

It is clear that this intensification of the TAA programme was necessary for the Trade Act to be passed. The limited wage insurance scheme reflected in part concerns about the implementation and effectiveness of such a scheme. The current provisions establish a demonstration project focused on older workers, although it is this group of workers who appear to be most affected in the adjustment to more open trade. If successful it is likely that there will be substantial pressure for wage insurance to be more broadly available to trade displaced workers.

In Europe, displaced workers are generally caught by a much more extensive welfare system than that in the US which has cushioned the impact of trade (and technology) on income inequality and poverty. These welfare systems are almost entirely administered and funded at the national level and there are some important variations in the nature and extent of provision between different EU member states. But, in the main, EU social protection systems are designed much more from an equity rather than an efficiency perspective, relative to the US approach (Sapir, 2000). Hence, whilst the increase in income inequality has been much less in Europe than in the US the level of unemployment in Europe has remained persistently higher. Even so there are no mechanisms in EU countries to directly identify and compensate trade displaced workers who find re-employment on less advantageous terms and therefore suffer permanent income losses.

National policies concerning taxes and transfers, including unemployment benefits, play a major role in reducing the extent of poverty in OECD countries. In the mid-1990s the pre-tax and transfer poverty rate[3] for the working-age population was about 23 per cent in Belgium, 25 per cent in France, 14 per cent in Germany and 23 and 24 per cent respectively in Sweden and the UK. However, the post-tax and transfer poverty rates for the working population were around 6 per cent in Belgium, 7 per cent in France, 9 per cent in Germany and 7 per cent and 12 per cent in Sweden and the UK respectively (Forster, 2000). In general the effectiveness of tax and transfer systems in OECD countries has increased in the period of globalisation. In a number of countries (Australia, Canada, Denmark, Ireland, US) pre-tax and transfer poverty rates increased between the mid-1980s and the mid-1990s whilst post-tax and transfer rates fell. For most other countries post-tax and transfer poverty rates increased by less than pre-tax and transfer poverty rates, the exceptions being Germany and the Netherlands. So in most countries the redistributive impact of the tax-transfer system increased in the late 1980s and 1990s.

EU policy was redefined by the extraordinary Luxembourg Summit on employment which took place at the end of 1997. Agreement was reached on a coordinated employment strategy (the Luxembourg Process) whereby each year the Commission submits a proposal for Employment Guidelines. Member states are obliged to take account of these guidelines in setting their employment policies and make annual reports on their implementation. The guidelines are developed around four pillars; employability, entrepreneurship, adaptability and equal opportunities. In the main the guidelines relate to active polices to increase the rate of employment and remove discrimination. Targets have been set for raising the employment rate to 70 per cent by 2010, from 62.2 per cent in 1999. Member states are also required to develop strategies with regard to the acquisition of skills to allow adjustment to economic changes. The guidelines also mention reform of tax and benefit systems although to date little progress has been made on this front. The Joint Employment Report for 2000 concludes that 'the development of comprehensive reforms addressing the combined incentive impact of tax and benefit schemes remains, therefore, a priority for most Member States'.[4]

Globalisation and the scope for adjustment assistance

A fear arising from globalisation is that the effectiveness of policies to deal with the adjustment implications of more open trade and free capital flows and the accompanying social exclusion that can arise will be eroded as, in the face of increasing mobility of some factors (primarily capital but also highly skilled labour to some extent), the ability to raise taxes to fund social programmes will be compromised. To maintain social spending, taxes on internationally immobile factors, most types of labour, will have to be continually increased. Thus governments in industrial economies face a dilemma: globalisation generates rising demand for social protection but at the same time limits the ability of the state to fulfil that role (Rodrik, 1997). Ultimately it has been suggested that this process will erode the social consensus underpinning open markets and we will see the re-emergence of the extensive protectionism which undermined economic welfare in the 1930s.

Rodrik (1997) seeks to support this proposition by suggesting that increased openness to trade has been associated with reductions in government activity in industrial countries. However, government expenditures on welfare and other programmes have been under review in many countries for reasons totally divorced from globalisation. Starting before the onset of the current wave of globalisation there has been a comprehensive and legitimate debate concerning how to reduce the burden of taxation in OECD countries. In Europe the debate has had a different flavour to that in the US, often in the context of how to raise the rate of employment creation in Europe, an issue which has been much less of a problem in the US. More recently, in Europe the debate surrounding the appropriate level of government support for welfare has become focused upon the problems caused by an ageing population. Many European countries are having to face up to the fact that a declining number of working-age adults will have to support an ever increasing number of elderly recipients of government support in the form of pensions and health care. Globalisation may exacerbate this problem if it becomes more difficult to tax those in employment.

Also trade between industrial and developing countries only really started to expand rapidly in the 1980s and 1990s. Prior to that most of the increasing import penetration of industrial country markets was accounted for by imports from other industrial countries. Two-way trade within industries, intra-industry trade, which tends to characterise trade between rich countries is less likely to generate permanent costs and temporary adjustment problems than imports of labour intensive products from low-income countries. Nevertheless, Martin (1998) reports OECD data which shows that government spending on labour market measures increased on average in industrial countries from 2 per cent of GDP in 1985 to 3 per cent of GDP in 1995. This spending covers both what are termed passive measures, unemployment and related social benefits and early retirement benefits, as well as active labour market policies, training, employment services and so on. With regard to the claim that globalisation has reduced the level of individual social protection for those suffering adverse employment developments, Martin concludes that 'few OECD countries have taken steps to roll back the generosity of their benefit systems in recent years in terms of cutting benefit levels and/or reducing the average duration of benefit payments'.

Further, the surge in import penetration from developing countries in the past two decades does not appear to have caused overwhelming difficulties in raising revenues to finance the welfare state and social protection systems in industrial countries. The proportion of taxes in GDP has continued to rise in most OECD countries[5] with tax reform and attention to tax loopholes generating a greater amount of taxation. Swank (1998) finds no evidence that international capital mobility is leading to a general retrenchment of the welfare state in industrial countries or to a movement towards a minimal system of social protection.

Although globalisation may not, to date, have led to any substantial deterioration in the welfare state, it could be argued that the inexorable integration of the global economy will sooner or later compromise current levels of social protection in OECD countries. There are however, two key reasons to doubt this is an inevitability. First, there is no evidence of such a process in highly integrated regions or in countries with federal systems and a degree of regional autonomy in setting taxes. The EU is one of the most integrated regional groupings of countries and has achieved a degree of integration considerably deeper than that which has been achieved in the world economy. The process of integration in Europe itself has not led to any apparent pressure on sources of government revenue in member states. Kerchgassner and Pommerehe (1996) find no evidence of tax competition amongst the cantons of Switzerland, where there is fiscal autonomy and a high degree of mobility of high-skilled workers.

Second, there is the issue of how much further the process of globalisation has to go? Will we eventually reach a state of perfectly integrated global markets? There are a number of reasons to believe that ultimately this integration will be constrained. Empirical applications of models which assume away constraints upon trade (such as the Heckscher–Ohlin model) vastly over-predict the amount of trade that actually takes place. This could be because there is a range of natural barriers to trade which imply that international commerce will be limited even if all man-made barriers to trade could be eliminated, which in itself is quite unlikely. These natural barriers include distance and something which economists have identified as 'home bias'.

Home bias implies that, other things being equal (mainly prices), consumers will still have a preference towards the purchase of domestically produced goods. To some extent this reflects history and culture but it appears to go much deeper than this. McCallum (1995) studied trade amongst Canadian provinces and trade between those provinces and US states and found that, after controlling for distance and economic factors such as size, trade between two provinces is typically 20 times more intensive than trade between a province and similar state on the other side of the border. This is perhaps strange given the apparent high level of economic integration and cultural similarity of Canada and the US. In this way; as McCallum concludes, national borders still matter. Further, Wolf (1997) finds evidence of home bias in trade amongst US states. So even when all trade policy variables are removed there remains a preference for products which are locally produced.

Why then do borders continue to matter? One of the main reasons is that movement across a national frontier, even those in the EU where, with the Single Market, there are no border formalities, only empty border posts, entails movements into a different legal, regulatory and cultural jurisdiction.[6] These borders 'proscribe, adjudicate and enforce a wide range of norms, rules, habits, networks and the like' (Thompson, 2000), which differentiate one geographical area from another, in terms of both consumers' preferences and the legal and institutional environment for doing business. It is most unlikely that globalisation will lead to the harmonisation of tastes across the world. For many modern quality differentiated products proximity to the market remains a crucial aspect of effective supply.

On the supply side Rauch (1999) has argued that differentiated manufactured products are often produced in an environment in which complex networks of contacts interact to establish markets and set prices, which usually involve extensive search costs. This can be compared to more standardised products, such as primary products which are traded on organised exchanges or intermediate products, such as chemicals, where trade is based upon 'references prices' quoted in specialist publications. Rauch suggests that trade rises much more slowly with production for the differentiated manufactured products relative to the standardised products. In addition, trade in standardised products has been declining in importance, so that differentiated manufactured products, where network costs are particularly important, are becoming increasingly dominant, but where growth is slower and trade may be ultimately constrained.

Similar arguments also pertain to international capital flows. Investors tend to hold a much smaller number of securities from other countries than one might expect in a well-diversified portfolio. Again, investors appear to exhibit home bias and imperfect information and transaction costs remain a barrier to cross-country investment flows. Thus, whilst globalisation will continue, it is most likely that the ultimate level of integration will be constrained. National governments will retain much of their ability to implement independent policies, with the choice of the scope and level of social protection remaining a national prerogative. The key challenges facing national welfare systems are internal rather than external with the greatest threat coming from the ageing structure of western populations and the way that the pension system in most OECD countries is funded.

In Europe, there are a number of reasons to believe that in some areas the limits to economic integration are close to being reached. Schmidt (2002) concludes from analyses of the integration of EU road transport and insurance markets that national markets in Europe continue to be 'shaped predominantly by national concerns'. Holmes and Young (2001) argue that a key feature of the EU's regulatory approach is that progress with market integration has been possible only by allowing members to pursue their own legitimate public policy objectives such that a significant degree of variation in rules between members is permitted.

They argue that the EU is reaching a 'logical limitation' in that market integration is only possible if some degree of national variation is permitted but such variation constrains integration. The further that integration progresses the more intractable will be the national variations that remain.

Is trade with developing countries fair trade: should labour standards be enforced through trade sanctions?[7]

In addition to discussions regarding the direct impact of trade on workers in trade sensitive sectors and the case for government intervention to assist with the costs of adjustment that are incurred, further demands for trade protection, particularly in the US, have been made on the basis that trade with developing countries is not 'fair trade'. Specifically, it is argued that US companies are at a disadvantage in competing with firms in the developing countries because the latter do not have to satisfy the same labour and environmental regulations. Here we concentrate on labour issues but similar arguments relate to trade protection to achieve environmental objectives.

Low wages in developing countries are seen by labour unions in industrial countries to be partly the result of a lack of basic labour rights. The decline in the wages, employment and employment stability of low-skilled workers in OECD countries is then seen to be due to trade which is unfair. In other words lack of enforcement of core labour standards leads to an unfair competitive advantage in international markets. Core labour standards are typically taken to be those specified by the 1998 ILO Declaration on fundamental principles and rights at work: freedom of association and recognition of the right to collective bargaining; elimination of forced and compulsory labour; abolition of child labour; and elimination of discrimination in respect of employment and occupation.

There are a number of issues which emanate from the debate over core labour standards. The first is whether lack of core labour rights significantly distorts comparative advantage and competitiveness? Here the theoretical analysis shows how under certain circumstances weak labour standards *can* lower wages in poor countries, increase exports from those countries and lower export prices and so reduce the wage of unskilled labour in rich countries relative to the returns paid to skilled workers. However, low labour standards *do not necessarily* lead to lower wages in the country with lax standards. For example, discrimination in employment is likely to lead to higher, not lower, wages by reducing the supply of workers. In fact, the links between low labour standards and competitiveness and trade are complex depending upon the nature of labour markets and production technologies. General statements on this issue are therefore impossible to make. It therefore follows that it would be nigh on impossible to identify any margin of competitiveness arising from lack of implementation of core labour standards. Thus, any attempt to countervail what some have called 'social dumping margins' would inevitably lead to arbitrary, and probably protectionist, levels of tariffs in industrial countries.

Further, there is a range of factors which suggest that the impact on workers in industrial countries of low wages in developing countries due to low labour standards will be limited (Maskus, 1997). For example, if the industrial countries are producing goods which differ from those produced in the developing countries, in terms of factor intensities, then the impact of low labour standards in the developing countries on wages in the industrial countries will be dampened. The impact will also be determined by the ease to which different factors of production can be substituted for one another and the sensitivity of demand for the product in the industrial countries to changes in price. The available empirical studies have yet to find any conclusive evidence that differences across countries in implementation of core labour standards has any significant impact upon the pattern of trade between developing and industrial countries.

More generally, it is erroneous to assume that differences in wages must be due to variation in labour standards. Many other factors contribute. In fact in the face of a large labour pool which is relatively responsive to changes in wages, the impact of low labour standards on wages in developing countries will probably be quite small. The OECD (1996) amongst others concludes that low labour standards are not an important competitive factor. This has two implications. First, that the impact of low labour standards in developing countries on workers in industrial countries is slight and secondly, that effective implementation of core labour standards will not undermine the ability of developing countries to compete on the world market.

The second key issue is whether failure to internationally enforce labour standards will lead to a global competitive race to the bottom in the extent of employment protection. The fear here is that international competition and the free movement of capital will make the maintenance of high labour standards untenable. Here again there are a number of reasons which suggest that this fear is, at least, exaggerated. First and foremost, the fear of a race to the bottom is based on the incorrect assumption that international competition will push standards down to their lowest level. Government regulations which improve employer–employee relations are unlikely to be watered down in a well-functioning democracy (Brown, 2000). Deregulation which leads to deterioration in labour relations will not improve firm performance.

In addition, some standards in industrial countries have emerged as part of the competitive process through negotiations between employers and employees. Thus, the overall package that the firm offers to the workers will comprise money wages, other benefits and working conditions. The precise outcome will reflect the particular preferences of the worker. Overall compensation will be related to the productivity of the individual and the market price of the product he or she produces. Firms which seek to reduce the compensation package on offer below that justified by the value of the workers productivity by reducing benefits or working conditions will find that they will lose workers to other employers. International competition will be important to the extent that it affects the value of the individual's productivity (either through a fall in the price of the final product or via an outflow of capital).

Even if international competition leads to some downward pressure on standards it is most unlikely that these will spiral downward to the lowest level observed in the international economy. The diversity of standards that we observe across the world reflects variations in incomes, preferences and technologies. Further, there are clearly cases, a notable example being the Netherlands, where very high labour standards have been maintained in the face of competition from low-wage countries whilst employment performance has dramatically improved. Thus, it is unlikely that increased global competition will inevitably lead to the downward convergence of labour standards.

Should trade sanctions be used to enforce core labour standards?

Thus, there is little convincing evidence to support fears in industrial countries that lack of basic labour rights in developing countries is the main source of employment and wage loss for unskilled workers or that current labour regulations in industrial countries will inevitably be eroded. Nevertheless, there is little dispute that implementation of core labour standards in developing countries is desirable. But what policies could be pursued to facilitate or encourage the adoption of basic labour rights throughout the world?

Trade sanctions by developed countries have often been touted as a response by labour unions in those countries and were even raised by the US President at the Seattle summit of the WTO in November 1999, which given the understandable sensitivity of developing countries on this issue, effectively doomed that meeting to failure. In general, trade sanctions are not an effective way of achieving adoption of core labour standards and indeed they may worsen the situation for those in the developing countries whom the proponents of sanctions may be seeking to help. Whalley and Wigle (1999) demonstrate that trade sanctions in industrial countries will tend to reduce wages in developing countries and reduce exports from all countries in the world.

The fact is that trade sanctions will in general benefit the scarce factor in the developed countries (unskilled labour) and will be to the detriment of the abundant factor (unskilled labour) in the developing countries. It is for this reason that the humanitarian motive for trade sanctions cannot easily be distinguished from the protectionist motive, so that a careful analysis of the impact of such policies is required before they can be considered for implementation. The analysis of appropriate policy towards labour standards varies somewhat according to the specific aspect of labour rights that is being addressed. We start by looking at the most emotive issue that of child labour.

Economic analysis shows the importance of not just considering whether possible policy choices reduce the amount of child labour but whether in addition the welfare of the children increases. Similarly, policies such as labelling to highlight that products are not produced with child labour whilst raising the well being of the concerned western consumers may not necessarily improve the lot of the child labourers. A complete ban on the employment of children is often proposed as a suitable response to this problem. This is the easiest response.

In models in which parents act in their own interest and take no account of the interests of their children it can be shown that a ban on child labour will benefit the children. However, the simple and popular description of selfish parents enjoying their leisure as their children work is not relevant to an explanation of the mass phenomenon of child labour that we observe in many of the least-developed countries. In this case it is not the attitude of the parents which forces children to work but poverty and the realisation by parents that sending their children to work is necessary for survival. Krueger (1996) demonstrates that there is a very strong correlation between child labour and poverty, as reflected in average GDP per capita. In countries where income per head exceeds $5,000 per year child labour is almost non-existent. It is in this sense that the problem of child labour can be identified as a problem of development rather than a trade problem. In cases where parents are altruistic but survival requires that children work a ban on child labour could harm the family if there are no accompanying measures to maintain and raise incomes.

If the response to the problem of child labour were trade sanctions by industrial countries then in cases where families cannot survive without child labour the sanctions would constrain trade and reduce growth in the developing country but would have no impact on the use of child labour. A trade prohibition would probably divert child workers into even more undesirable jobs in the import-competing or non-tradables sectors. Trade sanctions are likely to be effective only in cases where it can be clearly demonstrated that the interests of the children are not being fully reflected in the decisions of the household. This is very difficult to establish and, as noted earlier, will not be widespread. However, with bonded child labour, whereby an employer makes a lump-sum payment to the parents of a child and then provides food, clothing and shelter for the child, it can be demonstrated that there is a transfer from the child to the parents which suggests that the interests of the child are not valued within the family. However, specific import bans related to bonded labour will be difficult to monitor and to implement and better policies to tackle the problem will be available.

In fact, the importance of export oriented industries to the problems of child labour and discrimination at work is relatively small. It is estimated that 95 per cent of child labour is employed in the non-traded sectors in developing countries.[8] Trade sanctions will do little, nothing, or most likely have an adverse impact upon the majority of child labourers. More appropriate and effective responses to the problem of child labour are likely to lie in poverty alleviation schemes. There are also other more directly targeted policies which may reduce the use of child labour whilst per capita incomes remain below the level at which child labour disappears. The two main policies that have been identified are those which overcome capital market imperfections in developing countries and, most pertinently, targeted education subsidies. Both of these types of interventions provide a much more positive approach to overcoming the problem of child labour compared to bans and trade sanctions. There can be no guarantee that a ban on the use of child labour or trade sanctions will remove child exploitation, such policies could just force children into other 'undesirable' activities in the informal economy, such as living on the streets.

In industrial countries, families facing short-term financial difficulties can, in general, overcome these through access to the financial markets. In developing countries where financial markets are much less developed, families facing short-term difficulties but lacking collateral may be forced to sell their children as bonded labourers. Removing the causes of the failure of the capital markets in developing countries is not straightforward. In this case government grants to poor families or a policy of providing loans to families without collateral may be effective, but are likely to be difficult to implement.

The two main causes of child labour are, in general, poverty and lack of access to cheap education of suitable quality. Educational subsidies[9] tied to the child's attendance at school are a way of replacing the child's income in the home thus helping to ensure fuller educational participation and less child labour. 'The targeted educational subsidy dominates the use of sanctions, a ban on child labour and product labelling as a strategy for improving child welfare and lowering child employment' (Brown, 2000). However, funding such a subsidy scheme may be difficult in the least-developed countries where families cannot survive without child labour. Here international aid is likely to be necessary. In addition, it is likely that the subsidy would only need to be paid for one generation of children. When child labour is necessary for survival this reflects the low productivity and low wages of the adults in the family. Educational provision, by enhancing human capital, will raise productivity and wages of the next generation, thus confining child labour to history.

Moving on to discrimination at work, Maskus (1997) demonstrates that the impact of discrimination on exports and competitiveness is ambiguous but that in general discrimination against women, for example, by depressing the supply of workers, tends to raise wages. Hence, discrimination is costly and inefficient for the country which tolerates such practices and its elimination will be welfare improving. However, the power of special interest groups may be such that it is difficult for domestic governments acting alone to remove discrimination. Some groups in society may gain from being able to practice discrimination and they may be able to block proposals for reform.

In this case foreign action, in the form say of an import tariff on the good/country where discrimination takes place could assist reform but only if the threat of trade restrictions leads to the removal of the practice. If the country chooses to continue with discrimination and accept the trade sanction then the welfare of female workers may fall. This will arise if the imposition of the tariff reduces the cost of discrimination by reducing the ratio of the female to the male wage, that is by reducing the cost of preserving the existing male wage premium. Such a situation will occur if the export sector uses female workers intensively relative to male workers. Trade sanctions reduce the demand for female workers more proportionately than the fall in the demand for male workers and the female to male wage ratio will decline. Only if the export sector uses relatively more male labour will the trade sanction raise the costs of discrimination. Thus, the case for a trade sanction to help combat employment discrimination depends upon the precise circumstances of each case.

More generally, open trade, by increasing competitive pressures, is likely to lead to the abatement of what are costly, to the country tolerating them, discriminatory practices. Hence reducing import barriers in the country practising discrimination rather than higher trade barriers in the industrial countries is the easiest policy to implement and the one that is likely to be most successful. In this regard the WTO may, by providing for consistent and binding reductions in trade barriers, contribute to the long-term removal of discrimination.

The impact of trade sanctions when basic rights with regard to free association and collective bargaining are denied is also ambiguous. If the export sector of a developing country is dominated by a monopsonist and labour unions are suppressed then wages will be paid at a rate below that dictated by productivity. In this case the presence of a union would be welfare improving. However, if trade sanctions in overseas markets reduce the demand for the export good then there will be a decline in the demand for workers in the sector and the distortion caused by the single buyer of labour will be intensified. Again, only if the threat of trade sanctions leads to recognition of unions will the use of trade policies be successful. If the ban on association is maintained in the face of overseas trade restrictions then workers in the export sector will be worse off.

Thus, one can conclude from this discussion that the use of punitive trade measures in industrial countries to offset lack of compliance with core labour standards in developing countries will, under most plausible scenarios, not be the best way of intervening to encourage adoption of such standards. In many cases the use of trade sanctions may well have an adverse impact on the very people who are being denied their core labour rights.

The problem of child labour and lack of implementation of other core labour standards is one of development. There is a large body of work which suggests that trade and capital flows can play a major role in economic growth and the economic advancement of developing countries. Thus, the use of trade sanctions will most likely harm development prospects and undermine attempts to ensure effective implementation of core labour standards. The attempt to involve the WTO in the issue of core labour standards relates to the fact that the WTO has an effective enforcement mechanism, whilst the ILO does not. However, in many ways this has been rather futile. The developing countries, understandably fearful of the protectionist use of trade sanctions related to labour rights, will never agree to the linking of adoption of core labour standards to market access to industrial countries. Hence, attention has been diverted away from the important debate, which is how the ILO can be amended to help facilitate the effective implementation of core labour standards and how industrial countries can contribute to this process? The issue is not one of trade and labour standards, where there is an easy fix in the form of trade sanctions, but one of development and labour standards, where the solution is not as simple, but where open trade can play a significant positive role.

Conclusions

Whilst it is impossible to reject the assertion that globalisation has had a significant impact on wage and employment inequality in Europe and the US it is possible to dismiss trade protection and controls on long-term capital flows as an appropriate response in those countries. This is also the case for arguments based upon perceptions that trade with developing countries is unfair because of the lack of implementation of basic labour rights. This does not imply that governments should do nothing about the interests of low-skilled workers but that more effective policies for redistribution are available to compensate those who lose from trade liberalisation whilst preserving some of the gains that accrue from more open trade.

In the US there is a scheme targeted to assist trade displaced workers. This approach can be justified on the grounds that workers in trade sensitive sectors in the US possess a specific set of characteristics which entail that they face particular difficulties, relative to other displaced workers, in re-entering the job market and in maintaining previous levels of earnings. However, the presence of this scheme also reflects the particular political environment in the US and the leverage that trade sensitive sectors can bring upon decisions regarding trade policies. To date social protection systems in Europe have sought to catch displaced workers regardless of whether they have been affected by globalisation or by technological advance. There appears to have been little attempt in the EU countries to identify and study the characteristics of trade displaced workers and whether they vary from those of other displaced workers.

Assistance to trade displaced workers, whether targeted or not, seems to be an essential ingredient in maintaining support for open trade and capital flows in the EU and the US. The concerns that globalisation will undermine current social protection systems and will hamper the ability to deliver assistance to displaced workers appear excessive. Nevertheless, there is no strong evidence to suggest that to date governments have been dismantling systems of assistance for displaced workers in the face of globalisation. In the US such assistance has recently been intensified. In addition, there are a number of reasons to believe that borders will always matter and that the seamless world foreseen by some in which all scope for independent action by national governments is removed is most unlikely to materialise.

It is worth remembering here that developing countries are less able, if at all, to address the domestic distributional implications of globalisation. The consequences of trade expansion in the absence of social safety nets can be quite different from when there are guarantees that governments are able and willing 'to do their job' (Dasgupta, 2001: p. C19). In addition to the issue of redistribution within developing countries is the increasing perception held by many that globalisation is increasing inequality between rich and poor countries, leading to the questioning of globalisation and the role of the international institutions. At the global level redistribution between countries is tiny relative to redistribution within countries. At the global level globalisation has promulgated increased economic links and has been supported by the development of a clear and effectively enforced set of rules governing international exchange but, as political scientists emphasise, has not yet provided mechanisms for the establishment of a set of shared values and norms.

Acknowledgement

I am very grateful to Jacques Pelkmans for comments on an earlier draft. This research has been performed as part of the TSER project on 'Globalisation and Social Exclusion'. Financial support from the European Commission is gratefully acknowledged.

Notes

1 CEC (2000) p. 6.
2 Details are from 'Trade Promotion Authority: Background and Developments in the 107th Congress', Issue Brief for Congress, http://fpc.state.gov/documents/organization/16808.pdf (2000).
3 Proportion of persons in households with less than 50 per cent of median disposable income.
4 Joint Employment Report 2000, COM (2000), 551 final, 6.9.2000.
5 Financial times, 3.11.2000.
6 The following draws on Brenton (2002).
7 This section draws on the comprehensive review of the issue provided by Brown (2000).
8 See, for example, Memorandum submitted by the Department for International Development to the UK Commons Select Committee on International Development: http://www.parliament.the-stationary-office.co.uk/pa/cm199900/cmselect/cmintdev/uc227/uc22702.htm (1999).
9 The available evidence suggests that such subsidies may be more effective if paid to the mother, since increases in the mother's financial contribution to the family tend to raise the status of children in the household.

Bibliography

Abrego, L. (2000), 'Labour market institutions and decomposition of wage inequality outcomes', Centre for the Study of Globalisation and Regionalisation, University of Warwick, Mimeo.

Abrego, L. and J. Whalley (2000), 'The choice of structural model in trade–wages decompositions', *Review of International Economics*, 8: 462–477.

Abrego, L. and J. Whalley (2002), 'Decomposing wage inequality change using general equilibrium models', *NBER* Working Paper No. 9184.

Alic, J.A. and M.C. Harris (1991), 'Appendix: the NBER immigration, trade and labor markets data files', in G. Borjas and R. Freeman (eds), *Immigration, Trade and the Labour Market*, Chicago, IL: University of Chicago Press and the NBER, 407–420.

Anderton, R. (1999), 'UK trade performance and the role of product quality, variety, innovation and hysteresis: some preliminary results', *Scottish Journal of Political Economy*, 46, November, 553–570.

Anderton, R. and P. Brenton (1999a), 'Trade with the NICs and wage inequality: evidence from the UK and Germany', in P. Brenton and J. Pelkmans (eds), *Global Trade and European Workers*, London: Macmillan.

Anderton, R. and P. Brenton (1999b), 'Did outsourcing to low-wage countries hurt less-skilled workers in the UK?' in P. Brenton and J. Pelkmans (eds), *Global Trade and European Workers*, London: Macmillan.

Anderton, R. and P. Brenton (1999c), 'Outsourcing and low-skilled workers in the UK', *Bulletin of Economic Research*, 51: 267–286.

Anderton, R. and S. Schultz (1999), 'Explaining export success in the UK and Germany: a case study of the medical equipment industry', *Anglo-German Foundation Report*. London.

Anderton, R., P. Brenton and E. Oscarsson (2002), 'What's trade got to do with it? Relative demand for skills within Swedish manufacturing', *Weltwirtschaftliches Archiv*, Band 134, Heft 4: 629–651.

Baldwin, R. (1988), 'Hysteresis in import prices: the beachhead effect', *American Economic Review*, 78: 772–785.

Baldwin, R.E. (1995), 'The effect of trade and foreign direct investment on employment and relative wages,' *National Bureau of Economics*, Research Working Paper 5037.

Baldwin, R.E. and G.G. Cain (1997), 'Shifts in US relative wages: the role of trade, technology and factor endowments', *NBER* Working Paper No. 5934.

Bentivogli, Chiara and Patrizio Pagano (1999), 'Trade, job destruction and job creation in European manufacturing', *Open Economies Review*, 10: 165–184.

Berman, E., J. Bound and Z. Griliches (1993), 'Changes in the demand for skilled labor within US manufacturing industries: evidence from the Annual Survey of Manufactures', *NBER* Working Paper No. 4255.

Berman, E., J. Bound and Z. Griliches (1994), 'Changes in the demand for skilled labor within US manufacturing: evidence from the Annual Survey of Manufactures', *Quarterly Journal of Economics*, CIX(2), May.

Berndt, E.R. and D. Hesse (1986), 'Measuring and assessing capacity utilisation in the manufacturing sector of nine OECD countries', *European Economic Review*, 30(5): 961–989.

Bhattarai, K., M. Ghosh and J. Whalley (1999), 'On some properties of a trade closure widely used in numerical modeling', *Economics Letters*, 62: 13–21.

Blanchflower, David G., Simon M. Burgess (1996), 'Job creation and job destruction in Great Britain in the 1980s', *Industrial and Labor Relations Review*, 50(1): 1738.

Bleses, P. and C. Stahmer (2000), 'Input–output-rechnung 1995 und 1997', *Wirtschaft und Statistik*, Heft 12: 901–919.

Blim, Michael (1983), 'Positive adaptive responses of small Italian shoe producers to a changing European market: a case study of potential Italian adjustment problems to continuing European economic integration,' Temple University, Department of Anthropology.

Borjas, G., R. Freeman and L. Katz (1991), 'On the labour market effects of immigration and trade,' in G. Borjas and R. Freeman (eds), *Immigration and the Work Force*, Chicago, IL: The University of Chicago Press.

Brecher, R. (1974), 'Minimum wage rates and the pure theory of international trade', *Quarterly Journal of Economics*, 88: 98–116.

Brenton, P. (1999), 'Rising trade and falling wages: a review of the theory and the empirics', in P. Brenton and J. Pelkmans (eds), *Global Trade and European Workers*, Basingstoke: Macmillan.

Brenton, P. (2002), 'The limits to international trade and economic integration', *Journal of World Investment*, 3: 83–95.

Brenton, P. and J. Pelkmans (eds) (1999), *Global Trade and European Workers*, London: Macmillan.

Brenton, P. and A. Winters (1993), 'Voluntary export restraints and rationing: UK leather footwear imports from Eastern Europe', *Journal of International Economics*, 34: 289–308.

Brenton, P. and A.M. Pinna (2000), 'Trade and wages in Europe: what can disaggregated import and export price data tell us?' forthcoming working document, CEPS, Brussels.

Brenton, P., A.M. Pinna and M. Vancauteren (2000), 'Globalisation and social exclusion: a study of the footwear industry in Europe', mimeo, CEPS, Brussels.

Brown, D. (2000), 'International trade and core labour standards: a survey of recent literature', Occasional Paper 43, Directorate for Education, Employment, Labour and Social Affairs, *OECD*, Paris.

Brusco, Sebastiano (1996), 'Trust, social capital and local development: some lessons from the experience of the Italian districts', University of Modena.

Burtless, G. (1995), 'International trade and the rise in earnings inequality', *Journal of Economic Literature*, 33: 800–816.

Campa, J. and L.S. Goldberg (1997), 'The evolving external orientation of manufacturing: a profile of four countries', *Federal Reserve Bank of New York Economic Policy Review*, July: 53–81.

Cardoso, Ana Rute (2000), 'Wage differentials across firms: an application of multilevel modelling', *Journal of Applied Econometrics*, 15(4): 343–354.

Choi, E.K. and D. Greenaway (2001), *Globalisation and Labour Markets*, Oxford, UK: Blackwell Publishers Ltd.

Coe, D.T. and E. Helpman (1995), 'International R&D spillovers', *European Economic Review*, 39: 859–887.

Cohen, W. (1989), 'Empirical studies of innovative activity', in P. Stoneman (ed.), *Handbook of the Economics of Innovation and Technological Change*, Oxford, UK: Blackwell Handbooks in Economics.

Commission of the European Communities (CEC) (1989), 'The community footwear industry', Brussels.

CEC (2000), 'Communication from the commission: building and inclusive Europe', COM (2000) 79 final, *Commission of the European Communities*, Brussels.

Cuyvers, L., M.G. Rayp Dumont, K. Stevens and D. Van Den Bulcke (2001), 'Analysis of the influence of the trade flows between the community and the emerging economies, differentiated according to sectors and countries of origin and destination, on wage and employment developments in the EU, final report VC/2000/0012, *European Commission* (DG Employment, Industrial Relations and Social Affairs), Brussels.

Dasgupta, P. (2001), 'Valuing objects and evaluating policies in imperfect economies', *The Economic Journal*, 111: C1–C29.

Davis, D.H. (1998), 'Does European unemployment prop up American wages? National labor markets and global trade', *American Economic Review*, 88: 478–494.

Davis, S. (1992), 'Cross-country patterns of changes in relative wages', *NBER Macroeconomics Annual*, 239–291.

Davis, S.J. and J. Haltiwanger (1990), 'Gross job creation and destruction: microeconomic evidence and macroeconomic implications', *NBER Macroeconomics Annual*, 5: 123–168.

Davis, S.J., J. Haltiwanger and S. Scott (1996), *Job Creation and Destruction*, Cambridge, MA: MIT Press.

Deardorff, A. (1998a), *Fragmentation in Simple Trade Models*, RSIE Discussion Paper 422, Ann Arbor, MI: University of Michigan.

Deardorff, A. (1998b), 'Technology, trade and increasing inequality: does the cause matter for the cure?' Discussion Paper 428, Research Seminar in International Economics, University of Michigan, Michigan: http://www.spp.umich.edu/rsie/workingpapers/ wp.html

Deardorff, A. and D.S. Hakura (1994), 'Trade and wages: what are the questions', in Bhagwati, J. and M. Kosters (eds), *Trade and Wages: Levelling Wages Down?*, Washington, DC: AEI Press.

Desjonqueres, Thibaut, Stephen Machin, and John Van Reenen (1999), 'Another nail in the coffin? Or can the trade based explanation of changing skill structures be resurrected?' *Scandinavian Journal of Economics*, 101(4): 533–554.

Dewatripont, M., A. Sapir and K. Sekkat (1999), *Trade and Jobs in Europe: Much Ado about Nothing?*, Oxford: Oxford University Press.

Dicken, P. (1998), *Global Shift: Transforming the World Economy*, London: Chapman.

Diehl, M. (1999), The impact of international outsourcing on the skill structure of employment: empirical evidence from German manufacturing industries. *Kiel Working Paper* 946, Kiel: Institute of World Economics.

Dumont M., G. Rayp, O. Thas and P. Willemé (2005), 'Correcting standard errors in two-stage estimation procedures with generated regressands', *Oxford Bulletin of Economics and Statistics*, 67(3): 421–433.

Eden, L. and M.A. Molot (1993), 'Insiders and outsiders: defining "Who is Us" in the North American Automobile Industry', *Transnational Corporations*, 2(3): 31–64.

Edwards, H. and J. Whalley (2002), 'Short and long run decompositions of OECD wage inequality changes', *NBER* Working Paper.

EU-TARIC (1995), *Integrated Tariff System of the European Union*, Luxembourg.

European Commission (2000), *Trade in Goods: The Automotive Sector*, DG Trade, Brussels. Online, available at http://europa.eu.int/comm/trade/goods/auto/index_en.htm (accessed 20 September 2001).

Feenstra, R. (1999), *The Impact of International Trade on Wages*, Chicago, IL: The University of Chicago Press.

Feenstra, R. (2001), 'Special issue: trade and wages', *Journal of International Economics*, 54(1), June.

Feenstra, R.C. and G.H. Hanson (1995), 'Foreign investment, outsourcing and relative wages', *NBER* Working Paper No. 5121.

Feenstra, R.C. and G.H. Hanson (1996a), 'Globalization, outsourcing and wage inequality', *American Economic Review*, Papers and Proceedings, 86(2), May: 240–245.

Feenstra, R.C. and G.H. Hanson (1996b), 'Foreign investment, outsourcing and relative wages', in R.C. Feenstra, G.M. Grossman and D.A. Irwin (eds), *Political Economy of Trade Policy*, Cambridge, MA: MIT Press, 89–128.

Feenstra, R.C. and G.H. Hanson (1997a), 'Productivity measurement and the impact of trade and technology on wages: estimates for the US 1972–1990', *NBER* Working Paper No. 6052. Cambridge, MA: NBER.

Feenstra, R.C. and G.H. Hanson (1997b), 'Foreign direct investment and relative wages: evidence from Mexico's Maquiladora's', *Journal of International Economics*, 42: 371–393.

Feenstra, R.C. and G.H. Hanson (1999), 'The impact of outsourcing and high-technology capital on wages: estimates for the United States, 1979–1990', *Quarterly Journal of Economics*, 114(3), August: 907–940.

Forster, M. (2000), 'Trends and driving factors in income distribution and poverty in the OECD Area', Labour Market and Social Policy – Occasional Paper 42, OECD, Paris.

Francois, J. and D. Nelson (1998) 'Trade, technology and wages: general equilibrium mechanics', *Economic Journal*, 108: 1483–1499.

Freeman, R. and A. Revenga (1999), 'How Much Has LDC Trade Affected Western Job Markets?' in M. Dewatripont, A. Sapir and K. Sekkat (eds), *Trade and Jobs in Europe: Much Ado About Nothing?*, Oxford: Oxford University Press.

GATT (1993), *Trade Policy Review European Communities 1993*, Vol. I, Geneva.

GATT (1994), *Trade Policy Review United States 1994*, Vol. I, Geneva.

GATT (1995), *Trade Policy Review Japan 1994*, Vol. I, Geneva.

Gereffi, G. (1993), 'The role of big buyers in global commodity chains: how US retail networks affect overseas production patterns', in G. Gereffi and M. Korzeniewicz (eds), *Commodity Chains and Global Capitalism*, Westport, CT: Praeger, 95–122.

Glass, A.J. and K. Saggi (2001), 'Innovation and wage effects of international outsourcing', *European Economic Review*, 45: 67–86.

Greenaway, D. and D. Nelson (2000), 'Globalisation and labour market adjustment', in David Greenaway and Douglas Nelson (eds), in Special Issue of *Oxford Review of Economic Policy*, 16(3).

Grossman, G.M. and E. Helpman (1992), *Innovation and Growth in the Global Economy*, Cambridge, MA: MIT Press.

Grossman, G.M. and D. Irwin (eds) (1996), *Political Economy of Trade Policy*, Cambridge, MA: MIT Press.

Grossman, G.M. and D. Irwin (1997a), 'Productivity measurement and the impact of trade and technology on wages: estimates for the US 1972–1990', *NBER* Working Paper No. 6052. Cambridge, MA: NBER.

Grossman, G.M. and D. Irwin (1997b), 'Foreign direct investment and relative wages: evidence from Mexico's Maquiladora's', *Journal of International Economics*, 42: 371–393.

Grossman, G.M. and D. Irwin (1999), 'The impact of outsourcing and high-technology capital on wages: estimates for the US 1972–1990', *Quarterly Journal of Economics*, 114: 907–940.

Hanson, Gordon H. and Ann Harrison (1999), 'Trade liberalization and wage inequality in Mexico', *Industrial and Labor Relations Review*, 52(2): 271–288.

Härtel, H.-H. and R. Jungnickel (1996), *Grenzüberschreitende Produktion und Strukturwandel: Globalisierung der deutschen Wirtschaft*, Baden-Baden: Nomos.

Hartley, J. (1992), *Vehicle Manufacturing Technology: A Worldwide Review of Trends for the Future*, Special Report R304, London: Economist Intelligence Unit.

Haskel, J. (1996a), 'The decline in unskilled employment in UK manufacturing', *Centre for Economic Policy Research*, Discussion Paper No. 1356.

Haskel, J. (1996b), 'Small firms, contracting-out, computers and wage inequality: evidence from UK manufacturing', *Centre for Economic Policy Research*, Discussion Paper No. 1490.

Haskel, J. and M. Slaughter (1997), 'Does the sector bias of skill-biased technological change explain changing wage inequality?' unpublished paper.

Haskel, J. and M. Slaughter (2001), 'Trade, technology and UK wage inequality', *Economic Journal*, 111(468): 163–187.

Heitger, B., K. Schrader and J. Stehn (1999), *Handel, Technologie und Beschäftigung*, Kieler Studien 298, Tübingen: Mohr.

Helpman, Elhanan (1984), 'A simple theory of international trade with multinational corporations', *Journal of Political Economy*, 92: 451–472.

Helpman, Elhanan and Paul Krugman (1985), *Market Structure and Foreign Trade, Increasing Returns, Imperfect Competition and the International Economy*, Cambridge, MA: MIT Press.

Hijzen, A. (2003), 'Fragmentation, productivity and relative wages in the UK: A mandated wage approach', *University of Nottingham, Leverhulme Centre for Research on Globalisation and Economic Policy*, Discussion Paper No. 2003/17.

Hijzen, A., H. Gorg and R. Hine (2004), 'International outsourcing and the skill structure of labour demand in the United Kingdom', *University of Nottingham, Leverhulme Centre for Research on Globalisation and Economic Policy*, Discussion Paper No. 2004/24.

Hirsch, B.T. (1992), 'Firm investment behaviour and collective bargaining strategy', *Industrial Relations*, 31(1).

Holmes, P. and A. Young (2001), 'Emerging regulatory challenges to the EU's external economic relations', SEE Working Paper 42, *Sussex European Institute, University of Sussex*.

Hsing, You-Tsien (1998), 'Trading companies in Taiwan's fashion shoe networks', University of British Columbia, Department of Geography.

Hudson, R. (1995), 'The Japanese, the European market and the automobile industry in the United Kingdom', in R. Hudson and E.W. Schamp (eds), *Towards a New Map of Automobile Manufacturing in Europe? New Production Concepts and Spatial Restructuring*, Berlin, Heidelberg: Springer, 63–91.

Hummels, D., D. Rapoport and Kei-Mu Yi (1998), 'Vertical specialization and the changing nature of world trade', *Federal Reserve Bank of New York Economic Policy Review*, June: 79–99.

International Labour Organisation (ILO) (2000), *The Social and Labour Impact of Globalisation in the Manufacture of Transport Equipment*, Geneva: International Labour Office.

Jarvis, V. and S.J. Prais (1997), 'The quality of manufactured products in Britain and Germany', *International Review of Applied Economics*, 11(3): 421–438.

Jarvis, V., M. O'Mahony and H. Wessels (2002), 'Product quality, productivity and competitiveness: a study of the British and German ceramic tableware industries', *National Institute of Economic and Social Research*, Occasional Paper No. 55.

Jimeno, Juan F., Olga Cantó, Ana Rute Cardoso, Mario Izquierdo and Carlos Farinha Rodrigues (2000), 'Integration and inequality: lessons from the accessions of Portugal and Spain to the EU', in World Bank, *Making Transition Work for Everyone: Poverty and Inequality in Europe and Central Asia – Background Papers*, Washington, DC: World Bank, 1–47.

Johnson, H.G. (1966), 'Factor market distortions and the shape of the transformation frontier', *Econometrica*, 34: 686–698.

Jones, R.W. (1996), *Vertical Markets in International Trade*, Diskussionsbeiträge des SFB 'Internationalisierung der Wirtschaft' 318, University of Konstanz.

Katz, L. and K. Murphy (1992), 'Changes in relative wages, 1963–1987: supply and demand factors', *Quarterly Journal of Economics*, 107: 35–78.

Kerchgassner, G. and W. Pommerehe (1996), 'Tax harmonisation and tax competition in the European Union: lessons from Switzerland', *Journal of Public Economics*, 60: 351–371.

Kletzer, L. and R. Litan (2001), 'A Prescription to relieve worker anxiety', Policy Brief, No. 01–2, Institute for International Economics, www.iie.com/policybriefs/news01-2.htm

Kohler, W. (2004), 'International outsourcing and factor prices with multistage production', *Economic Journal*, 114 (March): C166–C185.

Kosters, M. (1994), 'An overview of changing wage patterns in the labour market', in J. Bhagwati and M. Kosters (eds), *Trade and Wages: Levelling Wages Down?*, Washington, DC: AEI Press.

Krueger, A. (1996), 'Observations on international labor standards and trade', *NBER* Working Paper No. 5355, Cambridge, MA.

Krugman, P. (1995a), 'Growing world trade: causes and consequences', *Brookings Papers on Economic Activity*, 1: 327–362.

Krugman, P. (1995b), Technology, trade and factor prices. *NBER* Working Paper No. 5355. NBER. Cambridge, MA.

Krugman, P. and R. Lawrence (1993), 'Trade, jobs and wages', *NBER* Working Paper No. 4478.

Lawrence, R. (1996), *Single World, Divided Nations?* Paris: OECD Development Centre.

Lawrence, R. and M. Slaughter (1993), 'International trade and American wages: giant sucking sound or small hiccup', *Brookings Papers of Economic Activity*, 161: 226.

Leamer, E. (1994), 'Trade, wages and revolving door ideas.' *NBER* Working Paper No. 4716.

Leamer, E. (1996), 'In search of Stolper–Samuelson effects on US wages', *National Bureau of Economic Research*, Working Paper No. 5427.

Leamer, E. (1998), 'In search of Stolper–Samuelson linkages between international trade and lower wages', in S.M. Collins (ed.), *Imports, Exports, and the American Worker*, Washington, DC: Brookings Institution Press.

Leamer, E.E. and J. Levinsohn (1995), 'International trade theory: the evidence', in Gene M. Grossman and Kenneth Rogoff (eds), *Handbook of International Economics*, 3. Amsterdam: North Holland, 1338–1394.

Legewie, J. (2000), 'Driving regional integration: Japanese firms and the development of the ASEAN automobile industry', in V. Blechinger and J. Legewie (eds), *Facing Asia: Japan's Role in the Political and Economic Dynamism of Regional Cooperation*, München: Ludicium-Verlag, 217–245.

Lewis, H. and J.D. Richardson (2001), *Why Global Commitment Really Matters*, Washington, DC: Institute for International Economics.

Lichtenberg, F. and B. Van Pottelsberghe de la Potterie (1996a), 'International R&D spillovers: a re-examination', *NBER* Working Paper No. 5668. Cambridge, MA: NBER.

Lucke, Matthias (1997), 'European trade with lower-income countries and the relative wages of the unskilled: an explanatory analysis for West Germany and the UK', Working Paper No. 819, Kiel Institute of World Economics.

Lücke, M. (1998), 'Trade with low-income countries and the relative wages and employment opportunities of the unskilled – an exploratory analysis for West-Germany and the UK', in P. Brenton and J. Pelkmans (eds.), *Global Trade and European Workers*. Basingstoke: Macmillan.

Lucke, Matthias (1999), 'Sectoral value added prices, TFP growth, and the low-skilled wage in high-income countries', Kiel Working Paper No. 923.

Machin, Stephen, Annette Ryan and John Van Reenen (1996), 'Changes in skill structure: evidence from an international panel of industries', CEPR Discussion Paper No. 1434.

Machin, Stephen and John Van Reenen (1998), 'Technology and changes in skill structure: evidence from seven OECD countries', *Quarterly Journal of Economics*, November 1998.

Marimon, Ramon, Fabrizio Zilibotti (1998), ' "Actual" versus "virtual" unemployment in Europe: is Spain different?' *European Economic Review*, 42: 123–153.

Marquez, J. (1994), 'The econometrics of elasticities or the elasticity of econometrics: an empirical analysis of the behavior of U.S. imports', *Review of Economics and Statistics*: 471–481.

Martin, J. (1998), 'What works among active labour market policies: evidence from OECD countries' experience', *Labour Market and Social Policy*, Occasional Paper 35, *OECD*, Paris.

Maskus, K. (1997), 'Should core labour standards be imposed through international trade policy', Policy Research Working Paper No. 1817, World Bank, Washington.

Mayer, W. (1974), 'Short-run and long-run equilibrium for a small open economy'. *Journal of Political Economy*, 82(5): 955–967.

McCallum, J. (1995), 'National borders matter: Canada–US regional trade patterns', *American Economic Review*, 85: 615–623.

Meissner, H.-R., K.P. Kisker, U. Bochum and J. Assmann (1994), *Die Teile und die Herrschaft: Die Reorganisation der Automobilproduktion und der Zulieferbeziehungen*, Berlin: Edition Sigma.

de Melo, J. and S. Robinson (1989), 'Product differentiation and the treatment of foreign trade in computable general equilibrium models of small economies', *Journal of International Economics*, 27: 47–67.

Minondo, Asier (1999), 'The labor market impact of trade in middle-income countries: a factor content analysis of Spain', *World Economy*, 22(8): 1095–1117.

Morrison, C. (1988), 'Quasi-fixed inputs in US and Japanese manufacturing: a generalized leontief restricted cost function approach', *Review of Economics and Statistics*, 70(2): 275–287.

Morrison-Paul, C. and D. Siegel (2001), 'The impacts of technology, trade and outsourcing on employment and labour composition', *The Scandinavian Journal of Economics* 103(2001): 241–264.

Murphy, K. and F. Welch (1991), 'The role of international trade in wage Differentials,' in M. Koster (ed.), *Workers and Their Wages: Changing Patterns in the United States*, Washington, DC: AEI Press.

Mussa, M. (1974), 'Tariffs and the distribution of income: the importance of factor specificity, subsitutability and intensity in the short and long run', *Journal of Political Economy*, 82: 1191–1204.

Neary, J.P. (1978), 'Short-run capital specificity and the pure theory of international trade', *Economic Journal*, 88(35): 488–510.

Ng, F. and A. Yeats (1999), *Production Sharing in East Asia: Who Does What for Whom and Why?*, Policy Research Working Paper No. 2197, Washington, DC: World Bank.

Nunnenkamp, P. (1998), 'Die deutsche automobilindustrie im prozeß der Globalisierung', *Die Weltwirtschaft*, Heft 3: 294–317.

Nunnenkamp, P. (2000), 'Globalisierung der automobilindustrie: neue standorte auf dem vormarsch, traditionelle anbieter unter druck?' Kiel Working Paper No. 1002, Kiel: Institute of World Economics.

Nunnenkamp, P. and J. Spatz (2002), *Globalisierung der Automobilindustrie: Wettbewerbsdruck, Arbeitsmarkteffekte und Anpassungsreaktionen*, Kieler Studie 217, Berlin: Springer.

Organization for Economic Co-operation and Development (OECD) (1992), *OECD Economic Surveys, Portugal, 1991/92*. Paris: OECD.

OECD (1994), 'The International sector database', *OECD Statistical Compendium on CD ROM*. Rheinberg: Data Service & Information (DSI).

OECD (1996), *Trade, Employment and Labour Standards: A Study of Core Workers' Rights and International Trade*, Paris: OECD.

OECD (1998), 'OECD Data on Skills: Employment by Industry and Occupation', *STI Working Paper* 1998/4. Paris: OECD.

OECD (2000), *International Trade by Commodities Statistics, Revision 2, 1990–1999.*

Office for National Statistics (ONS), UK (1998), *PRA 27 Household and Miscellaneous Ceramics*, 1998.

ONS, UK (1998), *Annual Census of Production, 1998.*

Orcutt, G. (1950), 'Measurement of price elasticities in international trade', *Review of Economics and Statistics*, 32(2): 117–132.

Oscarsson, E. (2000), 'Trade, employment and wages in Sweden 1975–1993', Working Paper No. 2000: 8. *Department of Economics*, Stockholm University.

Park, S., A. Holzhausen, G. Hennig and N. Haehling von Lanzenauer (1999), *Keiretsu am Ende? Die Neuordnung in der japanischen Automobilindustrie*, Berliner Ostasien-Studien 1, Hagen: ISL-Verlag.

Payne, M. and B. Payne (1990), *The US Automotive Components Industry. A Review of Leading Manufactures*, Special Report 2076, London: Economist Intelligence Unit.

Portugal, Ministério da Economia, Direcção-Geral das Relações Económicas Internacionais (1996, 1997, 1998, 2000), *Evolução do Comércio Internacional*.

Portugal, Ministério do Trabalho (1978), Decreto-Lei 121 de 2 Junho.

Portugal, Ministério do Trabalho e da Solidariedade, DETEFP (1985 to 1997), Quadros de Pessoal. Data in magnetic media.

Rabellotti, Roberta (1995), 'Is there an industrial district model? Footwear districts in Italy and Mexico compared', *World Development*, 23(1), January 1995: 29–41.

Rauch, J.E. (1999), 'Networks versus markets in international trade', *Journal of International Economics*, 48: 7–35.

Reinert, K. and D. Roland-Holst (1992), 'Armington elasticities for United States manufacturing sectors', *Journal of Policy Modelling*, 14: 631–639.

Rodrik, D. (1997), *Has International Economic Integration Gone Too Far?*, Washington, DC: Institute for International Economics.

Rosen, H. (2002), 'Reforming trade adjustment assistance: keeping a 40-year promise', *Institute for International Economics*, www.iie.com/papers/rosen0202.htm

Sachs, J. and H. Shatz (1994), 'Trade and jobs in US manufacturing', *Brookings Papers on Economic Activity*, 1: 1–69.

Sachs, J. and H. Shatz (1996), 'US trade with developing countries and wage inequality', *American Economic Review, Papers and Proceedings*, 86: 234–239.

Salvanes, Kjell G. (1995), 'The flexibility of the Norwegian labor market: job creation and job destruction in manufacturing 1977–86', Norwegian School of Economics and Business Administration, Institute of Economics Discussion Paper 12/95.

Samuel, H.D., L. Chimerine and M., Fooks (2000), 'Strengthening trade adjustment assistance', http://www.econstrat.org/taa.htm

Sapir, A. (2000), 'Who is afraid of globalization? The challenge of domestic adjustment in Europe and America', paper presented at the conference on *Efficiency, Equity and Legitimacy: The Multilateral Trading System at the Millennium*, Harvard University, June.

Schmidt, S. (2002), 'The impact of mutual recognition – in built limits and domestic responses to the single market', *Journal of European Public Policy*, 9: 935–953.

Schmitz, H. and P. Knorringa (1999), 'Learning from global buyers', Working Paper 100, IDS, University of Sussex.

Shiells, C. and K. Reinert (1993), 'Armington models and terms of trade effects: some econometric evidence for North America', *Canadian Journal of Economics*, 26: 299–316.

Slaughter, M.J. (1998), 'International trade and labour market outcomes: results, questions, and policy options', *Economic Journal*, 108: 1452–1462.

Slaughter, M.J. (2000), 'What are the results of product-price studies', in R.C. Feenstra (ed.), *The Impact of International Trade on Wages*, Chicago, IL: NBER-University of Chicago Press.

Sleigh, P.A.C. (1990), *Japan's Automotive Components Industry. A Review of Leading Manufactures*, Special Report 2057, London: Economist Intelligence Unit.

Sleigh, P.A.C. (1991), *The European Automotive Components Industry, 1991 edition*, Special Report 2107, London: Economist Intelligence Unit.

Smitka, M.J. (1991), *Competitive Ties: Subcontracting in the Japanese Automotive Industry*, New York: Columbia University Press.

Statistisches Bundesamt (1998a), *Produzierendes Gewerbe Fachserie 4 Reihe 4.1.1 Beschäftigung, Umsatz und Energieversorgung der Unternehmen und Betriebe im Bergbau und im verarbeitenden Gewerbe, 1998*.

Statistisches Bundesamt (1998b), *Produzierendes Gewerbe Fachserie 4 Reihe 4.3 Kostenstruktur der Unternehmen des Verarbeitenden Gewerbes sowie des Bergbaus und der Gewinnung von Steinen und Erden, 1998*.

Storper, Michael and Scott, Allen (1990), 'Work organization and local labor markets in an era of flexible production', *International Labor Review*, 129(5).

Strauss-Kahn, V. (2003), 'The role of globalisation in the within-industry shift away from unskilled workers in France', National Bureau of Economic Research, Working Paper 9716.

Swank, D. (1998), 'Funding the welfare state: globalisation and the taxation of business in advanced market economies', *Political Studies*, 46: 671–692.

Thompson, G. (2000), 'Taking economic borders seriously' prepared for the workshop on *Methodologies for Boundaries*, University of Surrey, May, http://www.surrey.ac.uk/LIS/MNP/may2000/Thompsonedited.htm

Tutak, R.J. (1999), 'The race is on: competition for the CEE car market', *Transition Newsletter*, May/June: 25–27.

Vainiomaki, Jari, Seppo Laaksonen (1999), 'Technology, job creation and job destruction in Finnish manufacturing', *Applied Economics Letters*, 6: 81–88.

Varaldo, Riccardo (1988) (ed.) Il Sistema delle Imprese Calzaturiere, Giappichelli, Milan.

Venables, A.J. (1999), 'Fragmentation and multinational production', *European Economic Review*, 43(5): 935–945.

Vickery, G. (1996), 'Globalization in the automobile industry', in OECD, *Globalization of Industry: Overview and Sector Reports*, Paris: OECD 153–205.

Waldinger, R.D. (1986), *Through the Eye of the Needle*, New York: New York University Press.

Winters, L.A. and W. Takacs (1991), 'Labor adjustment costs and British footwear protection', *Oxford Economic Papers*, 43: 471–501.

Wolf, H. (1997), 'Patterns of intra- and inter-state trade', Working Paper 5939, NBER, Cambridge, MA.

Womack, J.R., D.T. Jones and D. Roos (1990), *The Machine that Changed the World*, New York: Rawson.

Wood, A. (1994), *North-South Trade, Employment and Inequality: Changing Fortunes in a Skill-Driven World*, Oxford: Oxford University Press.

Wood, A. (1995), 'How trade hurt unskilled workers', *Journal of Economic Perspectives*, 9(3).

Wood, Adrian (1997), 'Openness and wage inequality in developing countries: the Latin American challenge to East Asian conventional wisdom', *World Bank Economic Review*, 11(1): 33–57.

Wood, Adrian (1998), 'Globalisation and the rise in labour market inequalities', *Economic Journal*, 108: 1463–1482.

World Trade Organization (WTO) (1997), *Trade Policy Review European Union*, Geneva.

WTO (1998), *Trade Policy Review Japan*, Geneva.

Whalley, J. and R. Wigle (1999), 'Quantifying the effects of labour sanctions on Trade', in P. Brenton and J. Pelkmans (eds), *Global Trade and European Workers*, Basingstoke: Macmillan.

Yeats, A.J. (1998), *Just How Big Is Global Production Sharing?*, Policy Research Working Paper 1871, Washington, DC: World Bank.

Yoffie, D.B. and B. Gomes-Casseres (1994), *International Trade and Competition*, New York: McGraw-Hill.

Index

Note: Page numbers in italics refer to tables and figures.

eBooks – at www.eBookstore.tandf.co.uk

A library at your fingertips!

eBooks are electronic versions of printed books. You can store them on your PC/laptop or browse them online.

They have advantages for anyone needing rapid access to a wide variety of published, copyright information.

eBooks can help your research by enabling you to bookmark chapters, annotate text and use instant searches to find specific words or phrases. Several eBook files would fit on even a small laptop or PDA.

NEW: Save money by eSubscribing: cheap, online access to any eBook for as long as you need it.

Annual subscription packages

We now offer special low-cost bulk subscriptions to packages of eBooks in certain subject areas. These are available to libraries or to individuals.

For more information please contact webmaster.ebooks@tandf.co.uk

We're continually developing the eBook concept, so keep up to date by visiting the website.

www.eBookstore.tandf.co.uk